The Valley of th

Peter B. Kyne

Alpha Editions

This edition published in 2024

ISBN : 9789362092502

Design and Setting By
Alpha Editions
www.alphaedis.com
Email - info@alphaedis.com

Contents

CHAPTER I

In the summer of 1850 a topsail schooner slipped into the cove under Trinidad Head and dropped anchor at the edge of the kelp-fields. Fifteen minutes later her small-boat deposited on the beach a man armed with long squirrel-rifle and an axe, and carrying food and clothing in a brown canvas pack. From the beach he watched the boat return and saw the schooner weigh anchor and stand out to sea before the northwest trades. When she had disappeared from his ken, he swung his pack to his broad and powerful back and strode resolutely into the timber at the mouth of a little river.

The man was John Cardigan; in that lonely, hostile land he was the first pioneer. This is the tale of Cardigan and Cardigan's son, for in his chosen land the pioneer leader in the gigantic task of hewing a path for civilization was to know the bliss of woman's love and of parenthood, and the sorrow that comes of the loss of a perfect mate; he was to know the tremendous joy of accomplishment and worldly success after infinite labour; and in the sunset of life he was to know the dull despair of failure and ruin. Because of these things there is a tale to be told, the tale of Cardigan's son, who, when his sire fell in the fray, took up the fight to save his heritage—a tale of life with its love and hate, its battle, victory, defeat, labour, joy, and sorrow, a tale of that unconquerable spirit of youth which spurred Bryce Cardigan to lead a forlorn hope for the sake not of wealth but of an ideal. Hark, then, to this tale of Cardigan's redwoods:

Along the coast of California, through the secret valleys and over the tumbled foothills of the Coast Range, extends a belt of timber of an average width of thirty miles. In approaching it from the Oregon line the first tree looms suddenly against the horizon—an outpost, as it were, of the host of giants whose column stretches south nearly four hundred miles to where the last of the rear-guard maintains eternal sentry go on the crest of the mountains overlooking Monterey Bay. Far in the interior of the State, beyond the fertile San Joaquin Valley, the allies of this vast army hold a small sector on the west slope of the Sierras.

These are the redwood forests of California, the only trees of their kind in the world and indigenous only to these two areas within the State. The coast timber is known botanically as sequoia sempervirens, that in the interior as sequoia gigantea. As the name indicates, the latter is the larger species of the two, although the fibre of the timber is coarser and the wood softer and consequently less valuable commercially than the sequoia sempervirens— which in Santa Cruz, San Mateo, Marin, and Sonoma counties has been almost wholly logged off, because of its accessibility. In northern

Mendocino, Humboldt, and Del Norte counties, however, sixty years of logging seems scarcely to have left a scar upon this vast body of timber. Notwithstanding sixty years of attrition, there remain in this section of the redwood belt thousands upon thousands of acres of virgin timber that had already attained a vigorous growth when Christ was crucified. In their vast, sombre recesses, with the sunlight filtering through their branches two hundred and fifty feet above, one hears no sound save the tremendous diapason of the silence of the ages; here, more forcibly than elsewhere in the universe, is one reminded of the littleness of man and the glory of his creator.

In sizes ranging from five to twenty feet in diameter, the brown trunks rise perpendicularly to a height of from ninety to a hundred and fifty feet before putting forth a single limb, which frequently is more massive than the growth which men call a tree in the forests of Michigan. Scattered between the giants, like subjects around their king, one finds noble fir, spruce, or pines, with some Valparaiso live oak, black oak, pepper-wood, madrone, yew, and cedar.

In May and June, when the twisted and cowering madrone trees are putting forth their clusters of creamy buds, when the white blossoms of the dogwoods line the banks of little streams, when the azaleas and rhododendrons, lovely and delicate as orchids, blaze a bed of glory, and the modest little oxalis has thrust itself up through the brown carpet of pine-needles and redwood-twigs, these wonderful forests cast upon one a potent spell. To have seen them once thus in gala dress is to yearn thereafter to see them again and still again and grieve always in the knowledge of their inevitable death at the hands of the woodsman.

John Cardigan settled in Humboldt County, where the sequoia sempervirens attains the pinnacle of its glory, and with the lust for conquest hot in his blood, he filed upon a quarter-section of the timber almost on the shore of Humboldt Bay—land upon which a city subsequently was to be built. With his double-bitted axe and crosscut saw John Cardigan brought the first of the redwood giants crashing to the earth above which it had towered for twenty centuries, and in the form of split posts, railroad ties, pickets, and shakes, the fallen giant was hauled to tidewater in ox-drawn wagons and shipped to San Francisco in the little two-masted coasting schooners of the period. Here, by the abominable magic of barter and trade, the dismembered tree was transmuted into dollars and cents and returned to Humboldt County to assist John Cardigan in his task of hewing an empire out of a wilderness.

At a period in the history of California when the treasures of the centuries were to be had for the asking or the taking, John Cardigan chose that which others elected to cast away. For him the fertile wheat and fruit-lands of California's smiling valleys, the dull placer gold in her foot-hill streams, and the free grass, knee deep, on her cattle and sheep-ranges held no lure; for he had been first among the Humboldt redwoods and had come under the spell of the vastness and antiquity, the majesty and promise of these epics of a planet. He was a big man with a great heart and the soul of a dreamer, and in such a land as this it was fitting he should take his stand.

In that wasteful day a timber-claim was not looked upon as valuable. The price of a quarter-section was a pittance in cash and a brief residence in a cabin constructed on the claim as evidence of good faith to a government none too exacting in the restrictions with which it hedged about its careless dissipation of the heritage of posterity. Hence, because redwood timber-claims were easy to acquire, many men acquired them; but when the lure of greener pastures gripped these men and the necessity for ready money oppressed, they were wont to sell their holdings for a few hundred dollars. Gradually it became the fashion in Humboldt to "unload" redwood timber-claims on thrifty, far-seeing, visionary John Cardigan who appeared to be always in the market for any claim worth while.

Cardigan was a shrewd judge of stumpage; with the calm certitude of a prophet he looked over township after township and cunningly checkerboarded it with his holdings. Notwithstanding the fact that hillside timber is the best, John Cardigan in those days preferred to buy valley timber, for he was looking forward to the day when the timber on the watersheds should become available. He knew that when such timber should be cut it would have to be hauled out through the valleys where his untouched holdings formed an impenetrable barrier to the exit! Before long the owners of timber on the watersheds would come to realize this and sell to John Cardigan at a reasonable price.

Time passed. John Cardigan no longer swung an axe or dragged a cross-cut saw through a fallen redwood. He was an employer of labour now, well known in San Francisco as a manufacturer of split-redwood products, the purchasers sending their own schooners for the cargo. And presently John Cardigan mortgaged all of his timber holdings with a San Francisco bank, made a heap of his winnings, and like a true adventurer staked his all on a new venture—the first sawmill in Humboldt County. The timbers for it were hewed out by hand; the boards and planking were whipsawed.

It was a tiny mill, judged by present-day standards, for in a fourteen-hour working day John Cardigan and his men could not cut more than twenty thousand feet of lumber. Nevertheless, when Cardigan looked at his mill, his great heart would swell with pride. Built on tidewater and at the mouth of a large slough in the waters of which he stored the logs his woods-crew cut and peeled for the bull-whackers to haul with ox-teams down a mile-long skid-road, vessels could come to Cardigan's mill dock to load and lie safely in twenty feet of water at low tide. Also this dock was sufficiently far up the bay to be sheltered from the heavy seas that rolled in from Humboldt Bar, while the level land that stretched inland to the timber-line constituted the only logical townsite on the bay.

"Here," said John Cardigan to himself exultingly when a long-drawn wail told him his circular saw was biting into the first redwood log to be milled since the world began, "I shall build a city and call it Sequoia. By to-morrow I shall have cut sufficient timber to make a start. First I shall build for my employees better homes than the rude shacks and tent-houses they now occupy; then I shall build myself a fine residence with six rooms, and the room that faces on the bay shall be the parlour. When I can afford it, I shall build a larger mill, employ more men, and build more houses. I shall encourage tradesmen to set up in business in Sequoia, and to my city I shall present a church and a schoolhouse. We shall have a volunteer fire department, and if God is good, I shall, at a later date, get out some long-length fir-timber and build a schooner to freight my lumber to market. And she shall have three masts instead of two, and carry half a million feet of lumber instead of two hundred thousand. First, however, I must build a steam tugboat to tow my schooner in and out over Humboldt Bar. And after that—ah, well! That is sufficient for the present."

CHAPTER II

Thus did John Cardigan dream, and as he dreamed he worked. The city of Sequoia was born with the Argonaut's six-room mansion of rough redwood boards and a dozen three-room cabins with lean-to kitchens; and the tradespeople came when John Cardigan, with something of the largeness of his own redwood trees, gave them ground and lumber in order to encourage the building of their enterprises. Also the dream of the schoolhouse and the church came true, as did the steam tugboat and the schooner with three masts. The mill was enlarged until it could cut forty thousand feet on a twelve-hour shift, and a planer and machines for making rustic siding and tongued-and-grooved flooring and ceiling were installed. More ox-teams appeared upon the skid-road, which was longer now; the cry of "Timber-r-r!" and the thunderous roar of a falling redwood grew fainter and fainter as the forest receded from the bay shore, and at last the whine of the saws silenced these sounds forever in Sequoia.

At forty John Cardigan was younger than most men at thirty, albeit he worked fourteen hours a day, slept eight, and consumed the remaining two at his meals. But through all those fruitful years of toil he had still found time to dream, and the spell of the redwoods had lost none of its potency. He was still checker-boarding the forested townships with his adverse holdings—the key-positions to the timber in back of beyond which some day should come to his hand. Also he had competition now: other sawmills dotted the bay shore; other three-masted schooners carried Humboldt redwood to the world beyond the bar, over which they were escorted by other and more powerful steam-tugs. This competition John Cardigan welcomed and enjoyed, however, for he had been first in Humboldt, and the townsite and a mile of tidelands fronting on deep water were his; hence each incoming adventurer merely helped his dream of a city to come true.

At forty-two Cardigan was the first mayor of Sequoia. At forty-four he was standing on his dock one day, watching his tug kick into her berth the first square-rigged ship that had ever come to Humboldt Bay to load a cargo of clear redwood for foreign delivery. She was a big Bath-built clipper, and her master a lusty down-Easter, a widower with one daughter who had come with him around the Horn. John Cardigan saw this girl come up on the quarter-deck and stand by with a heaving-line in her hand; calmly she fixed her glance upon him, and as the ship was shunted in closer to the dock, she made the cast to Cardigan. He caught the light heaving-line, hauled in the heavy Manila stern-line to which it was attached, and slipped the loop of the mooring-cable over the dolphin at the end of the dock.

"Some men wanted aft here to take up the slack of the stern-line on the windlass, sir," he shouted to the skipper, who was walking around on top of the house. "That girl can't haul her in alone."

"Can't. I'm short-handed," the skipper replied. "Jump aboard and help her."

Cardigan made a long leap from the dock to the ship's rail, balanced there lightly a moment, and sprang to the deck. He passed the bight of the stern-line in a triple loop around the drum of the windlass, and without awaiting his instructions, the girl grasped the slack of the line and prepared to walk away with it as the rope paid in on the windlass. Cardigan inserted a belaying-pin in the windlass, paused and looked at the girl. "Raise a chantey," he suggested. Instantly she lifted a sweet contralto in that rollicking old ballad of the sea—"Blow the Men Down."

For tinkers and tailors and lawyers and all,

Way! Aye! Blow the men down!

They ship for real sailors aboard the Black Ball,

Give me some time to blow the men down.

Round the windlass Cardigan walked, steadily and easily, and the girl's eyes widened in wonder as he did the work of three powerful men. When the ship had been warped in and the slack of the line made fast on the bitts, she said:

"Please run for'd and help my father with the bow-lines. You're worth three foremast hands. Indeed, I didn't expect to see a sailor on this dock."

"I had to come around the Horn to get here, Miss," he explained, "and when a man hasn't money to pay for his passage, he needs must work it."

"I'm the second mate," she explained. "We had a succession of gales from the Falklands to the Evangelistas, and there the mate got her in irons and she took three big ones over the taffrail and cost us eight men. Working short-handed, we couldn't get any canvas on her to speak of—long voyage, you know, and the rest of the crew got scurvy."

"You're a brave girl," he told her.

"And you're a first-class A. B.," she replied. "If you're looking for a berth, my father will be glad to ship you."

"Sorry, but I can't go," he called as he turned toward the companion ladder. "I'm Cardigan, and I own this sawmill and must stay here and look after it."

There was a light, exultant feeling in his middle-aged heart as he scampered along the deck. The girl had wonderful dark auburn hair and brown eyes, with a milk-white skin that sun and wind had sought in vain to blemish. And for all her girlhood she was a woman—bred from a race (his own people) to whom danger and despair merely furnished a tonic for their courage. What a mate for a man! And she had looked at him pridefully.

They were married before the ship was loaded, and on a knoll of the logged-over lands back of the town and commanding a view of the bay, with the dark-forested hills in back and the little second-growth redwoods flourishing in the front yard, he built her the finest home in Sequoia. He had reserved this building-site in a vague hope that some day he might utilize it for this very purpose, and here he spent with her three wonderfully happy years. Here his son Bryce was born, and here, two days later, the new-made mother made the supreme sacrifice of maternity.

For half a day following the destruction of his Eden John Cardigan sat dumbly beside his wife, his great, hard hand caressing the auburn head whose every thought for three years had been his happiness and comfort. Then the doctor came to him and mentioned the matter of funeral arrangements.

Cardigan looked up at him blankly. "Funeral arrangements?" he murmured. "Funeral arrangements?" He passed his gnarled hand over his leonine head. "Ah, yes, I suppose so. I shall attend to it."

He rose and left the house, walking with bowed head out of Sequoia, up the abandoned and decaying skid-road through the second-growth redwoods to the dark green blur that marked the old timber. It was May, and Nature was renewing herself, for spring comes late in Humboldt County. From an alder thicket a pompous cock grouse boomed intermittently; the valley quail, in pairs, were busy about their household affairs; from a clump of manzanita a buck watched John Cardigan curiously. On past the landing where the big bull donkey-engine stood (for with the march of progress, the logging donkey-engine had replaced the ox-teams, while the logs were hauled out of the woods to the landing by means of a mile-long steel cable, and there loaded on the flat-cars of a logging railroad to be hauled to the mill and dumped in the log-boom) he went, up the skid-road recently swamped from the landing to the down timber where the crosscut men and barkpeelers were at work, on into the green timber where the woods-boss and his men were chopping.

"Come with me, McTavish," he said to his woods-boss. They passed through a narrow gap between two low hills and emerged in a long narrow valley where the redwood grew thickly and where the smallest tree was not less than fifteen feet in diameter and two hundred and fifty feet tall. McTavish followed at the master's heels as they penetrated this grove, making their way with difficulty through the underbrush until they came at length to a little amphitheatre, a clearing perhaps a hundred feet in diameter, oval-shaped and surrounded by a wall of redwoods of such dimensions that even McTavish, who was no stranger to these natural marvels, was struck with wonder. The ground in this little amphitheatre was covered to a depth of a foot with brown, withered little redwood twigs to which the dead leaves still clung, while up through this aromatic covering delicate maidenhair ferns and oxalis had thrust themselves. Between the huge brown boles of the redwoods woodwardia grew riotously, while through the great branches of these sentinels of the ages the sunlight filtered. Against the prevailing twilight of the surrounding forest it descended like a halo, and where it struck the ground John Cardigan paused.

"McTavish," he said, "she died this morning."

"I'm sore distressed for you, sir," the woods-boss answered. "We'd a whisper in the camp yesterday that the lass was like to be in a bad way."

Cardigan scuffed with his foot a clear space in the brown litter. "Take two men from the section-gang, McTavish," he ordered, "and have them dig her grave here; then swamp a trail through the underbrush and out to the donkey-landing, so we can carry her in. The funeral will be private."

McTavish nodded. "Any further orders, sir?"

"Yes. When you come to that little gap in the hills, cease your logging and bear off yonder." He waved his hand. "I'm not going to cut the timber in this valley. You see, McTavish, what it is. The trees here—ah, man, I haven't the heart to destroy God's most wonderful handiwork. Besides, she loved this spot, McTavish, and she called the valley her Valley of the Giants. I—I gave it to her for a wedding present because she had a bit of a dream that some day the town I started would grow up to yonder gap, and when that time came and we could afford it, 'twas in her mind to give her Valley of the Giants to Sequoia for a city park, all hidden away here and unsuspected.

"She loved it, McTavish. It pleased her to come here with me; she'd make up a lunch of her own cooking and I would catch trout in the stream by the dogwoods yonder and fry the fish for her. Sometimes I'd barbecue a venison steak and—well, 'twas our playhouse, McTavish, and I who am no longer young—I who never played until I met her—I—I'm a bit foolish, I fear, but I found rest and comfort here, McTavish, even before I met her, and I'm thinking I'll have to come here often for the same. She—she was a very superior woman, McTavish—very superior. Ah, man, the soul of her! I cannot bear that her body should rest in Sequoia cemetery, along with the rag tag and bobtail o' the town. She was like this sunbeam, McTavish. She—she—"

"Aye," murmured McTavish huskily. "I ken. Ye wouldna gie her a common or a public spot in which to wait for ye. An' ye'll be shuttin' down the mill an' loggin'-camps an' layin' off the hands in her honour for a bit?"

"Until after the funeral, McTavish. And tell your men they'll be paid for the lost time. That will be all, lad."

When McTavish was gone, John Cardigan sat down on a small sugar-pine windfall, his head held slightly to one side while he listened to that which in the redwoods is not sound but rather the absence of it. And as he listened, he absorbed a subtle comfort from those huge brown trees, so emblematic of immortality; in the thought he grew closer to his Maker, and presently found that peace which he sought. Love such as theirs could never die... The tears came at last.

At sundown he walked home bearing an armful of rhododendrons and dogwood blossoms, which he arranged in the room where she lay. Then he sought the nurse who had attended her.

"I'd like to hold my son," he said gently. "May I?"

She brought him the baby and placed it in his great arms that trembled so; he sat down and gazed long and earnestly at this flesh of his flesh and blood of his blood. "You'll have her hair and skin and eyes," he murmured. "My son, my son, I shall love you so, for now I must love for two. Sorrow I shall keep from you, please God, and happiness and worldly comfort shall I leave you when I go to her." He nuzzled his grizzled cheek against the baby's face. "Just you and my trees," he whispered, "just you and my trees to help me hang on to a plucky finish."

For love and paternity had come to him late in life, and so had his first great sorrow; wherefore, since he was not accustomed to these heritages of all flesh, he would have to adjust himself to the change. But his son and his trees—ah, yes, they would help. And he would gather more redwoods now!

CHAPTER III

A young half-breed Digger woman, who had suffered the loss of the latest of her numerous progeny two days prior to Mrs. Cardigan's death, was installed in the house on the knoll as nurse to John Cardigan's son whom he called Bryce, the family name of his mother's people. A Mrs. Tully, widow of Cardigan's first engineer in the mill, was engaged as housekeeper and cook; and with his domestic establishment reorganized along these simple lines, John Cardigan turned with added eagerness to his business affairs, hoping between them and his boy to salvage as much as possible from what seemed to him, in the first pangs of his loneliness and desolation, the wreckage of his life.

While Bryce was in swaddling clothes, he was known only to those females of Sequoia to whom his half-breed foster mother proudly exhibited him when taking him abroad for an airing in his perambulator. With his advent into rompers, however, and the assumption of his American prerogative of free speech, his father developed the habit of bringing the child down to the mill office, to which he added a playroom that connected with his private office. Hence, prior to his second birthday, Bryce divined that his father was closer to him than motherly Mrs. Tully or the half-breed girl, albeit the housekeeper sang to him the lullabys that mothers know while the Digger girl, improvising blank verse paeans of praise and prophecy, crooned them to her charge in the unmusical monotone of her tribal tongue. His father, on the contrary, wasted no time in singing, but would toss him to the ceiling or set him astride his foot and swing him until he screamed in ecstasy. Moreover, his father took him on wonderful journeys which no other member of the household had even suggested. Together they were wont to ride to and from the woods in the cab of the logging locomotive, and once they both got on the log carriage in the mill with Dan Keyes, the head sawyer, and had a jolly ride up to the saw and back again, up and back again until the log had been completely sawed; and because he had refrained from crying aloud when the greedy saw bit into the log with a shrill whine, Dan Keyes had given him a nickel to put in his tin bank.

Of all their adventures together, however, those which occurred on their frequent excursions up to the Valley of the Giants impressed themselves imperishably upon Bryce's memory. How well he remembered their first trip, when, seated astride his father's shoulders with his sturdy little legs around Cardigan's neck and his chubby little hands clasping the old man's ears, they had gone up the abandoned skid-road and into the semi-darkness of the forest, terminating suddenly in a shower of sunshine that fell in an open space where a boy could roll and play and never get dirty. Also there were several dozen gray squirrels there waiting to climb on his shoulder and search his pockets for pine-nuts, a supply of which his father always furnished.

Bryce always looked forward with eagerness to those frequent trips with his father "to the place where Mother dear went to heaven." From his perch on his father's shoulders he could look vast distances into the underbrush and catch glimpses of the wild life therein; when the last nut had been distributed to the squirrels in the clearing, he would follow a flash of blue that was a jay high up among the evergreen branches, or a flash of red that was a woodpecker hammering a home in the bark of a sugar-pine. Eventually, however, the spell of the forest would creep over the child; intuitively he would become one with the all-pervading silence, climb into his father's arms as the latter sat dreaming on the old sugar-pine windfall, and presently drop off to sleep.

When Bryce was six years old, his father sent him to the public school in Sequoia with the children of his loggers and mill-hands, thus laying the foundation for a democratic education all too infrequent with the sons of men rated as millionaires. At night old Cardigan (for so men had now commenced to designate him!) would hear his boy's lessons, taking the while an immeasurable delight in watching the lad's mind develop. As a pupil Bryce was not meteoric; he had his father's patient, unexcitable nature; and, like the old man, he possessed the glorious gift of imagination. Never mediocre, he was never especially brilliant, but was seemingly content to maintain a steady, dependable average in all things. He had his mother's dark auburn hair, brown eyes, and fair white skin, and quite early in life he gave promise of being as large and powerful a man as his father.

Bryce's boyhood was much the same as that of other lads in Sequoia, save that in the matter of toys and, later guns, fishing-rods, dogs, and ponies he was a source of envy to his fellows. After his tenth year his father placed him on the mill pay-roll, and on payday he was wont to line up with the mill-crew to receive his modest stipend of ten dollars for carrying in kindling to the cook in the mill kitchen each day after school.

This otherwise needless arrangement was old Cardigan's way of teaching his boy financial responsibility. All that he possessed he had worked for, and he wanted his son to grow up with the business to realize that he was a part of it with definite duties connected with it developing upon him—duties which he must never shirk if he was to retain the rich redwood heritage his father had been so eagerly storing up for him.

When Bryce Cardigan was about fourteen years old there occurred an important event in his life. In a commendable effort to increase his income he had laid out a small vegetable garden in the rear of his father's house, and here on a Saturday morning, while down on his knees weeding carrots, he chanced to look up and discovered a young lady gazing at him through the picket fence. She was a few years his junior, and a stranger in Sequoia. Ensued the following conversation: "Hello, little boy."

"Hello yourself! I ain't a little boy."

She ignored the correction. "What are you doing?"

"Weedin' carrots. Can't you see?"

"What for?"

Bryce, highly incensed at having been designated a little boy by this superior damsel, saw his opportunity to silence her. "Cat's fur for kitten breeches," he retorted—without any evidence of originality, we must confess. Whereat she stung him to the heart with a sweet smile and promptly sang for him this ancient ballad of childhood:

> *"What are little boys made of?*
>
> *What are little boys made of?*
>
> *Snakes and snails,*
>
> *And puppy dog's tails,*
>
> *And that's what little boys are made of."*

Bryce knew the second verse and shrivelled inwardly in anticipation of being informed that little girls are made of sugar and spice and everything nice. Realizing that he had begun something which might not terminate with credit to himself, he hung his head and for the space of several minutes gave all his attention to his crop. And presently the visitor spoke again.

"I like your hair, little boy. It's a pretty red."

That settled the issue between them. To be hailed as little boy was bad enough, but to be reminded of his crowning misfortune was adding insult to injury. He rose and cautiously approached the fence with the intention of pinching the impudent stranger, suddenly and surreptitiously, and sending her away weeping. As his hand crept between the palings on its wicked mission, the little miss looked at him in friendly fashion and queried:

"What's your name?"

Bryce's hand hesitated. "Bryce Cardigan," he answered gruffly.

"I'm Shirley Sumner," she ventured, "Let's be friends."

"When did you come to live in Sequoia?" he demanded.

"I don't live here. I'm just visiting here with my aunt and uncle. We're staying at the hotel, and there's nobody to play with. My uncle's name is Pennington. So's my aunt's. He's out here buying timber, and we live in Michigan. Do you know the capital of Michigan?"

"Of course I do," he answered. "The capital of Michigan is Chicago."

"Oh, you big stupid! It isn't. It's Detroit."

"'Tain't neither. It's Chicago."

"I live there—so I guess I ought to know. So there!"

Bryce was vanquished, and an acute sense of his imperfections in matters geographical inclined him to end the argument. "Well, maybe you're right," he admitted grudgingly. "Anyhow, what difference does it make?"

She did not answer. Evidently she was desirous of avoiding an argument if possible. Her gaze wandered past Bryce to where his Indian pony stood with her head out the window of her box-stall contemplating her master.

"Oh, what a dear little horse!" Shirley Sumner exclaimed. "Whose is he?"

"'Tain't a he. It's a she. And she belongs to me."

"Do you ride her?"

"Not very often now. I'm getting too heavy for her, so Dad's bought me a horse that weighs nine hundred pounds. Midget only weighs five hundred." He considered her a moment while she gazed in awe upon this man with two horses. "Can you ride a pony?" he asked, for no reason that he was aware of.

She sighed, shaking her head resignedly. "We haven't any room to keep a pony at our house in Detroit," she explained, and added hopefully: "But I'd love to ride on Midget. I suppose I could learn to ride if somebody taught me how."

He looked at her again. At that period of his existence he was inclined to regard girls as a necessary evil. For some immutable reason they existed, and perforce must be borne with, and it was his hope that he would get through life and see as little as possible of the exasperating sex. Nevertheless, as Bryce surveyed this winsome miss through the palings, he was sensible of a sneaking desire to find favour in her eyes—also equally sensible of the fact that the path to that desirable end lay between himself and Midget. He swelled with the importance of one who knows he controls a delicate situation. "Well, I suppose if you want a ride I'll have to give it to you," he grumbled, "although I'm mighty busy this morning."

"Oh, I think you're so nice," she declared.

A thrill shot through him that was akin to pain; with difficulty did he restrain an impulse to dash wildly into the stable and saddle Midget in furious haste. Instead he walked to the barn slowly and with extreme dignity. When he reappeared, he was leading Midget, a little silverpoint runt of a Klamath Indian pony, and Moses, a sturdy pinto cayuse from the cattle ranges over in Trinity County. "I'll have to ride with you," he announced. "Can't let a tenderfoot like you go out alone on Midget."

All aflutter with delightful anticipation, the young lady climbed up on the gate and scrambled into the saddle when Bryce swung the pony broadside to the gate. Then he adjusted the stirrups to fit her, passed a hair rope from Midget's little hackamore to the pommel of Moses' saddle, mounted the pinto, and proceeded with his first adventure as a riding-master. Two hours of his valuable time did he give that morning before the call of duty brought him back to the house and his neglected crop of carrots. When he suggested tactfully, however, that it was now necessary that his guest and Midget separate, a difficulty arose. Shirley Sumner refused point blank to leave the premises. She liked Bryce for his hair and because he had been so kind to her; she was a stranger in Sequoia, and now that she had found an agreeable companion, it was far from her intention to desert him.

So Miss Sumner stayed and helped Bryce weed his carrots, and since as a voluntary labourer she was at least worth her board, at noon Bryce brought her in to Mrs. Tully with a request for luncheon. When he went to the mill to carry in the kindling for the cook, the young lady returned rather sorrowfully to the Hotel Sequoia, with a fervent promise to see him the next day. She did, and Bryce took her for a long ride up into the Valley of the Giants and showed her his mother's grave. The gray squirrels were there, and Bryce gave Shirley a bag of pine-nuts to feed them. Then they put some flowers on the grave, and when they returned to town and Bryce was unsaddling the ponies, Shirley drew Midget's nose down to her and kissed it. Then she commenced to weep rather violently.

"What are you crying about?" Bryce demanded. Girls were so hard to understand.

"I'm go-going h-h-h-home to-morrow," she howled.

He was stricken with dismay and bade her desist from her vain repinings. But her heart was broken, and somehow—Bryce appeared to act automatically—he had his arm around her. "Don't cry, Shirley," he pleaded. "It breaks my heart to see you cry. Do you want Midget? I'll give her to you."

Between sobs Shirley confessed that the prospect of parting with him and not Midget was provocative of her woe. This staggered Bryce and pleased him immensely. And at parting she kissed him good-bye, reiterating her opinion that he was the nicest, kindest boy she had ever met or hoped to meet.

When Shirley and her uncle and aunt boarded the steamer for San Francisco, Bryce stood disconsolate on the dock and waved to Shirley until he could no longer discern her on the deck. Then he went home, crawled up into the haymow and wept, for he had something in his heart and it hurt. He thought of his elfin companion very frequently for a week, and he lost his appetite, very much to Mrs. Tully's concern. Then the steelhead trout began to run in Eel River, and the sweetest event that can occur in any boy's existence—the sudden awakening to the wonder and beauty of life so poignantly realized in his first love-affair—was lost sight of by Bryce. In a month he had forgotten the incident; in six months he had forgotten Shirley Sumner.

CHAPTER IV

The succeeding years of Bryce Cardigan's life, until he completed his high-school studies and went East to Princeton, were those of the ordinary youth in a small and somewhat primitive country town. He made frequent trips to San Francisco with his father, taking passage on the steamer that made bi-weekly trips between Sequoia and the metropolis—as The Sequoia Sentinel always referred to San Francisco. He was an expert fisherman, and the best shot with rifle or shot-gun in the county; he delighted in sports and, greatly to the secret delight of his father showed a profound interest in the latter's business.

Throughout the happy years of Bryce's boyhood his father continued to enlarge and improve his sawmill, to build more schooners, and to acquire more redwood timber. Lands, the purchase of which by Cardigan a decade before had caused his neighbours to impugn his judgment, now developed strategical importance. As a result those lands necessary to consolidate his own holdings came to him at his own price, while his adverse holdings that blocked the logging operations of his competitors went from him—also at his own price. In fact, all well-laid plans matured satisfactorily with the exception of one, and since it has a very definite bearing on the story, the necessity for explaining it is paramount.

Contiguous to Cardigan's logging operations to the east and north of Sequoia, and comparatively close in, lay a block of two thousand acres of splendid timber, the natural, feasible, and inexpensive outlet for which, when it should be logged, was the Valley of the Giants. For thirty years John Cardigan had played a waiting game with the owner of that timber, for the latter was as fully obsessed with the belief that he was going to sell it to John Cardigan at a dollar and a half per thousand feet stumpage as Cardigan was certain he was going to buy it for a dollar a thousand—when he should be ready to do so and not one second sooner. He calculated, as did the owner of the timber, that the time to do business would be a year or two before the last of Cardigan's timber in that section should be gone.

Eventually the time for acquiring more timber arrived. John Cardigan, meeting his neighbour on the street, accosted him thus:

"Look here, Bill: isn't it time we got together on that timber of yours? You know you've been holding it to block me and force me to buy at your figure."

"That's why I bought it," the other admitted smilingly. "Then, before I realized my position, you checkmated me with that quarter-section in the valley, and we've been deadlocked ever since."

"I'll give you a dollar a thousand stumpage for your timber, Bill."

"I want a dollar and a half."

"A dollar is my absolute limit."

"Then I'll keep my timber."

"And I'll keep my money. When I finish logging in my present holdings, I'm going to pull out of that country and log twenty miles south of Sequoia. I have ten thousand acres in the San Hedrin watershed. Remember, Bill, the man who buys your timber will have to log it through my land—and I'm not going to log that quarter-section in the valley. Hence there will be no outlet for your timber in back."

"Not going to log it? Why, what are you going to do with it?"

"I'm just going to let it stay there until I die. When my will is filed for probate, your curiosity will be satisfied—but not until then."

The other laughed. "John," he declared, "you just haven't got the courage to pull out when your timber adjoining mine is gone, and move twenty miles south to the San Hedrin watershed. That will be too expensive a move, and you'll only be biting off your nose to spite your face. Come through with a dollar and a half, John."

"I never bluff, Bill. Remember, if I pull out for the San Hedrin, I'll not abandon my logging-camps there to come back and log your timber. One expensive move is enough for me. Better take a dollar, Bill. It's a good, fair price, as the market on redwood timber is now, and you'll be making an even hundred per cent, on your investment. Remember, Bill, if I don't buy your timber, you'll never log it yourself and neither will anybody else. You'll be stuck with it for the next forty years—and taxes aren't getting any lower. Besides, there's a good deal of pine and fir in there, and you know what a forest fire will do to that."

"I'll hang on a little longer, I think."

"I think so, too," John Cardigan replied. And that night, as was his wont, even though he realized that it was not possible for Bryce to gain a profound understanding of the business problems to which he was heir, John Cardigan discussed the Squaw Creek timber with his son, relating to him the details of his conversation with the owner.

"I suppose he thinks you're bluffing," Bryce commented.

"I'm not, Bryce. I never bluff—that is, I never permit a bluff of mine to be called, and don't you ever do it, either. Remember that, boy. Any time you deliver a verdict, be sure you're in such a position you won't have to reverse yourself. I'm going to finish logging in that district this fall, so if I'm to keep the mill running, I'll have to establish my camps on the San Hedrin watershed right away."

Bryce pondered. "But isn't it cheaper to give him his price on Squaw Creek timber than go logging in the San Hedrin and have to build twenty miles of logging railroad to get your logs to the mill?"

"It would be, son, if I HAD to build the railroad. Fortunately, I do not. I'll just shoot the logs down the hillside to the San Hedrin River and drive them down the stream to a log-boom on tidewater."

"But there isn't enough water in the San Hedrin to float a redwood log, Dad. I've fished there, and I know."

"Quite true—in the summer and fall. But when the winter freshets come on and the snow begins to melt in the spring up in the Yola Bolas, where the San Hedrin has its source, we'll have plenty of water for driving the river. Once we get the logs down to tide-water, we'll raft them and tow them up to the mill. So you see, Bryce, we won't be bothered with the expense of maintaining a logging railroad, as at present."

Bryce looked at his father admiringly. "I guess Dan Keyes is right, Dad," he said. "Dan says you're crazy—like a fox. Now I know why you've been picking up claims in the San Hedrin watershed."

"No, you don't, Bryce. I've never told you, but I'll tell you now the real reason. Humboldt County has no rail connection with the outside world, so we are forced to ship our lumber by water. But some day a railroad will be built in from the south—from San Francisco; and when it comes, the only route for it to travel is through our timber in the San Hedrin Valley. I've accumulated that ten thousand acres for you, my son, for the railroad will never be built in my day. It may come in yours, but I have grown weary waiting for it, and now that my hand is forced, I'm going to start logging there. It doesn't matter, son. You will still be logging there fifty years from now. And when the railroad people come to you for a right of way, my boy, give it to them. Don't charge them a cent. It has always been my policy to encourage the development of this county, and I want you to be a forward-looking, public-spirited citizen. That's why I'm sending you East to college. You've been born and raised in this town, and you must see more of the world. You mustn't be narrow or provincial, because I'm saving up for you, my son, a great many responsibilities, and I want to educate you to meet them bravely and sensibly."

He paused, regarding the boy gravely and tenderly. "Bryce, lad," he said presently, "do you ever wonder why I work so hard and barely manage to spare the time to go camping with you in vacation time?"

"Why don't you take it easy, Dad? You do work awfully hard, and I have wondered about it."

"I have to work hard, my son, because I started something a long time ago, when work was fun. And now I can't let go. I employ too many people who are dependent on me for their bread and butter. When they plan a marriage or the building of a home or the purchase of a cottage organ, they have to figure me in on the proposition. I didn't have a name for the part I played in these people's lives until the other night when I was helping you with your algebra. I'm the unknown quantity."

"Oh, no," Bryce protested. "You're the known quantity."

Cardigan smiled. "Well, maybe I am," he admitted. "I've always tried to be. And if I have succeeded, then you're the unknown quantity, Bryce, because some day you'll have to take my place; they will have to depend upon you when I am gone. Listen to me, son. You're only a boy, and you can't understand everything I tell you now, but I want you to remember what I tell you, and some day understanding will come to you. You mustn't fail the people who work for you—who are dependent upon your strength and brains and enterprises to furnish them with an opportunity for life, liberty, and the pursuit of happiness. When you are the boss of Cardigan's mill, you must keep the wheels turning; you must never shut down the mill or the logging-camps in dull times just to avoid a loss you can stand better than your employees."

His hard, trembling old hand closed over the boy's. "I want you to be a brave and honourable man," he concluded.

True to his word, when John Cardigan finished his logging in his old, original holdings adjacent to Sequoia and Bill Henderson's Squaw Creek timber, he quietly moved south with his Squaw Creek woods-gang and joined the crew already getting out logs in the San Hedrin watershed. Not until then did Bill Henderson realize that John Cardigan had called his bluff—whereat he cursed himself for a fool and a poor judge of human nature. He had tried a hold-up game and had failed; a dollar a thousand feet stumpage was a fair price; for years he had needed the money; and now, when it was too late, he realized his error. Luck was with Henderson, however; for shortly thereafter there came again to Sequoia one Colonel Seth Pennington, a millionaire white-pine operator from Michigan. The Colonel's Michigan lands had been logged off, and since he had had one taste of cheap timber, having seen fifty-cent stumpage go to five dollars, the Colonel, like Oliver Twist, desired some more of the same. On his previous visit to Sequoia he had seen his chance awaiting him in the gradually decreasing market for redwood lumber and the corresponding increase of melancholia in the redwood operators; hence he had returned to Michigan, closed out his business interests there, and returned to Sequoia on the alert for an investment in redwood timber. From a chair-warmer on the porch of the Hotel Sequoia, the Colonel had heard the tale of how stiff-necked old John Cardigan had called the bluff of equally stiff-necked old Bill Henderson; so for the next few weeks the Colonel, under pretense of going hunting or fishing on Squaw Creek, managed to make a fairly accurate cursory cruise of the Henderson timber—following which he purchased it from the delighted Bill for a dollar and a quarter per thousand feet stumpage and paid for it with a certified check. With his check in his hand, Henderson queried:

"Colonel, how do you purpose logging that timber?"

The Colonel smiled. "Oh, I don't intend to log it. When I log timber, it has to be more accessible. I'm just going to hold on and outgame your former prospect, John Cardigan. He needs that timber; he has to have it—and one of these days he'll pay me two dollars for it."

Bill Henderson raised an admonitory finger and shook it under the Colonel's nose. "Hear me, stranger," he warned. "When you know John Cardigan as well as I do, you'll change your tune. He doesn't bluff."

"He doesn't?" The Colonel laughed derisively. "Why, that move of his over to the San Hedrin was the most monumental bluff ever pulled off in this country."

"All right, sir. You wait and see."

"I've seen already. I know."

"How do you know?"

"Well, for one thing, Henderson, I noticed Cardigan has carefully housed his rolling-stock—and he hasn't scrapped his five miles of logging railroad and three miles of spurs."

Old Bill Henderson chewed his quid of tobacco reflectively and spat at a crack in the sidewalk. "No," he replied, "I'll admit he ain't started scrappin' it yet, but I happen to know he's sold the rollin'-stock an' rails to the Freshwater Lumber Company, so I reckon they'll be scrappin' that railroad for him before long."

The Colonel was visibly moved. "If your information is authentic," he said slowly, "I suppose I'll have to build a mill on tidewater and log the timber."

"'Twon't pay you to do that at the present price of redwood lumber."

"I'm in no hurry. I can wait for better times."

"Well, when better times arrive, you'll find that John Cardigan owns the only water-front property on this side of the bay where the water's deep enough to let a ship lie at low tide and load in safety."

"There is deep water across the bay and plenty of water-front property for sale. I'll find a mill-site there and tow my logs across."

"But you've got to dump 'em in the water on this side. Everything north of Cardigan's mill is tide-flat; he owns all the deep-water frontage for a mile south of Sequoia, and after that come more tide-flats. If you dump your logs on these tide-flats, they'll bog down in the mud, and there isn't water enough at high tide to float 'em off or let a tug go in an' snake 'em off."

"You're a discouraging sort of person," the Colonel declared irritably. "I suppose you'll tell me now that I can't log my timber without permission from Cardigan."

Old Bill spat at another crack; his faded blue eyes twinkled mischievously. "No, that's where you've got the bulge on John, Colonel. You can build a logging railroad from the southern fringe of your timber north and up a ten per cent. grade on the far side of the Squaw Creek watershed, then west three miles around a spur of low hills, and then south eleven miles through the level country along the bay shore. If you want to reduce your Squaw Creek grade to say two per cent., figure on ten additional miles of railroad and a couple extra locomotives. You understand, of course, Colonel, that no Locomotive can haul a long trainload of redwood logs up a long, crooked, two per cent. grade. You have to have an extry in back to push."

"Nonsense! I'll build my road from Squaw Creek gulch south through that valley where those whopping big trees grow. That's the natural outlet for the timber. See here:" [graphic]

Colonel Pennington took from his pocket the rough sketch-map of the region which we have reproduced herewith and pointed to the spot numbered "11."

"But that valley ain't logged yet," explained Henderson.

"Don't worry. Cardigan will sell that valley to me—also a right of way down his old railroad grade and through his logged-over lands to tidewater."

"Bet you a chaw o' tobacco he won't. Those big trees in that valley ain't goin' to be cut for no railroad right o' way. That valley's John Cardigan's private park; his wife's buried up there. Why, Colonel, that's the biggest grove of the biggest sequoia sempervirens in the world, an' many's the time I've heard John say he'd almost as lief cut off his right hand as fell one o' his giants, as he calls 'em. I tell you, Colonel, John Cardigan's mighty peculiar about them big trees. Any time he can get a day off he goes up an' looks 'em over."

"But, my very dear sir," the Colonel protested, "if the man will not listen to reason, the courts will make him. I can condemn a right of way, you know."

"We-ll," said old Bill, wagging his head sagely, "mebbe you can, an' then again mebbe you can't. It took me a long time to figger out just where I stood, but mebbe you're quicker at figgers than I am. Anyhow, Colonel, good luck to you, whichever way the cat jumps."

This illuminating conversation had one effect on Colonel Seth Pennington. It decided him to make haste slowly; so without taking the trouble to make the acquaintance of John Cardigan, he returned to Detroit, there to await the next move in this gigantic game of chess.

CHAPTER V

No man is infallible, and in planning his logging operations in the San Hedrin watershed, John Cardigan presently made the discovery that he had erred in judgment. That season, from May to November, his woods-crew put thirty million feet of logs into the San Hedrin River, while the mill sawed on a reserve supply of logs taken from the last of the old choppings adjacent to Squaw Creek. That year, however, the rainfall in the San Hedrin country was fifty per cent. less than normal, and by the first of May of the following year Cardigan's woods-crew had succeeded in driving slightly less than half of the cut of the preceding year to the boom on tidewater at the mouth of the river.

"Unless the Lord'll gi' us a lot more water in the river," the woods-boss McTavish complained, "I dinna see how I'm to keep the mill runnin'." He was taking John Cardigan up the riverbank and explaining the situation. "The heavy butt-logs hae sunk to the bottom," he continued. "Wie a normal head o' water, the lads'll move them, but wi' the wee drappie we have the noo—" He threw up his hamlike hands despairingly.

Three days later a cloud-burst filled the river to the brim; it came at night and swept the river clean of Cardigan's clear logs, An army of Juggernauts, they swept down on the boiling torrent to tidewater, reaching the bay shortly after the tide had commenced to ebb.

Now, a chain is only as strong as its weakest link, and a log-boom is a chaplet of a small logs, linked end to end by means of short chains; hence when the vanguard of logs on the lip of that flood reached the log-boom, the impetus of the charge was too great to be resisted. Straight through the weakest link in this boom the huge saw-logs crashed and out over Humboldt Bar to the broad Pacific. With the ebb tide some of them came back, while others, caught in cross-currents, bobbed about the Bay all night and finally beached at widely scattered points. Out of the fifteen million feet of logs less than three million feet were salvaged, and this task in itself was an expensive operation.

John Cardigan received the news calmly. "Thank God we don't have a cloud-burst more than once in ten years," he remarked to his manager. "However, that is often enough, considering the high cost of this one. Those logs were worth eight dollars a thousand feet, board measure, in the millpond, and I suppose we've lost a hundred thousand dollars' worth."

He turned from the manager and walked away through the drying yard, up the main street of Sequoia, and on into the second-growth timber at the edge of the town. Presently he emerged on the old, decaying skid-road and continued on through his logged-over lands, across the little divide and down into the quarter-section of green timber he had told McTavish not to cut. Once in the Valley of the Giants, he followed a well-worn foot-path to the little amphitheatre, and where the sunlight filtered through like a halo and fell on a plain little white marble monument, he paused and sat down on the now almost decayed sugar-pine windfall.

"I've come for a little comfort, sweetheart," he murmured to her who slept beneath the stone. Then he leaned back against a redwood tree, removed his hat, and closed his eyes, holding his great gray head the while a little to one side in a listening attitude. Long he sat there, a great, time-bitten devotee at the shrine of his comfort; and presently the harried look left his strong, kind face and was replaced by a little prescient smile—the sort of smile worn by one who through bitter years has sought something very, very precious and has at length discovered it.

CHAPTER VI

It was on the day that John Cardigan received the telegram from Bryce saying that, following four years at Princeton and two years of travel abroad, he was returning to Sequoia to take over his redwood heritage—that he discovered that a stranger and not the flesh of his flesh and the blood of his blood was to reap the reward of his fifty years of endeavour. Small wonder, then, that he laid his leonine head upon his desk and wept, silently, as the aged and helpless weep.

For a long time he sat there lethargic with misery. Eventually he roused himself, reached for the desk telephone, and pressed a button on the office exchange-station. His manager, one Thomas Sinclair, answered. "Thomas," he said calmly, "you know, of course, that Bryce is coming home. Tell George to take the big car and go over to Red Bluff for him."

"I'll attend to it, Mr Cardigan. Anything else?"

"Yes, but I'll wait until Bryce gets home."

George Sea Otter, son of Bryce Cardigan's old half-breed nurse, was a person in whose nature struggled the white man's predilection for advertisement and civic pride and the red man's instinct for adornment. For three years he had been old man Cardigan's chauffeur and man-of-all-work about the latter's old-fashioned home, and in the former capacity he drove John Cardigan's single evidence of extravagance—a Napier car, which was very justly regarded by George Sea Otter as the king of automobiles, since it was the only imported car in the county. Upon receipt of orders, therefore, from Sinclair, to drive the Napier over to Red Bluff and meet his future boss and one-time playfellow, George Sea Otter arrayed himself in a pair of new black corduroy trousers, yellow button shoes, a blue woollen shirt with a large scarlet silk handkerchief tied around the neck, a pair of beaded buckskin gloves with fringe dependent from the gauntlet, and a broad white beaver hat with a rattlesnake-skin band. Across the windshield of the Napier he fastened an orange-coloured pennant bearing in bright green letters the legend: MY CITY—SEQUOIA. As a safety-first precaution against man and beast en route, he buckled a gun-scabbard to the spare tires on the running-board and slipped a rifle into the scabbard within quick and easy reach of his hand; and arrayed thus, George descended upon Red Bluff at the helm of the king of automobiles.

When the overland train coasted into Red Bluff and slid to a grinding halt, Bryce Cardigan saw that the Highest Living Authority had descended from the train also. He had elected to designate her thus in the absence of any information anent her Christian and family names, and for the further reason that quite obviously she was a very superior person. He had a vague suspicion that she was the kind of girl in whose presence a man always feels that he must appear on parade—one of those alert, highly intelligent young women so extremely apt to reduce an ordinarily intelligent young man to a state of gibbering idiocy or stupid immobility.

Bryce had travelled in the same car with the Highest Living Authority from Chicago and had made up his mind by observation that with a little encouragement she could be induced to mount a soap-box and make a speech about Women's Rights; that when her native State should be granted equal suffrage she would run for office or manage somebody's political campaign; that she could drive an automobile and had probably been arrested for speeding; that she could go around any golf links in the country in ninety and had read Maeterlinck and enjoyed it.

Bryce could see that she was the little daughter of some large rich man. The sparsity of jewellery and the rich simplicity of her attire proved that, and moreover she was accompanied by a French maid to whom she spoke French in a manner which testified that before acquiring the French maid she had been in the custody of a French nurse. She possessed poise. For the rest, she had wonderful jet-black hair, violet eyes, and milk-white skin, a correct nose but a somewhat generous mouth, Bryce guessed she was twenty or twenty-one years old and that she had a temper susceptible of being aroused. On the whole, she was rather wonderful but not dazzling—at least, not to Bryce Cardigan. He told himself she merely interested him as a type—whatever he meant by that.

The fact that this remarkable young woman had also left the train at Red Bluff further interested him, for he knew Red Bluff and while giving due credit to the many lovely damsels of that ambitious little city, Bryce had a suspicion that no former Red Bluff girl would dare to invade the old home town with a French maid. He noted, as further evidence of the correctness of his assumption, that the youthful baggage-smasher at the station failed to recognize her and was evidently dazzled when, followed by the maid struggling with two suit-cases, she approached him and in pure though alien English (the Italian A predominated) inquired the name and location of the best hotel and the hour and point of departure of the automobile stage for San Hedrin. The youth had answered her first question and was about to answer the second when George Sea Otter, in all his barbaric splendour, came pussy-footing around the corner of the station in old man Cardigan's regal touring-car.

The Highest Living Authority, following the gaze of the baggage-smasher, turned and beheld George Sea Otter. Beyond a doubt he was of the West westward. She had heard that California stage-drivers were picturesque fellows, and in all probability the displacing of the old Concord coach of the movie-thriller in favour of the motor-stage had not disturbed the idiosyncrasies of the drivers in their choice of raiment. She noted the rifle-stock projecting from the scabbard, and a vision of a stage hold-up flashed across her mind. Ah, yes, of course—the express messenger's weapon, no doubt! And further to clinch her instant assumption that here was the Sequoia motor-stage, there was the pennant adorning the wind-shield!

Dismissing the baggage-smasher with a gracious smile, the Highest Living Authority approached George Sea Otter, noting, the while, further evidence that this car was a public conveyance, for the young man who had been her fellow-passenger was heading toward the automobile also. She heard him say:

"Hello, George, you radiant red rascal! I'm mighty glad to see you, boy. Shake!"

They shook, George Sea Otter's dark eyes and white teeth flashing pleasurably. Bryce tossed his bag into the tonneau; the half-breed opened the front door; and the young master had his foot on the running-board and was about to enter the car when a soft voice spoke at his elbow:

"Driver, this is the stage for Sequoia, is it not?"

George Sea Otter could scarcely credit his auditory nerves. "This car?" he demanded bluntly, "this—the Sequoia stage! Take a look, lady. This here's a Napier imported English automobile. It's a private car and belongs to my boss here."

"I'm so sorry I slandered your car," she replied demurely. "I observed the pennant on the wind-shield, and I thought—"

Bryce Cardigan turned and lifted his hat.

"Quite naturally, you thought it was the Sequoia stage," he said to her. He turned a smoldering glance upon George Sea Otter. "George," he declared ominously, but with a sly wink that drew the sting from his words, "if you're anxious to hold down your job the next time a lady speaks to you and asks you a simple question, you answer yes or no and refrain from sarcastic remarks. Don't let your enthusiasm for this car run away with you." He faced the girl again. "Was it your intention to go out to Sequoia on the next trip of the stage?"

She nodded.

"That means you will have to wait here three days until the stage returns from Sequoia," Bryce replied.

"I realized, of course, that we would arrive here too late to connect with the stage if it maintained the customary schedule for its departure," she explained, "but it didn't occur to me that the stage-driver wouldn't wait until our train arrived. I had an idea his schedule was rather elastic."

"Stage-drivers have no imagination, to speak of," Bryce assured her. To himself he remarked: "She's used to having people wait on her."

A shade of annoyance passed over the classic features of the Highest Living Authority. "Oh, dear," she complained, "how fearfully awkward! Now I shall have to take the next train to San Francisco and book passage on the steamer to Sequoia—and Marcelle is such a poor sailor. Oh, dear!"

Bryce had an inspiration and hastened to reveal it.

"We are about to start for Sequoia now, although the lateness of our start will compel us to put up tonight at the rest-house on the south fork of Trinity River and continue the journey in the morning. However, this rest-house is eminently respectable and the food and accommodations are extraordinarily good for mountains; so, if an invitation to occupy the tonneau of my car will not be construed as an impertinence, coming as it does from a total stranger, you are at liberty to regard this car as to all intents and purposes the public conveyance which so scandalously declined to wait for you this morning."

She looked at him searchingly for a brief instant: then with a peculiarly winning smile and a graceful inclination of her head she thanked him and accepted his hospitality—thus:

"Why, certainly not! You are very kind, and I shall be eternally grateful."

"Thank you for that vote of confidence. It makes me feel that I have your permission to introduce myself. My name is Bryce Cardigan, and I live in Sequoia when I'm at home."

"Of Cardigan's Redwoods?" she questioned. He nodded. "I've heard of you, I think," she continued. "I am Shirley Sumner."

"You do not live in Sequoia."

"No, but I'm going to hereafter. I was there about ten years ago."

He grinned and thrust out a great hand which she surveyed gravely for a minute before inserting hers in it. "I wonder," he said, "if it is to be my duty to give you a ride every time you come to Sequoia? The last time you were there you wheedled me into giving you a ride on my pony, an animal known as Midget. Do you, by any chance, recall that incident?"

She looked up at him wonderingly. "Why—why you're the boy with the beautiful auburn hair," she declared. He lifted his hat and revealed his thick thatch in all its glory. "I'm not so sensitive about it now," he explained. "When we first met, reference to my hair was apt to rile me." He shook her little hand with cordial good-nature. "What a pity it wasn't possible for us to renew acquaintance on the train, Miss Sumner!"

"Better late than never, Mr. Cardigan, considering the predicament in which you found me. What became of Midget?"

"Midget, I regret to state, made a little pig of herself one day and died of acute indigestion. She ate half a sack of carrots, and knowing full well that she was eating forbidden fruit, she bolted them, and for her failure to Fletcherize—but speaking of Fletcherizing, did you dine aboard the train?"

She nodded. "So did I, Miss Sumner; hence I take it that you are quite ready to start."

"Quite, Mr. Cardigan."

"Then we'll drift. George, suppose you pile Miss Sumner's hand-baggage in the tonneau and then pile in there yourself and keep Marcelle company. I'll drive; and you can sit up in front with me, Miss Sumner, snug behind the wind-shield where you'll not be blown about."

"I'm sure this is going to be a far pleasanter journey than the stage could possibly have afforded," she said graciously as Bryce slipped in beside her and took the wheel.

"You are very kind to share the pleasure with me, Miss Sumner." He went through his gears, and the car glided away on its journey. "By the way," he said suddenly as he turned west toward the distant blue mountains of Trinity County, "how did you happen to connect me with Cardigan's redwoods?"

"I've heard my uncle, Colonel Seth Pennington, speak of them."

"Colonel Seth Pennington means nothing in my young life. I never heard of him before; so I dare say he's a newcomer in our country. I've been away six years," he added in explanation.

"We're from Michigan. Uncle was formerly in the lumber business there, but he's logged out now."

"I see. So he came West, I suppose, and bought a lot of redwood timber cheap from some old croaker who never could see any future to the redwood lumber industry. Personally, I don't think he could have made a better investment. I hope I shall have the pleasure of making his acquaintance when I deliver you to him. Perhaps you may be a neighbour of mine. Hope so."

At this juncture George Sea Otter, who had been an interested listener to the conversation, essayed a grunt from the rear seat. Instantly, to Shirley

Sumner's vast surprise, her host grunted also; whereupon George Sea Otter broke into a series of grunts and guttural exclamations which evidently appeared quite intelligible to her host, for he slowed down to five miles an hour and cocked one ear to the rear; apparently he was profoundly interested in whatever information his henchman had to impart. When George Sea Otter finished his harangue, Bryce nodded and once more gave his attention to tossing the miles behind him.

"What language was that?" Shirley Sumner inquired, consumed with curiosity.

"Digger Indian," he replied. "George's mother was my nurse, and he and I grew up together. So I can't very well help speaking the language of the tribe."

They chattered volubly on many subjects for the first twenty miles; then the road narrowed and commenced to climb steadily, and thereafter Bryce gave all of his attention to the car, for a deviation of a foot from the wheel-rut on the outside of the road would have sent them hurtling over the grade into the deep-timbered canons below. Their course led through a rugged wilderness, widely diversified and transcendently beautiful, and the girl was rather glad of the opportunity to enjoy it in silence. Also by reason of the fact that Bryce's gaze never wavered from the road immediately in front of the car, she had a chance to appraise him critically while pretending to look past him to the tumbled, snow-covered ranges to their right.

She saw a big, supple, powerful man of twenty-five or six, with the bearing and general demeanour of one many years his elder. His rich, dark auburn hair was wavy, and a curling lock of it had escaped from the band of his cap at the temple; his eyes were brown to match his hair and were the striking feature of a strong, rugged countenance, for they were spaced at that eminently proper interval which proclaims an honest man. His nose was high, of medium thickness and just a trifle long—the nose of a thinker. His ears were large, with full lobes—the ears of a generous man. The mouth, full-lipped but firm, the heavy jaw and square chin, the great hands (most amazingly free from freckles) denoted the man who would not avoid a fight worth while. Indeed, while the girl was looking covertly at him, she saw his jaw set and a sudden, fierce light leap up in his eyes, which at first sight had seemed to her rather quizzical. Subconsciously he lifted one hand from the wheel and clenched it; he wagged his head a very little bit; consequently she knew his thoughts were far away, and for some reason, not quite clear to her, she would have preferred that they weren't. As a usual thing, young men did not go wool-gathering in her presence; so she sought to divert his thoughts to present company.

"What a perfectly glorious country!" she exclaimed. "Can't we stop for just a minute to appreciate it?"

"Yes," he replied abstractedly as he descended from the car and sat at her feet while she drank in the beauty of the scene, "it's a he country; I love it, and I'm glad to get back to it."

Upon their arrival at the rest-house, however, Bryce cheered up, and during dinner was very attentive and mildly amusing, although Shirley's keen wits assured her that this was merely a clever pose and sustained with difficulty. She was confirmed in this assumption when, after sitting with him a little on the porch after dinner, she complained of being weary and bade him good-night. She had scarcely left him when he called:

"George!"

The half-breed slid out of the darkness and sat down beside him. A moment later, through the open window of her room just above the porch where Bryce and George Sea Otter sat, Shirley heard the former say:

"George, when did you first notice that my father's sight was beginning to fail?"

"About two years ago, Bryce."

"What made you notice it?"

"He began to walk with his hands held out in front of him, and sometimes he lifted his feet too high."

"Can he see at all now, George?"

"Oh, yes, a little bit—enough to make his way to the office and back."

"Poor old governor! George, until you told me this afternoon, I hadn't heard a word about it. If I had, I never would have taken that two-year jaunt around the world."

George Sea Otter grunted. "That's what your father said, too. So he wouldn't tell you, and he ordered everybody else to keep quiet about it. Myself—well, I didn't want you to go home and not know it until you met him."

"That was mighty kind and considerate of you, George. And you say this man Colonel Pennington and my father have been having trouble?"

"Yes—" Here George Sea Otter gracefully unburdened himself of a fervent curse directed at Shirley's avuncular relative; whereupon that young lady promptly left the window and heard no more.

They were on the road again by eight o'clock next morning, and just as Cardigan's mill was blowing the six o'clock whistle, Bryce stopped the car at the head of the street leading down to the water-front. "I'll let you drive now, George," he informed the silent Sea Otter. He turned to Shirley Sumner. "I'm going to leave you now," he said. "Thank you for riding over from Red Bluff with me. My father never leaves the office until the whistle blows, and so I'm going to hurry down to that little building you see at the end of the street and surprise him."

He stepped out on the running-board, stood there a moment, and extended his hand. Shirley had commenced a due and formal expression of her gratitude for having been delivered safely in Sequoia, when George Sea Otter spoke:

"Here comes John Cardigan," he said.

"Drive Miss Sumner around to Colonel Pennington's house," Bryce ordered, and even while he held Shirley's hand, he turned to catch the first glimpse of his father. Shirley followed his glance and saw a tall, powerfully built old man coming down the street with his hands thrust a little in front of him, as if for protection from some invisible assailant.

"Oh, my poor old father!" she heard Bryce Cardigan murmur. "My dear old pal! And I've let him grope in the dark for two years!"

He released her hand and leaped from the car. "Dad!" he called. "It is I— Bryce. I've come home to you at last."

The slightly bent figure of John Cardigan straightened with a jerk; he held out his arms, trembling with eagerness, and as the car continued on to the Pennington house Shirley looked back and saw Bryce folded in his father's embrace. She did not, however, hear the heart-cry with which the beaten old man welcomed his boy.

"Sonny, sonny—oh, I'm so glad you're back. I've missed you. Bryce, I'm whipped—I've lost your heritage. Oh, son! I'm old—I can't fight any more. I'm blind—I can't see my enemies. I've lost your redwood trees—even your mother's Valley of the Giants."

And he commenced to weep for the third time in fifty years. And when the aged and helpless weep, nothing is more terrible. Bryce Cardigan said no word, but held his father close to his great heart and laid his cheek gently against the old man's, tenderly as a woman might. And presently, from that silent communion of spirit, each drew strength and comfort. As the shadows fell in John Cardigan's town, they went home to the house on the hill.

CHAPTER VII

Shirley Sumner's eyes were still moist when George Sea Otter, in obedience to the instructions of his youthful master, set her, the French maid, and their hand-baggage down on the sidewalk in front of Colonel Seth Pennington's house. The half-breed hesitated a moment, undecided whether he would carry the hand-baggage up to the door or leave that task for a Pennington retainer; then he noted the tear-stains on the cheeks of his fair passenger. Instantly he took up the hand-baggage, kicked open the iron gate, and preceded Shirley up the cement walk to the door.

"Just wait a moment, if you please, George," Shirley said as he set the baggage down and started back for the car. He turned and beheld her extracting a five-dollar bill from her purse. "For you, George," she continued. "Thank you so much."

In all his life George Sea Otter had never had such an experience—he, happily, having been raised in a country where, with the exception of waiters, only a pronounced vagrant expects or accepts a gratuity from a woman. He took the bill and fingered it curiously; then his white blood asserted itself and he handed the bill back to Shirley.

"Thank you," he said respectfully. "If you are a man—all right. But from a lady—no. I am like my boss. I work for you for nothing."

Shirley did not understand his refusal, but her instinctive tact warned her not to insist. She returned the bill to her purse, thanked him again, and turned quickly to hide the slight flush of annoyance. George Sea Otter noted it.

"Lady," he said with great dignity, "at first I did not want to carry your baggage. I did not want to walk on this land." And with a sweeping gesture he indicated the Pennington grounds. "Then you cry a little because my boss is feeling bad about his old man. So I like you better. The old man—well, he has been like father to me and my mother—and we are Indians. My brothers, too—they work for him. So if you like my boss and his old man, George Sea Otter would go to hell for you pretty damn' quick. You bet you my life!"

"You're a very good boy, George," she replied, with difficulty repressing a smile at his blunt but earnest avowal. "I am glad the Cardigans have such an honest, loyal servant."

George Sea Otter's dark face lighted with a quick smile. "Now you pay me," he replied and returned to the car.

The door opened, and a Swedish maid stood in the entrance regarding her stolidly. "I'm Miss Sumner," Shirley informed her. "This is my maid

- 33 -

Marcelle. Help her in with the hand-baggage." She stepped into the hall and called: "Ooh-hooh! Nunky-dunk!"

"Ship ahoy!" An answering call came to her from the dining room, across the entrance-hall, and an instant later Colonel Seth Pennington stood in the doorway, "Bless my whiskers! Is that you, my dear?" he cried, and advanced to greet her. "Why, how did you get here, Shirley? I thought you'd missed the stage."

She presented her cheek for his kiss. "So I did, Uncle, but a nice red-haired young man named Bryce Cardigan found me in distress at Red Bluff, picked me up in his car, and brought me here." She sniffed adorably. "I'm so hungry," she declared, "and here I am, just in time for dinner. Is my name in the pot?"

"It isn't, Shirley, but it soon will be. How perfectly bully to have you with me again, my dear! And what a charming young lady you've grown to be since I saw you last! You're—why, you've been crying! By Jove, I had no idea you'd be so glad to see me again."

She could not forego a sly little smile at his egoism.

"You're looking perfectly splendid, Uncle Seth," she parried.

"And I'm feeling perfectly splendid. This is a wonderful country, Shirley, and everything is going nicely with me here. By the way, who did you say picked you up in his car?"

"Bryce Cardigan. Do you know him?"

"No, we haven't met. Son of old John Cardigan, I dare say. I've heard of him. He's been away from Sequoia for quite a while, I believe."

"Yes; he was abroad for two years after he was graduated from Princeton."

"Hum-m-m! Well, it's about time he came home to take care of that stiff-necked old father of his." He stepped to the bell and pressed it, and the butler answered. "Set a place at dinner for Miss Shirley, James," he ordered. "Thelma will show you your rooms, Shirley. I was just about to sit down to dinner. I'll wait for you."

While Shirley was in the living room Colonel Pennington's features wore an expression almost pontifical, but when she had gone, the atmosphere of paternalism and affection which he radiated faded instantly. The Colonel's face was in repose now—cold, calculating, vaguely repellent. He scowled slightly.

"Now, isn't that the devil's luck?" he soliloquized. "Young Cardigan is probably the only man in Sequoia—dashed awkward if they should become interested in each other—at this time. Everybody in town, from lumberjacks to bankers, has told me what a fine fellow Bryce Cardigan is. They say he's good-looking; certainly he is educated and has acquired some worldly polish—just the kind of young fellow Shirley will find interesting and welcome company in a town like this. Many things can happen in a year— and it will be a year before I can smash the Cardigans. Damn it!"

CHAPTER VII

Along the well-remembered streets of Sequoia Bryce Cardigan and his father walked arm in arm, their progress continuously interrupted by well-meaning but impulsive Sequoians who insisted upon halting the pair to shake hands with Bryce and bid him welcome home. In the presence of those third parties the old man quickly conquered the agitation he had felt at this long-deferred meeting with his son, and when presently they left the business section of the town and turned into a less-frequented street, his emotion assumed the character of a quiet joy, evidenced in a more erect bearing and a firmer tread, as if he strove, despite his seventy-six years, not to appear incongruous as he walked beside his splendid son.

"I wish I could see you more clearly," he said presently. His voice as well as his words expressed profound regret, but there was no hint of despair or heartbreak now.

Bryce, who up to this moment had refrained from discussing his father's misfortunes, drew the old man a little closer to his side.

"What's wrong with your eyes, pal?" he queried. He did not often address his parent, after the fashion of most sons, as "Father," "Dad" or "Pop." They were closer to each other than that, and a rare sense of perfect comradeship found expression, on Bryce's part, in such salutations as "pal," "partner" and, infrequently, "old sport." When arguing with his father, protesting with him or affectionately scolding him, Bryce, with mock seriousness, sometimes called the old man John Cardigan.

"Cataracts, son," his father answered. "Merely the penalty of old age."

"But can't something be done about it?" demanded Bryce. "Can't they be cured somehow or other?"

"Certainly they can. But I shall have to wait until they are completely matured and I have become completely blind; then a specialist will perform an operation on my eyes, and in all probability my sight will be restored for a few years. However, I haven't given the matter a great deal of consideration. At my age one doesn't find very much difficulty in making the best of everything. And I am about ready to quit now. I'd like to, in fact; I'm tired."

"Oh, but you can't quit until you've seen your redwoods again," Bryce reminded him. "I suppose it's been a long time since you've visited the Valley of the Giants; your long exile from the wood-goblins has made you a trifle gloomy, I'm afraid."

John Cardigan nodded. "I haven't seen them in a year and a half, Bryce. Last time I was up, I slipped between the logs on the old skid-road and like to broke my old fool neck. But even that wasn't warning enough for me. I cracked right on into the timber and got lost."

"Lost? Poor old partner! And what did you do about it?"

"The sensible thing, my boy. I just sat down under a tree and waited for George Sea Otter to trail me and bring me home."

"And did he find you? Or did you have to spend the night in the woods?"

John Cardigan smiled humorously. "I did not. Along about sunset George found me. Seems he'd been following me all the time, and when I sat down he waited to make certain whether I was lost or just taking a rest where I could be quiet and think."

"I've been leaving to an Indian the fulfillment of my duty," Bryce murmured bitterly.

"No, no, son. You have never been deficient in that," the old man protested.

"Why didn't you have the old skid-road planked with refuse lumber so you wouldn't fall through? And you might have had the woods-boss swamp a new trail into the timber and fence it on both sides, in order that you might feel your way along."

"Yes, quite true," admitted the old man. "But then, I don't spend money quite as freely as I used to, Bryce. I consider carefully now before I part with a dollar."

"Pal, it wasn't fair of you to make me stay away so long. If I had only known—if I had remotely suspected—"

"You'd have spoiled everything—of course. Don't scold me, son. You're all I have now, and I couldn't bear to send for you until you'd had your fling." His trembling old hand crept over and closed upon his boy's hand, so firm but free from signs of toil. "It was my pleasure, Bryce," he continued, "and you wouldn't deny me my choice of sport, would you? Remember, lad, I never had a boyhood; I never had a college education, and the only real travel I have ever had was when I worked my way around Cape Horn as a foremast hand, and all I saw then was water and hardships; all I've seen since is my little world here in Sequoia and in San Francisco."

"You've sacrificed enough—too much—for me, Dad."

"It pleased me to give you all the advantages I wanted and couldn't afford until I was too old and too busy to consider them. Besides, it was your mother's wish. We made plans for you before you were born, and I promised her—ah, well, why be a cry-baby? I knew I could manage until you were ready to settle down to business. And you HAVE enjoyed your little run, haven't you?" he concluded wistfully.

"I have, Dad." Bryce's great hand closed over the back of his father's neck; he shook the old man with mock ferocity. "Stubborn old lumberjack!" he chided.

John Cardigan shook with an inward chuckle, for the loving abuse his boy had formed a habit of heaping on him never failed to thrill him. Instinctively Bryce had realized that to-night obvious sympathy copiously expressed was not the medicine for his father's bruised spirit; hence he elected to regard the latter's blindness as a mere temporary annoyance, something to be considered lightly, if at all; and it was typical of him now that the subject had been discussed briefly, to resolve never to refer to it again. He released his hold on the old man's neck and tapped the latter's gray head lightly, while with his tongue he made hollow-sounding noises against the roof of his mouth.

"Ha! I thought so," he declared. "After your fifty-odd years in the lumber business your head has become packed with sawdust—"

"Be serious and talk to me, Bryce."

"I ought to send you to bed without your supper. Talk to you? You bet I'll talk to you, John Cardigan; and I'll tell you things, too, you scandalous bunko-steerer. To-morrow morning I'm going to put a pair of overalls on you, arm you with a tin can and a swab, and set you to greasing the skidways. Partner, you've deceived me."

"Oh, nonsense. If I had whimpered, that would only have spoiled everything."

"Nevertheless, you were forced to cable me to hurry home."

"I summoned you the instant I realized I was going to need you."

"No, you didn't, John Cardigan. You summoned me because, for the first time in your life, you were panicky and let yourself get out of hand."

His father nodded slowly. "And you aren't over it yet," Bryee continued, his voice no longer bantering but lowered affectionately. "What's the trouble, Dad? Trot out your old panic and let me inspect it. Trouble must be very real when it gets my father on the run."

"It is, Bryce, very real indeed. As I remarked before, I've lost your heritage for you." He sighed. "I waited till you would be able to come home and settle down to business; now you're home, and there isn't any business to settle down to."

Bryce chuckled, for he was indeed far from being worried over business matters, his consideration now being entirely for his father's peace of mind. "All right," he retorted, "Father has lost his money and we'll have to let the servants go and give up the old home. That part of it is settled; and weak, anemic, tenderly nurtured little Bryce Cardigan must put his turkey on his back and go into the woods looking for a job as lumberjack ... Busted, eh? Did I or did I not hear the six o'clock whistle blow at the mill? Bet you a dollar I did."

"Oh, I have title to everything—yet."

"How I do have to dig for good news! Then it appears we still have a business; indeed, we may always have a business, for the very fact that it is going but not quite gone implies a doubt as to its ultimate departure, and perhaps we may yet scheme a way to retain it."

"Oh, my boy, when I think of my years of toil and scheming, of the big dreams I dreamed—"

"Belay all! If we can save enough out of the wreck to insure you your customary home comforts, I shan't cry, partner. I have a profession to fall back on. Yes, sirree. I own a sheep-skin, and it says I'm an electrical and civil engineer."

"What!"

"I said it. An electrical and civil engineer. Slipped one over on you at college, John Cardigan, when all the time you thought I was having a good time. Thought I'd come home and surprise you."

"Bu-bu-but—"

"It drives me wild to have a man sputter at me. I'm an electrical and civil engineer, I tell you, and my two years of travel have been spent studying the installation and construction of big plants abroad." He commenced to chuckle softly. "I've known for years that our sawmill was a debilitated old coffee-grinder and would have to be rebuilt, so I wanted to know how to rebuild it. And I've known for years that some day I might have to build a logging railroad—"

"My dear boy! And you've got your degree?"

"Partner, I have a string of letters after my name like the tail of a comet."

"You comfort me," the old man answered simply. "I have reproached myself with the thought that I reared you with the sole thought of making a lumberman out of you—and when I saw your lumber business slipping through my fingers—"

"You were sorry I didn't have a profession to fall back on, eh? Or were you fearful lest you had raised the usual rich man's son? If the latter, you did not compliment me, pal. I've never forgotten how hard you always strove to impress me with a sense of the exact weight of my responsibility as your successor."

"How big are you now?" his father queried suddenly.

"Well, sir," Bryce answered, for his father's pleasure putting aside his normal modesty, "I'm six feet two inches tall, and I weigh two hundred pounds in the pink of condition. I have a forty-eight-inch chest, with five and a half inches chest-expansion, and a reach as long as a gorilla's. My underpinning is good, too; I'm not one of these fellows with spidery legs and a barrel-chest. I can do a hundred yards in ten seconds; I'm no slouch of a swimmer; and at Princeton they say I made football history. And in spite of it all, I haven't an athletic heart."

"That is very encouraging, my boy—very. Ever do any boxing?"

"Quite a little. I'm fairly up in the manly art of self-defence."

"That's good. And I suppose you did some wrestling at your college gymnasium, did you not?"

"Naturally. I went in for everything my big carcass could stand."

The old man wagged his head approvingly, and they had reached the gate of the Cardigan home before he spoke again. "There's a big buck woods-boss up in Pennington's camp," he remarked irrelevantly. "He's a French Canadian imported from northern Michigan by Colonel Pennington. I dare say he's the only man in this country who measures up to you physically. He can fight with his fists and wrestle right cleverly, I'm told. His name is Jules Rondeau, and he's top dog among the lumberjacks. They say he's the strongest man in the county." He unlatched the gate. "Folks used to say that about me once," he continued wistfully. "Ah, if I could have my eyes to see you meet Jules Rondeau!"

The front portal of the quaint old Cardigan residence opened, and a silver-haired lady came out on the porch and hailed Bryce. She was Mrs. Tully, John Cardigan's old housekeeper, and almost a mother to Bryce. "Oh, here's my boy!" she cried, and a moment later found herself encircled by Bryce's arms and saluted with a hearty kiss.

As he stepped into the familiar entrance-hall, Bryce paused, raised his head and sniffed suspiciously, like a bird-dog. Mrs. Tully, arms akimbo, watched him pleasurably. "I smell something," he declared, and advanced a step down the hall for another sniff; then, in exact imitation of a foxhound, he gave tongue and started for the kitchen. Mrs. Tully, waddling after, found him "pointing" two hot blackberry pies which had but a few minutes previous been taken from the oven. He was baying lugubriously.

"They're wild blackberries, too," Mrs. Tully announced pridefully. "I remembered how fond you used to be of wild-blackberry pie—so I phoned up to the logging-camp and had the woods-boss send a man out to pick them."

"I'm still a pie-hound, Mrs. Tully, and you're still the same dear, thoughtful soul. I'm so glad now that I had sense enough to think of you before I turned my footsteps toward the setting sun." He patted her gray head. "Mrs. T.," he declared, "I've brought you a nice big collar of Irish lace—bought it in Belfast, b'gosh. It comes down around your neck and buckles right here with an old ivory cameo I picked up in Burma and which formerly was the property of a Hindu queen."

Mrs. Tully simpered with pleasure and protested that her boy was too kind. "You haven't changed a single speck," she concluded proudly.

"Has the pie?"

"I should say not."

"How many did you make?"

"Two."

"May I have one all for myself, Mrs. Tully?"

"Indeed you may, my dear."

"Thank you, but I do not want it for myself. Mrs. Tully, will you please wrap one of those wonderful pies in a napkin and the instant George Sea Otter comes in with the car, tell him to take the pie over to Colonel Pennington's house and deliver it to Miss Sumner? There's a girl who doubtless thinks she has tasted pie in her day, and I want to prove to her that she hasn't." He selected a card from his card-case, sat down, and wrote:

Dear Miss Sumner:

Here is a priceless hot wild-blackberry pie, especially manufactured in my honour. It is so good I wanted you to have some. In all your life you have never tasted anything like it.

Sincerely, BRYCE CARDIGAN.

He handed the card to Mrs. Tully and repaired to his old room to remove the stains of travel before joining his father at dinner.

Some twenty minutes later his unusual votive offering was delivered by George Sea Otter to Colonel Pennington's Swedish maid, who promptly brought it in to the Colonel and Shirley Sumner, who were even then at dinner in the Colonel's fine burl-redwood-panelled dining room. Miss Sumner's amazement was so profound that for fully a minute she was mute, contenting herself with scrutinizing alternately the pie and the card that accompanied it. Presently she handed the card to her uncle, who affixed his pince-nez and read the epistle with deliberation.

"Isn't this young Cardigan a truly remarkable young man, Shirley?" he declared. "Why, I have never heard of anything like his astounding action. If he had sent you over an armful of American Beauty roses from his father's old-fashioned garden, I could understand it, but an infernal blackberry pie! Good heavens!"

"I told you he was different," she replied. To the Colonel's amazement she did not appear at all amused.

Colonel Pennington poked a fork through the delicate brown crust. "I wonder if it is really as good as he says it is, Shirley."

"Of course. If it wasn't, he wouldn't have sent it."

"How do you know?"

"By intuition," she replied. And she cut into the pie and helped the Colonel to a quadrant of it.

"That was a genuine hayseed faux-pas," announced the Colonel a few moments later as Shirley was pouring coffee from a samovar-shaped percolator in the library. "The idea of anybody who has enjoyed the advantages that fellow has, sending a hot blackberry pie to a girl he has just met!"

"Yes, the idea!" she echoed. "I find it rather charming."

"You mean amusing."

"I said 'charming.' Bryce Cardigan is a man with the heart and soul of a boy, and I think it was mighty sweet of him to share his pie with me. If he had sent roses, I should have suspected him of trying to 'rush' me, but the fact that he sent a blackberry pie proves that he's just a natural, simple, sane, original citizen—just the kind of person a girl can have for a dear friend without incurring the risk of having to marry him."

"I repeat that this is most extraordinary."

"Only because it is an unusual thing for a young man to do, although, after all, why shouldn't he send me a blackberry pie if he thought a blackberry pie would please me more than an armful of roses? Besides, he may send the roses to-morrow."

"Most extraordinary!" the Colonel reiterated.

"What should one expect from such an extraordinary creature? He's an extraordinary fine-looking young man, with an extraordinary scowl and an extraordinary crinkly smile that is friendly and generous and free from masculine guile. Why, I think he's just the kind of man who WOULD send a girl a blackberry pie."

The Colonel noticed a calm little smile fringing her generous mouth. He wished he could tell, by intuition, what she was thinking about—and what effect a hot wild-blackberry pie was ultimately to have upon the value of his minority holding in the Laguna Grande Lumber Company.

CHAPTER IX

Not until dinner was finished and father and son had repaired to the library for their coffee and cigars did Bryce Cardigan advert to the subject of his father's business affairs.

"Well, John Cardigan," he declared comfortably, "to-day is Friday. I'll spend Saturday and Sunday in sinful sloth and the renewal of old acquaintance, and on Monday I'll sit in at your desk and give you a long-deferred vacation. How about that programme, pard?"

"Our affairs are in such shape that they could not possibly be hurt or bettered, no matter who takes charge of them now," Cardigan replied bitterly. "We're about through. I waited too long and trusted too far; and now—well, in a year we'll be out of business."

"Suppose you start at the beginning and tell me everything right to the end. George Sea Otter informed me that you've been having trouble with this Johnny-come-lately, Colonel Pennington. Is he the man who has us where the hair is short?"

The old man nodded.

"The Squaw Creek timber deal, eh?" Bryce suggested.

Again the old man nodded. "You wrote me all about that," Bryce continued. "You had him blocked whichever way he turned—so effectually blocked, in fact, that the only pleasure he has derived from his investment since is the knowledge that he owns two thousand acres of timber with the exclusive right to pay taxes on it, walk in it, look at it and admire it—in fact, do everything except log it, mill it, and realize on his investment. It must make him feel like a bally jackass."

"On the other hand," his father reminded him, "no matter what the Colonel's feeling on that score may be, misery loves company, and not until I had pulled out of the Squaw Creek country and started logging in the San Hedrin watershed, did I realize that I had been considerable of a jackass myself."

"Yes," Bryce admitted, "there can be no doubt but that you cut off your nose to spite your face."

There was silence between them for several minutes. Bryce's thoughts harked back to that first season of logging in the San Hedrin, when the cloud-burst had caught the river filled with Cardigan logs and whirled them down to the bay, to crash through the log-boom at tidewater and continue out to the open sea. In his mind's eye he could still see the red-ink figures on the profit-and-loss statement Sinclair, his father's manager, had presented at the end of that year.

The old man appeared to divine the trend of his son's thoughts. "Yes, Bryce, that was a disastrous year," he declared. "The mere loss of the logs was a severe blow, but in addition I had to pay out quite a little money to settle with my customers. I was loaded up with low-priced orders that year, although I didn't expect to make any money. The orders were merely taken to keep the men employed. You understand, Bryce! I had a good crew, the finest in the country; and if I had shut down, my men would have scattered and—well, you know how hard it is to get that kind of a crew together again. Besides, I had never failed my boys before, and I couldn't bear the thought of failing them then. Half the mills in the country were shut down at the time, and there was a lot of distress among the unemployed. I couldn't do it, Bryce."

Bryce nodded. "And when you lost the logs, you couldn't fill those low-priced orders. Then the market commenced to jump and advanced three dollars in three months—"

"Exactly, my son. And my customers began to crowd me to fill those old orders. Praise be, my regular customers knew I wasn't the kind of lumberman who tries to crawl out of filling low-priced orders after the market has gone up. Nevertheless I couldn't expect them to suffer with me; my failure to perform my contracts, while unavoidable, nevertheless would have caused them a severe loss, and when they were forced to buy elsewhere, I paid them the difference between the price they paid my competitors and the price at which they originally placed their orders with me. And the delay in delivery caused them further loss."

"How much?"

"Nearly a hundred thousand—to settle for losses to my local customers alone. Among my orders I had three million feet of clear lumber for shipment to the United Kingdom, and these foreign customers, thinking I was trying to crawfish on my contracts, sued me and got judgment for actual and exemplary damages for my failure to perform, while the demurrage on the ships they sent to freight the lumber sent me hustling to the bank to borrow money."

He smoked meditatively for a minute. "I've always been land-poor," he explained apologetically. "Never kept much of a reserve working-capital for emergencies, you know. Whenever I had idle money, I put it into timber in the San Hedrin watershed, because I realized that some day the railroad would build in from the south, tap that timber, and double its value. I've not as yet found reason to doubt the wisdom of my course; but"—he sighed— "the railroad is a long time coming!"

John Cardigan here spoke of a most important factor in the situation. The crying need of the country was a feeder to some transcontinental railroad. By reason of natural barriers, Humboldt County was not easily accessible to the outside world except from the sea, and even this avenue of ingress and egress would be closed for days at a stretch when the harbour bar was on a rampage. With the exception of a strip of level, fertile land, perhaps five miles wide and thirty miles long and contiguous to the seacoast, the heavily timbered mountains to the north, east, and south rendered the building of a railroad that would connect Humboldt County with the outside world a profoundly difficult and expensive task. The Northwestern Pacific, indeed, had been slowly building from San Francisco Bay up through Marin and Sonoma counties to Willits in Mendocino County. But there it had stuck to await that indefinite day when its finances and the courage of its board of directors should prove equal to the colossal task of continuing the road two hundred miles through the mountains to Sequoia on Humboldt Bay. For twenty years the Humboldt pioneers had lived in hope of this; but eventually they had died in despair or were in process of doing so.

"Don't worry, Dad. It will come," Bryce assured his father. "It's bound to."

"Yes, but not in my day. And when it comes, a stranger may own your San Hedrin timber and reap the reward of my lifetime of labour."

Again a silence fell between them, broken presently by the old man. "That was a mistake—logging in the San Hedrin," he observed. "I had my lesson that first year, but I didn't heed it. If I had abandoned my camps there, pocketed my pride, paid Colonel Pennington two dollars for his Squaw Creek timber, and rebuilt my old logging-road, I would have been safe to-day. But I was stubborn; I'd played the game so long, you know—I didn't want to let that man Pennington outgame me. So I tackled the San Hedrin again. We put thirty million feet of logs into the river that year, and when the freshet came, McTavish managed to make a fairly successful drive. But he was all winter on the job, and when spring came and the men went into the woods again, they had to leave nearly a million feet of heavy butt logs permanently stranded in the slack water along the banks, while perhaps another million feet of lighter logs had been lifted out of the channel by the overflow and left high and dry when the water receded. There they were, Bryce, scattered up and down the river, far from the cables and logging-donkeys, the only power we could use to get those monsters back into the river again, and I was forced to decide whether they should be abandoned or split during the summer into railroad ties, posts, pickets, and shakes—commodities for which there was very little call at the time and in which, even when sold, there could be no profit after deducting the cost of the twenty-mile wagon haul to Sequoia, and the water freight from Sequoia to market. So I abandoned them."

"I remember that phase of it, partner."

"To log it the third year only meant that more of those heavy logs would jam and spell more loss. Besides, there was always danger of another cloud-burst which would put me out of business completely, and I couldn't afford the risk."

"That was the time you should have offered Colonel Pennington a handsome profit on his Squaw Creek timber, pal."

"If my hindsight was as good as my foresight, and I had my eyesight, I wouldn't be in this dilemma at all," the old man retorted briskly. "It's hard to teach an old dog new tricks, and besides, I was obsessed with the need of protecting your heritage from attack in any direction."

John Cardigan straightened up in his chair and laid the tip of his right index finger in the centre of the palm of his left hand. "Here was the situation, Bryce: The centre of my palm represents Sequoia; the end of my fingers represents the San Hedrin timber twenty miles south. Now, if the railroad built in from the south, you would win. But if it built in from Grant's Pass, Oregon, on the north from the base of my hand, the terminus of the line would be Sequoia, twenty miles from your timber in the San Hedrin watershed!"

Bryce nodded. "In which event," he replied, "we, would be in much the same position with our San Hedrin timber as Colonel Pennington is with his Squaw Creek timber. We would have the comforting knowledge that we owned it and paid taxes on it but couldn't do a dad-burned thing with it!"

"Right you are! The thing to do, then, as I viewed the situation, Bryce, was to acquire a body of timber NORTH of Sequoia and be prepared for either eventuality. And this I did."

Silence again descended upon them; and Bryce, gazing into the open fireplace, recalled an event in that period of his father's activities: Old Bill Henderson had come up to their house to dinner one night, and quite suddenly, in the midst of his soup, the old fox had glared across at his host and bellowed:

"John, I hear you've bought six thousand acres up in Township Nine."

John Cardigan had merely nodded, and Henderson had continued:

"Going to log it or hold it for investment?"

"It was a good buy," Cardigan had replied enigmatically; "so I thought I'd better take it at the price. I suppose Bryce will log it some day."

"Then I wish Bryce wasn't such a boy, John. See here, now, neighbour. I'll 'fess up. I took that money Pennington gave me for my Squaw Creek timber and put it back into redwood in Township Nine, slam-bang up against your holdings there. John, I'd build a mill on tidewater if you'd sell me a site, and I'd log my timber if—"

"I'll sell you a mill-site, Bill, and I won't stab you to the heart, either. Consider that settled."

"That's bully, John; but still, you only dispose of part of my troubles. There's twelve miles of logging-road to build to get my logs to the mill, and I haven't enough ready money to make the grade. Better throw in with me, John, and we'll build the road and operate it for our joint interest."

"I'll not throw in with you, Bill, at my time of life, I don't want to have the worry of building, maintaining, and operating twelve miles of private railroad. But I'll loan you, without security—"

"You'll have to take an unsecured note, John. Everything I've got is hocked."

"—the money you need to build and equip the road," finished Cardigan. "In return you are to shoulder all the grief and worry of the road and give me a ten-year contract at a dollar and a half per thousand feet, to haul my logs down to tidewater with your own. My minimum haul will be twenty-five million feet annually, and my maximum fifty million—"

"Sold!" cried Henderson. And it was even so.

Bryce came out of his reverie. "And now?" he queried of his father.

"I mortgaged the San Hedrin timber in the south to buy the timber in the north, my son; then after I commenced logging in my new holdings, came several long, lean years of famine. I stuck it out, hoping for a change for the better; I couldn't bear to close down my mill and logging-camps, for the reason that I could stand the loss far more readily than the men who worked for me and depended upon me. But the market dragged in the doldrums, and Bill Henderson died, and his boys got discouraged, and—"

A sudden flash of inspiration illumined Bryce Cardigan's brain. "And they sold out to Colonel Pennington," he cried.

"Exactly. The Colonel took over my contract with Henderson's company, along with the other assets, and it was incumbent upon him, as assignee, to fulfill the contract. For the past two years the market for redwood has been most gratifying, and if I could only have gotten a maximum supply of logs over Pennington's road, I'd have worked out of the hole, but—"

"He manages to hold you to a minimum annual haul of twenty-five million feet, eh?"

John Cardigan nodded. "He claims he's short of rolling-stock—that wrecks and fires have embarrassed the road. He can always find excuses for failing to spot in logging-trucks for Cardigan's logs. Bill Henderson never played the game that way. He gave me what I wanted and never held me to the minimum haulage when I was prepared to give him the maximum."

"What does Colonel Pennington want, pard?"

"He wants," said John Cardigan slowly, "my Valley of the Giants and a right of way through my land from the valley to a log-dump on deep water."

"And you refused him?"

"Naturally. You know my ideas on that big timber." His old head sank low on his breast. "Folks call them Cardigan's Redwoods now," he murmured. "Cardigan's Redwoods—and Pennington would cut them! Oh, Bryce, the man hasn't a soul!"

"But I fail to see what the loss of Cardigan's Redwoods has to do with the impending ruin of the Cardigan Redwood Lumber Company," his son reminded him. "We have all the timber we want."

"My ten-year contract has but one more year to run, and recently I tried to get Pennington to renew it. He was very nice and sociable, but—he named me a freight-rate, for a renewal of the contract for five years, of three dollars per thousand feet. That rate is prohibitive and puts us out of business."

"Not necessarily," Bryce returned evenly. "How about the State railroad commission? Hasn't it got something to say about rates?"

"Yes—on common carriers. But Pennington's load is a private logging-road; my contract will expire next year, and it is not incumbent upon Pennington to renew it. And one can't operate a sawmill without logs, you know."

"Then," said Bryce calmly, "we'll shut the mill down when the log-hauling contract expires, hold our timber as an investment, and live the simple life until we can sell it or a transcontinental road builds into Humboldt County and enables us to start up the mill again."

John Cardigan shook his head. "I'm mortgaged to the last penny," he confessed, "and Pennington has been buying Cardigan Redwood Lumber Company first-mortgage bonds until he is in control of the issue. He'll buy in the San Hedrin timber at the foreclosure sale, and in order to get it back and save something for you out of the wreckage, I'll have to make an unprofitable trade with him. I'll have to give him my timber adjoining his north of Sequoia, together with my Valley of the Giants, in return for the

San Hedrin timber, to which he'll have a sheriff's deed. But the mill, all my old employees, with their numerous dependents—gone, with you left land-poor and without a dollar to pay your taxes. Smashed—like that!" And he drove his fist into the palm of his hand.

"Perhaps—but not without a fight," Bryce answered, although he knew their plight was well-nigh hopeless. "I'll give that man Pennington a run for his money, or I'll know the reason."

The telephone on the table beside him tinkled, and he took down the receiver and said "Hello!"

"Mercy!" came the clear, sweet voice of Shirley Sumner over the wire. "Do you feel as savage as all that, Mr. Cardigan?"

For the second time in his life the thrill that was akin to pain came to Bryce Cardigan. He laughed. "If I had known you were calling, Miss Sumner," he said, "I shouldn't have growled so."

"Well, you're forgiven—for several reasons, but principally for sending me that delicious blackberry pie. Of course, it discoloured my teeth temporarily, but I don't care. The pie was worth it, and you were awfully dear to think of sending it. Thank you so much."

"Glad you liked it, Miss Sumner. I dare to hope that I may have the privilege of seeing you soon again."

"Of course. One good pie deserves another. Some evening next week, when that dear old daddy of yours can spare his boy, you might be interested to see our burl-redwood-panelled dining room Uncle Seth is so proud of. I'm too recent an arrival to know the hour at which Uncle Seth dines, but I'll let you know later and name a definite date. Would Thursday night be convenient?"

"Perfectly. Thank you a thousand times."

She bade him good-night. As he turned from the telephone, his father looked up. "What are you going to do to-morrow, lad?" he queried.

"I have to do some thinking to-morrow," Bryce answered. "So I'm going up into Cardigan's Redwoods to do it. Up there a fellow can get set, as it were, to put over a thought with a punch in it."

"The dogwoods and rhododendron are blooming now," the old man murmured wistfully. Bryce knew what he was thinking of. "I'll attend to the flowers for Mother," he assured Cardigan, and he added fiercely: "And I'll attend to the battle for Father. We may lose, but that man Pennington will know he's been in a fight before we fin——"

He broke off abruptly, for he had just remembered that he was to dine at the Pennington house the following Thursday—and he was not the sort of man who smilingly breaks bread with his enemy.

CHAPTER X

For many years there had been installed in Cardigan's mill a clock set to United States observatory time and corrected hourly by the telegraph company. It was the only clock of its kind in Sequoia; hence folk set their watches by it, or rather by the whistle on Cardigan's mill. With a due appreciation of the important function of this clock toward his fellow-citizens, old Zeb Curry, the chief engineer and a stickler for being on time, was most meticulous in his whistle-blowing. With a sage and prophetic eye fixed upon the face of the clock, and a particularly greasy hand grasping the whistle-cord, Zeb would wait until the clock registered exactly six-fifty-nine and a half—whereupon the seven o'clock whistle would commence blowing, to cease instantly upon the stroke of the hour. It was old Zeb's pride and boast that with a single exception, during the sixteen years the clock had been in service, no man could say that Zeb had been more than a second late or early with his whistle-blowing. That exception occurred when Bryce Cardigan, invading the engine room while Zeb was at luncheon, looped the whistle-cord until the end dangled seven feet above ground. As a consequence Zeb, who was a short, fat little man, was forced to leap at it several times before success crowned his efforts and the whistle blew. Thereafter for the remainder of the day his reason tottered on its throne, due to the fact that Bryce induced every mill employee to call upon the engineer and remind him that he must be growing old, since he was no longer dependable!

On the morning following Bryce Cardigan's return to Sequoia, Zeb Curry, as per custom, started his engine at six-fifty-eight. That gave the huge bandsaws two minutes in which to attain their proper speed and afforded Dan Kenyon, the head sawyer, ample time to run his steam log-carriage out to the end of the track; for Daniel, too, was a reliable man in the matter of starting his daily uproar on time.

At precisely six fifty-nine and a half, therefore, the engineer's hand closed over the handle of the whistle-cord, and Dan Kenyon, standing on the steam-carriage with his hand on the lever, took a thirty-second squint through a rather grimy window that gave upon the drying-yard and the mill-office at the head of it.

The whistle ceased blowing, but still Dan Kenyon stood at his post, oblivious of the hungry saws. Ten seconds passed; then Zeb Curry, immeasurably scandalized at Daniel's tardiness, tooted the whistle sharply twice; whereupon Dan woke up, threw over the lever, and walked his log up to the saw.

For the next five hours Zeb Curry had no opportunity to discuss the matter with the head sawyer. After blowing the twelve o'clock whistle, however, he hurried over to the dining-hall, where the mill hands already lined the benches, shovelling food into their mouths as only a lumberman or a miner can. Dan Kenyon sat at the head of the table in the place of honour sacred to the head sawyer, and when his mouth would permit of some activity other than mastication, Zeb Curry caught his eye.

"Hey, you, Dan Kenyon," he shouted across the table, "what happened to you this mornin'? It was sixteen seconds between the tail end o' my whistle an' the front end o' your whinin'. First thing you know, you'll be gettin' so slack an' careless-like some other man'll be ridin' that log-carriage o' yourn."

"I was struck dumb," Dan Kenyon replied. "I just stood there like one o' these here graven images. Last night on my way home from work I heerd the young feller was back—he got in just as we was knockin' off for the day; an' this mornin' just as you cut loose, Zeb, I'll be danged if he didn't show up in front o' the office door, fumblin' for the keyhole. Yes, sirree! That boy gets in at six o'clock last night an' turns to on his paw's job when the whistle blows this mornin' at seven."

"You mean young Bryce Cardigan?" Zeb queried incredulously.

"I shore do."

"'Tain't possible," Zeb declared. "You seen a new bookkeeper, mebbe, but you didn't see Bryce. He aint no such hog for labour as his daddy before him, I'm tellin' you. Not that there's a lazy bone in his body, for there ain't, but because that there boy's got too much sense to come bollin' down to work at seven o'clock the very first mornin' he's back from Yurrup."

"I'm layin' you ten to one I seen him," Dan replied defiantly, "an' what's more, I'll bet a good cigar—a ten-center straight—the boy don't leave till six o'clock to-night."

"You're on," answered the chief engineer. "Them's lumberjack hours, man. From seven till six means work—an' only fools an' hosses keeps them hours."

The head sawyer leaned across the table and pounded with the handle of his knife until he had the attention of all present. "I'm a-goin' to tell you young fellers somethin'," he announced. "Ever since the old boss got so he couldn't look after his business with his own eyes, things has been goin' to blazes round this sawmill, but they ain't a-goin' no more. How do I know? Well, I'll tell you. All this forenoon I kept my eye on the office door—I can see it through a mill winder; an' I'm tellin' you the old boss didn't show up till ten o'clock, which the old man ain't never been a ten o'clock business man at no time. Don't that prove the boy's took his place?"

Confused murmurs of affirmation and negation ran up and down the long table. Dan tapped with his knife again. "You hear me," he warned. "Thirty year I've been ridin' John Cardigan's log-carriages; thirty year I've been gettin' everythin' out of a log it's possible to git out, which is more'n you fellers at the trimmers can git out of a board after I've sawed it off the cant. There's a lot o' you young fellers that've been takin' John Cardigan's money under false pretenses, so if I was you I'd keep both eyes on my job hereafter. For a year I've been claimin' that good No. 2 stock has been chucked into the slab-fire as refuge lumber." (Dan meant refuse lumber.) "But it won't be done no more. The raftsman tells me he seen Bryce down at the end o' the conveyin' belt givin' that refuge the once-over—so step easy."

"What does young Cardigan know about runnin' a sawmill?" a planer-man demanded bluntly. "They tell me he's been away to college an' travellin' the past six years."

"Wa-ll," drawled the head sawyer, "you git to talkin' with him some day an' see how much he knows about runnin' a sawmill. What he knows will surprise you. Yes, indeed, you'll find he knows considerable. He's picked up loose shingles around the yard an' bundled 'em in vacation times, an' I want to see the shingle-weaver that can teach him some tricks. Also, I've had him come up on the steam carriage more'n once an' saw up logs, while at times I've seen him put in a week or two on the sortin' table. In a pinch, with a lot o' vessels loadin' here at the dock an' the skippers raisin' Cain because they wasn't gettin' their cargo fast enough, I've seen him work nights an' Sundays tallyin' with the best o' them. Believe me that boy can grade lumber."

"An' I'll tell you somethin' else," Zeb Curry cut in. "If the new boss ever tells you to do a thing his way, you do it an' don't argue none as to whether he knows more about it than you do or not."

"A whole lot o' dagos an' bohunks that's come into the woods since the blue-noses an' canucks an' wild Irish went out had better keep your eyes open," Dan Kenyon warned sagely. "There ain't none o' you any better'n you ought to be, an' things have been pretty durned slack around Cardigan's mill since the old man went blind, but—you watch out. There's a change due. Bryce Cardigan is his father's son. He'll do things."

"Which he's big enough to throw a bear uphill by the tail," Zeb Curry added, "an' you fellers all know how much tail a bear has."

"Every mornin' for thirty years, 'ceptin' when we was shut down for repairs," Dan continued, "I've looked through that winder, when John Cardigan wasn't away from Sequoia, to watch him git to his office on time. He's there when the whistle blows, clear up to the time his eyes go back on him, an' then he arrives late once or twice on account o' havin' to go careful. This mornin', for the first time in fifty year, he stays in bed; but—his son has the key in the office door when the whistle blows, an'—"

Dan Kenyon paused abruptly; the hum of conversation ceased, and silence fell upon the room as Bryce Cardigan strolled in the door, nodded to the men, and slid in on the bench to a seat beside the head sawyer.

"Hello, Dan—hello, Zeb," he said and shook hands with each. "I'm mighty glad to see you both again. Hello, everybody. I'm the new boss, so I suppose I'd better introduce myself—there are so many new faces here. I'm Bryce Cardigan."

"Yes," Zeb Curry volunteered, "an' he's like his daddy. He ain't ashamed to work with his men, an' he ain't ashamed to eat with his men, nuther. Glad you're back with us again, boy—mighty glad. Dan, here, he's gittin' slacker'n an old squaw with his work an' needs somebody to jerk him up, while the rest o' these here—"

"I noticed that about Dan," Bryce interrupted craftily. "He's slowing up, Zeb. He must have been fifteen seconds late this morning—or perhaps," he added "you were fifteen seconds earlier than the clock."

Dan grinned, and Bryce went on seriously: "I'm afraid you're getting too old to ride the log-carriage, Dan. You've been at it a long time; so, with the utmost good will in the world toward you, you're fired. I might as well tell you now. You know me, Dan. I always did dislike beating about the bush."

"Fired!" Dan Kenyon's eyes popped with amazement and horror. "Fired— after thirty years!" he croaked.

"Fired!" There was unmistakable finality in Bryce's tones. "You're hired again, however, at a higher salary, as mill-superintendent. You can get away with that job, can't you, Dan? In fact," he added without waiting for the overjoyed Dan to answer him, "you've got to get away with it, because I discharged the mill-superintendent I found on the job when I got down here this morning. He's been letting too many profits go into the slab-fire. In fact, the entire plant has gone to glory. Fire-hose old and rotten—couldn't stand a hundred-pound pressure; fire-buckets and water-barrels empty, axes not in their proper places, fire-extinguishers filled with stale chemical—why, the smallest kind of a fire here would get beyond our control with that man on the job. Besides, he's changed the grading-rules. I found the men putting clear boards with hard-grained streaks in them in with the No. 1 clear. The customer may not kick at a small percentage of No. 2 in his No. 1 but it's only fair to give it to him at two dollars a thousand less."

"Well," purred Zeb Curry, "they don't grade lumber as strict nowadays as they used to before you went away. Colonel Pennington says we're a lot o' back numbers out this way an' too generous with our grades. First thing he did was to call a meetin' of all the Humboldt lumber manufacturers an' organize 'em into an association. Then he had the gradin'-rules changed. The retailers hollered for a while, but bimeby they got used to it."

"Did my father join that association?" Bryce demanded quickly.

"Yes. He told Pennington he wasn't goin' to be no obstructionist in the trade, but he did kick like a bay steer on them new gradin'-rules an' refused to conform to 'em. Said he was too old an' had been too long in business to start gougin' his customers at his time o' life. So he got out o' the association."

"Bully for John Cardigan!" Bryce declared. "I suppose we could make a little more money by cheapening our grade, but the quality of our lumber is so well known that it sells itself and saves us the expense of maintaining a corps of salesmen."

"From what I hear tell o' the Colonel," Dan observed sagely, "the least he ever wants is a hundred and fifty per cent. the best of it."

"Yes," old Zeb observed gravely, "an' so fur as I can see, he ain't none too perticular how he gets it." He helped himself to a toothpick, and followed by the head sawyer, abruptly left the room—after the fashion of sawmill men and woodsmen, who eat as much as they can as quickly as they can and eventually die of old age rather than indigestion. Bryce ate his noonday meal in more leisurely fashion and at its conclusion stepped into the kitchen.

"Where do you live, cook?" he demanded of that functionary; and upon being informed, he retired to the office and called up the Sequoia meat-market.

"Bryce Cardigan speaking," he informed the butcher. "Do you ever buy any pigs from our mill cook?"

"Not any more," the butcher answered. "He stung me once with a dozen fine shoats. They looked great, but after I had slaughtered them and had them dressed, they turned out to be swill-fed hogs—swill and alfalfa."

"Thank you." Bryce hung up. "I knew that cook was wasteful," he declared, turning to his father's old manager, one Thomas Sinclair. "He wastes food in order to take the swill home to his hogs—and nobody watches him. Things have certainly gone to the devil," he continued.

"No fault of mine," Sinclair protested. "I've never paid any attention to matters outside the office. Your father looked after everything else."

Bryce looked at Sinclair. The latter was a thin, spare, nervous man in the late fifties, and though generally credited with being John Cardigan's manager, Bryce knew that Sinclair was in reality little more than a glorified bookkeeper—and a very excellent bookkeeper indeed. Bryce realized that in the colossal task that confronted him he could expect no real help from Sinclair.

"Yes," he replied, "my father looked after everything else—while he could."

"Oh, you'll soon get the business straightened out and running smoothly again," Sinclair declared confidently.

"Well, I'm glad I started on the job to-day, rather than next Monday, as I planned to do last night."

He stepped to the window and looked out. At the mill-dock a big steam schooner and a wind-jammer lay; in the lee of the piles of lumber, sailors and long-shoremen, tallymen and timekeeper lounged, enjoying the brief period of the noon hour still theirs before the driving mates of the lumber-vessels should turn them to on the job once more. To his right and left stretched the drying yard, gangway on gangway formed by the serried rows of lumber-piles, the hoop-horses placidly feeding from their nosebags while the strong-armed fellows who piled the lumber sat about in little groups conversing with the mill-hands.

As Bryce looked, a puff of white steam appeared over the roof of the old sawmill, and the one o'clock whistle blew. Instantly that scene of indolence and ease turned to one of activity. The mill-hands lounging in the gangways scurried for their stations in the mill; men climbed to the tops of the lumber-piles, while other men passed boards and scantlings up to them; the donkey-engines aboard the vessels rattled; the cargo-gaffs of the steam schooner swung outward, and a moment later two great sling-loads of newly sawed lumber rose in the air, swung inward, and descended to the steamer's decks.

All about Bryce were scenes of activity, of human endeavour; and to him in that moment came the thought: "My father brought all this to pass—and now the task of continuing it is mine! All those men who earn a living in Cardigan's mill and on Cardigan's dock—those sailors who sail the ships that carry Cardigan's lumber into the distant marts of men—are dependent upon me; and my father used to tell me not to fail them. Must my father have wrought all this in vain? And must I stand by and see all this go to satisfy the overwhelming ambition of a stranger?" His big hands clenched. "No!" he growled savagely.

"If I stick around this office a minute longer, I'll go crazy," Bryce snarled then. "Give me your last five annual statements, Mr. Sinclair, please."

The old servitor brought forth the documents in question. Bryce stuffed them into his pocket and left the office. Three quarters of an hour later he entered the little amphitheatre in the Valley of the Giants and paused with an expression of dismay. One of the giants had fallen and lay stretched across the little clearing. In its descent it had demolished the little white stone over his mother's grave and had driven the fragments of the stone deep into the earth.

The tremendous brown butt quite ruined the appearance of the amphitheatre by reason of the fact that it constituted a barrier some fifteen feet high and of equal thickness athwart the centre of the clearing, with fully three quarters of the length of the tree lost to sight where the fallen monarch had wedged between its more fortunate fellows. The fact that the tree was down, however, was secondary to the fact that neither wind nor lightning had brought it low, but rather the impious hand of man; for the great jagged stump showed all too plainly the marks of cross-cut saw and axe; a pile of chips four feet deep littered the ground.

For fully a minute Bryce stood dumbly gazing upon the sacrilege before his rage and horror found vent in words. "An enemy has done this thing," he cried aloud to the wood-goblins. "And over her grave!"

Presently, smothering his emotion, he walked the length of the dead giant, and where the top tapered off to a size that would permit of his stepping across it, he retraced his steps on the other side of the tree until he had reached a point some fifty feet from the butt—when the vandal's reason for felling the monster became apparent.

It was a burl tree. At the point where Bryce paused a malignant growth had developed on the trunk of the tree, for all the world like a tremendous wart. This was the burl, so prized for table-tops and panelling because of the fact that the twisted, wavy, helter-skelter grain lends to the wood an extraordinary beauty when polished. Bryee noted that the work of removing this excrescence had been accomplished very neatly. With a cross-cut saw the growth, perhaps ten feet in diameter, had been neatly sliced off much as a housewife cuts slice after slice from a loaf of bread. He guessed that these slices, practically circular in shape, had been rolled out of the woods to some conveyance waiting to receive them.

What Bryce could not understand, however, was the stupid brutality of the raiders in felling the tree merely for that section of burl. By permitting the tree to stand and merely building a staging up to the burl, the latter could have been removed without vital injury to the tree—whereas by destroying the tree the wretches had evidenced all too clearly to Bryce a wanton desire to add insult to injury.

Bryce inspected the scars on the stump carefully. They were weather-stained to such an extent that to his experienced eye it was evident the outrage had been committed more than a year previously; and the winter rains, not to mention the spring growth of grasses and underbrush, had effectually destroyed all trace of the trail taken by the vandals with their booty.

"Poor old Dad!" he murmured. "I'm glad now he has been unable to get up here and see this. It would have broken his heart. I'll have this tree made into fence-posts and the stump dynamited and removed this summer. After he is operated on and gets back his sight, he will come up here—and he must never know. Perhaps he will have forgotten how many trees stood in this circle. And I'll fill in the hole left by the stump and plant some manzanita there to hide the—"

He paused. Peeping out from under a chip among the litter at his feet was the moldy corner of a white envelope. In an instant Bryce had it in his hand. The envelope was dirty and weather-beaten, but to a certain extent the redwood chips under which it had lain hidden had served to protect it, and the writing on the face was still legible. The envelope was empty and addressed to Jules Rondeau, care of the Laguna Grande Lumber Company, Sequoia, California.

Bryce read and reread that address. "Rondeau!" he muttered. "Jules Rondeau! I've heard that name before—ah, yes! Dad spoke of him last night. He's Pennington's woods-boss—"

He paused. An enemy had done this thing—and in all the world John Cardigan had but one enemy—Colonel Seth Pennington. Had Pennington sent his woods-boss to do this dirty work out of sheer spite? Hardly. The section of burl was gone, and this argued that the question of spite had been purely a matter of secondary consideration.

Evidently, Bryce reasoned, someone had desired that burl redwood greatly, and that someone had not been Jules Rondeau, since a woods-boss would not be likely to spend five minutes of his leisure time in consideration of the beauties of a burl table-top or panel. Hence, if Rondeau had superintended the task of felling the tree, it must have been at the behest of a superior; and since a woods-boss acknowledges no superior save the creator of the pay-roll, the recipient of that stolen burl must have been Colonel Pennington.

Suddenly he thrilled. If Jules Rondeau had stolen that burl to present it to Colonel Pennington, his employer, then the finished article must be in Pennington's home! And Bryce had been invited to that home for dinner the following Thursday by the Colonel's niece.

"I'll go, after all," he told himself. "I'll go—and I'll see what I shall see."

He was too wrought up now to sit calmly down in the peace and quietude of the giants, and digest the annual reports Sinclair had given him. He hastened back to the mill-office and sought Sinclair.

"At what hour does the logging-train leave the Laguna Grande Lumber Company's yard for our log-landing in Township Nine?" he demanded.

"Eight a.m. and one p.m. daily, Bryce."

"Have you any maps of the holdings of Pennington and ourselves in that district?"

"Yes."

"Let me have them, please. I know the topography of that district perfectly, but I am not familiar with the holdings in and around ours."

Sinclair gave him the maps, and Bryce retired to his father's private office and gave himself up to a study of them.

CHAPTER XI

When Shirley Sumner descended to the breakfast room on the morning following her arrival in Sequoia, the first glance at her uncle's stately countenance informed her that during the night something had occurred to irritate Colonel Seth Pennington and startle him out of his customary bland composure. He greeted her politely but coldly, and without even the perfunctory formality of inquiring how she had passed the night, he came directly to the issue,

"Shirley," he began, "did I hear you calling young Cardigan on the telephone after dinner last night or did my ears deceive me?"

"Your ears are all right, Uncle Seth. I called Mr. Cardigan up to thank him for the pie he sent over, and incidentally to invite him over here to dinner on Thursday night."

"I thought I heard you asking somebody to dinner, and as you don't know a soul in Sequoia except young Cardigan, naturally I opined that he was to be the object of our hospitality."

The Colonel coughed slightly. From the manner in which he approached the task of buttering his hot cakes Shirley knew he had something more to say and was merely formulating a polite set of phrases in which to express himself. She resolved to help him along.

"I dare say it's quite all right to have invited him; isn't it, Uncle Seth?"

"Certainly, certainly, my dear. Quite all right, but er—ah, slightly inconvenient."

"Oh, I'm so sorry. If I had known—Perhaps some other night—"

"I am expecting other company Thursday night—unfortunately, Brayton, the president of the Bank of Sequoia, is coming up to dine and discuss some business affairs with me afterward; so if you don't mind, my dear, suppose you call young Cardigan up and ask him to defer his visit until some later date."

"Certainly, Uncle. There is no particular reason why I should have Mr. Cardigan on Thursday if his presence would mean the slightest interference with your plans. What perfectly marvellous roses! How did you succeed in growing them, Uncle Seth?"

He smiled sourly. "I didn't raise them," he replied. "That half-breed Indian that drives John Cardigan's car brought them around about an hour ago, along with a card. There it is, beside your plate."

She blushed ever so slightly. "I suppose Bryce Cardigan is vindicating himself," she murmured as she withdrew the card from the envelope. As she had surmised, it was Bryce Cardigan's. Colonel Pennington was the proprietor of a similar surmise.

"Fast work, Shirley," he murmured banteringly. "I wonder what he'll send you for luncheon. Some dill pickles, probably."

She pretended to be very busy with the roses, and not to have heard him. Her uncle's sneer was not lost on her, however; she resented it but chose to ignore it for the present; and when at length she had finished arranging the flowers, she changed the conversation adroitly by questioning her relative anent the opportunities for shopping in Sequoia. The Colonel, who could assimilate a hint quicker than most ordinary mortals, saw that he had annoyed her, and he promptly hastened to make amends by permitting himself to be led readily into this new conversational channel. As soon as he could do so, however, he excused himself on the plea of urgent business at the office, and left the room.

Shirley, left alone at the breakfast-table, picked idly at the preserved figs the owlish butler set before her. Vaguely she wondered at her uncle's apparent hostility to the Cardigans; she was as vaguely troubled in the knowledge that until she should succeed in eradicating this hostility, it must inevitably act as a bar to the further progress of her friendship with Bryce Cardigan. And she told herself she did not want to lose that friendship. She wasn't the least bit in love with him albeit she realized he was rather lovable. The delight which she had experienced in his society lay in the fact that he was absolutely different from any other man she had met. His simplicity, his utter lack of "swank," his directness, his good nature, and dry sense of humour made him shine luminously in comparison with the worldly, rather artificial young men she had previously met—young men who said and did only those things which time, tradition, and hallowed memory assured them were done by the right sort of people. Shirley had a suspicion that Bryce Cardigan could—and would—swear like a pirate should his temper be aroused and the circumstances appear to warrant letting off steam. Also she liked him because he was imaginative—because he saw and sensed and properly understood without a diagram or a blueprint. And lastly, he was a good, devoted son and was susceptible of development into a congenial and wholly acceptable comrade to a young lady absolutely lacking in other means of amusement.

She finished her breakfast in thoughtful silence; then she went to the telephone and called up Bryce at his home. Mrs. Tully, all aflutter with curiosity, was quite insistent that Shirley should leave her name and telephone number, but failing to carry her point, consented to inform the latter that Mr. Bryce was at the office. She gave Shirley the telephone number.

When the girl called the Cardigan Redwood Lumber Company, Bryce answered. He recognized her voice instantly and called her name before she had opportunity to announce her identity.

"Thank you so much for the beautiful roses, Mr. Cardigan," she began.

"I'm glad you liked them. Nobody picks flowers out of our garden, you know. I used to, but I'll be too busy hereafter to bother with the garden."

"Very well. Then I am not to expect any more roses?"

"I'm a stupid clodhopper. Of course you may. By the way, Miss Sumner, does your uncle own a car?"

"I believe he does—a little old rattletrap which he drives himself."

"Then I'll send George over with the Napier this afternoon. You might care to take a spin out into the surrounding country. By the way, Miss Sumner, you are to consider George and that car as your personal property. I fear you're going to find Sequoia a dull place; so whenever you wish to go for a ride, just call me up, and I'll have George report to you."

"But think of all the expensive gasoline and tires!"

"Oh, but you mustn't look at things from that angle after you cross the Rocky Mountains on your way west. Moreover, mine is the only real car in the country, and I know you like it. What are you going to do this afternoon?"

"I don't know. I haven't thought that far ahead."

"For some real sport I would suggest that you motor up to Laguna Grande. That's Spanish for Big Lagoon, you know. Take a rod with you. There are some land-locked salmon in the lagoon—that is, there used to be; and if you hook one you'll get a thrill."

"But I haven't any rod."

"I'll send you over a good one."

"But I have nobody to teach me how to use it," she hinted daringly.

"I appreciate that compliment," he flashed back at her, "but unfortunately my holidays are over for a long, long time. I took my father's place in the business this morning."

"So soon?"

"Yes. Things have been happening while I was away. However, speaking of fishing, George Sea Otter will prove an invaluable instructor. He is a good boy and you may trust him implicitly. On Thursday evening you can tell me what success you had with the salmon."

"Oh, that reminds me, Mr. Cardigan. You can't come Thursday evening, after all." And she explained the reason.

"By Jove," he replied, "I'm mighty glad you tipped me off about that. I couldn't possibly remain at ease in the presence of a banker-particularly one who will not lend me money."

"Suppose you come Wednesday night instead."

"We'll call that a bet. Thank you."

She chuckled at his frank good humour. "Thank YOU, Mr Cardigan, for all your kindness and thoughtfulness; and if you WILL persist in being nice to me, you might send George Sea Otter and the car at one-thirty. I'll be glad to avail myself of both until I can get a car of my own sent up from San Francisco. Till Wednesday night, then. Good-bye."

As Bryce Cardigan hung up, he heaved a slight sigh, and a parody on a quatrain from "Lalla Rookh" ran through his mind:

I never loved a dear gazelle, To glad me with its limpid eye, But when I learned to love it well, The gol-darned thing was sure to die!

It was difficult to get out of the habit of playing; he found himself the possessor of a very great desire to close down the desk, call on Shirley Sumner, and spend the remainder of the day basking in the sunlight of her presence.

CHAPTER XII

The days passed swiftly, as they have a habit of passing after one has discovered one's allotted task in life and has proceeded to perform it. Following his discovery of the outrage committed on his father's sanctuary, Bryce wasted considerable valuable time and effort in a futile endeavour to gather some further hint of the identity of the vandals; but despairing at last, he dismissed the matter from his mind, resolving only that on Thursday he would go up into Pennington's woods and interview the redoubtable Jules Rondeau. Bryce's natural inclination was to wait upon M. Rondeau immediately, if not sooner, but the recollection of his dinner engagement at the Pennington home warned him to proceed cautiously; for while harbouring no apprehensions as to the outcome of a possible clash with Rondeau, Bryce was not so optimistic as to believe he would escape unscathed from an encounter. Experience had impressed upon him the fact that in a rough-and-tumble battle nobody is quite so thoroughly at home as a lumberjack; once in a clinch with such a man, even a champion gladiator of the prize ring may well feel apprehensive of the outcome.

Wednesday evening at five o'clock Mr. Sinclair, the manager, came into Bryce's office with a handful of folded papers. "I have here," he announced in his clerky voice with a touch of solemnity to it, "a trial balance. I have not had time to make an exact inventory; but in order to give you some idea of the condition of your father's affairs, I have used approximate figures and prepared a profit-and-loss account."

Bryce reached for the papers.

"You will note the amount charged off to profit and loss under the head of 'Pensions,'" Sinclair continued. "It amounts approximately to two thousand dollars a month, and this sum represents payments to crippled employees and the dependent families of men killed in the employ of the Company."

"In addition to these payments, your father owns thirty-two thirty-acre farms which he has cleared from his logged-over lands. These little farms are equipped with bungalows and outbuildings built by your father and represent a considerable investment. As you know, these farms are wonderfully rich, and are planted in apples and berries. Other lands contiguous to them sell readily at two hundred dollars an acre, and so you will see that your father has approximately two hundred thousand dollars tied up in these little farms."

"But he has given a life-lease at nothing a year for each farm to former employees who have been smashed beyond the possibility of doing the hard work of the mill and woods," Bryce reminded the manager. "Hence you must not figure those farms among our assets."

"Why not?" Sinclair replied evenly. "Formal leases have never been executed, and the tenants occupy the property at your father's pleasure."

"I think that will be about as far as the discussion on that point need proceed," Bryce replied smilingly. "My father's word has always been considered sufficient in this country; his verbal promise to pay has always been collateral enough for those who know him."

"But my dear boy," Sinclair protested, "while that sort of philanthropy is very delightful when one can afford the luxury, it is scarcely practical when one is teetering on the verge of financial ruin. After all, Bryce, self-preservation is the first law of human nature, and the sale of those farms would go a long way toward helping the Cardigan Redwood Lumber Company out of the hole it is in at present."

"And we're really teetering on the edge of financial ruin, eh?" Bryce queried calmly.

"That is expressing your condition mildly. The semi-annual payment of interest on the bonded indebtedness falls due on July first—and we're going to default on it, sure as death and taxes. Colonel Pennington holds a majority of our bonds, and that means prompt suit for foreclosure."

"Well, then, Sinclair," Bryce retorted, carefully pigeon-holing the documents the manager had handed him, "I'll tell you what we'll do. For fifty years my father has played the game in this community like a sport and a gentleman, and I'll be damned if his son will dog it now, at the finish. I gather from your remarks that we could find ready sale for those thirty-two little farms?"

"I am continually receiving offers for them."

"Then they were not included in the list of properties covered by our bonded indebtedness?"

"No, your father refused to include them. He said he would take a chance on the financial future of himself and his boy, but not on his helpless dependents."

"Good old John Cardigan! Well, Sinclair, I'll not take a chance on them either; so to-morrow morning you will instruct our attorney to draw up formal life-leases on those farms, and to make certain they are absolutely unassailable. Colonel Pennington may have the lands sold to satisfy a deficiency judgment against us, but while those life-leases from the former owner are in force, my father's proteges cannot be dispossessed. After they are dead, of course, Pennington may take the farms—and be damned to him."

Sinclair stared in frank amazement at his youthful superior. "You are throwing away two hundred thousand dollars," he said distinctly.

"I haven't thrown it away—yet. You forget, Sinclair, that we're going to fight first—and fight like fiends; then if we lose—well, the tail goes with the hide, By the way, Sinclair, are any of those farms untenanted at the present time?"

"Yes. Old Bill Tarpey, who lost his three boys in a forest fire over on the San Hedrin, passed out last week. The Tarpey boys died in the Cardigan employ, and so your father gave Bill the use of a farm out near Freshwater."

"Well, you'd better be his successor, Sinclair. You're no longer a young man, and you've been thirty years in this office. Play safe, Sinclair, and include yourself in one of those life-leases."

"My dear boy—"

"Nonsense! United we stand, divided we fall, Sinclair; and let there be no moaning of the bar when a Cardigan puts out to sea."

Smiling, he rose from his desk, patted the bewildered Sinclair on the latter's grizzled head, and then reached for his hat. "I'm dining out to-night, Sinclair, and I wouldn't be a kill-joy at the feast, for a ripe peach. Your confounded figures might make me gloomy; so we'll just reserve discussion of them till to-morrow morning. Be a sport, Sinclair, and for once in your life beat the six o'clock whistle. In other words, I suggest that you go home and rest for once."

He left Sinclair staring at him rather stupidly.

CHAPTER XIII

Colonel Pennington's imported British butler showed Bryce into the Pennington living room at six-thirty, announcing him with due ceremony. Shirley rose from the piano where she had been idly fingering the keys and greeted him with every appearance of pleasure—following which, she turned to present her visitor to Colonel Pennington, who was standing in his favourite position with his back to the fireplace.

"Uncle Seth, this is Mr. Cardigan, who was so very nice to me the day I landed in Red Bluff."

The Colonel bowed. "I have to thank you, sir, for your courtesy to my niece." He had assumed an air of reserve, of distinct aloofness, despite his studied politeness. Bryce stepped forward with extended hand, which the Colonel grasped in a manner vaguely suggestive of that clammy-palmed creation of Charles Dickens—Uriah Heep. Bryce was tempted to squeeze the lax fingers until the Colonel should bellow with pain; but resisting the ungenerous impulse, he replied instead:

"Your niece, Colonel, is one of those fortunate beings the world will always clamour to serve."

"Quite true, Mr. Cardigan. When she was quite a little girl I came under her spell myself."

"So did I, Colonel. Miss Sumner has doubtless told you of our first meeting some twelve years ago?"

"Quite so. May I offer you a cocktail, Mr. Cardigan?"

"Thank you, certainly. Dad and I have been pinning one on about this time every night since my return."

"Shirley belongs to the Band of Hope," the Colonel explained. "She's ready at any time to break a lance with the Demon Rum. Back in Michigan, where we used to live, she saw too many woodsmen around after the spring drive. So we'll have to drink her share, Mr. Cardigan. Pray be seated."

Bryce seated himself. "Well, we lumbermen are a low lot and naturally fond of dissipation," he agreed. "I fear Miss Sumner's Prohibition tendencies will be still further strengthened after she has seen the mad-train."

"What is that?" Shirley queried.

"The mad-train runs over your uncle's logging railroad up into Township Nine, where his timber and ours is located. It is the only train operated on Sunday, and it leaves Sequoia at five p.m. to carry the Pennington and Cardigan crews back to the woods after their Saturday-night celebration in town. As a usual thing, all hands, with the exception of the brakeman, engineers, and fireman, are singing, weeping or fighting drunk."

"But why do you provide transportation for them to come to town Saturday nights?" Shirley protested.

"They ride in on the last trainload of logs, and if we didn't let them do it, they'd ask for their time. It's the way of the gentle lumberjack. And of course, once they get in, we have to round them up on Sunday afternoon and get them back on the job. Hence the mad-train."

"Do they fight, Mr. Cardigan?"

"Frequently. I might say usually. It's quite an inspiring sight to see a couple of lumberjacks going to it on a flat-car travelling thirty miles an hour."

"But aren't they liable to fall off and get killed?"

"No. You see, they're used to fighting that way. Moreover, the engineer looks back, and if he sees any signs of Donnybrook Fair, he slows down."

"How horrible!"

"Yes, indeed. The right of way is lined with empty whiskey bottles."

Colonel Pennington spoke up. "We don't have any fighting on the mad-train any more," he said blandly.

"Indeed! How do you prevent it?" Bryce asked.

"My woods-boss, Jules Rondeau, makes them keep the peace," Pennington replied with a small smile. "If there's any fighting to be done, he does it."

"You mean among his own crew, of course," Bryce suggested.

"No, he's in charge of the mad-train, and whether a fight starts among your men or ours, he takes a hand. He's had them all behaving mildly for quite a while, because he can whip any man in the country, and everybody realizes it. I don't know what I'd do without Rondeau. He certainly makes those bohunks of mine step lively."

"Oh-h-h! Do you employ bohunks, Colonel?"

"Certainly. They cost less; they are far less independent than most men and more readily handled. And you don't have to pamper them—particularly in the matter of food. Why, Mr Cardigan, with all due respect to your father, the way he feeds his men is simply ridiculous! Cake and pie and doughnuts at the same meal!" The Colonel snorted virtuously.

"Well, Dad started in to feed his men the same food he fed himself, and I suppose the habits one forms in youth are not readily changed in old age, Colonel."

"But that makes it hard for other manufacturers," the Colonel protested. "I feed my men good plain food and plenty of it—quite better food than they were used to before they came to this country; but I cannot seem to satisfy them. I am continuously being reminded, when I do a thing thus and so, that John Cardigan does it otherwise. Your respected parent is the basis for comparison in this country, Cardigan, and I find it devilish inconvenient." He laughed indulgently and passed his cigarette-case to Bryce.

"Uncle Seth always grows restless when some other man is the leader," Shirley volunteered with a mischievous glance at Pennington. "He was the Great Pooh-Bah of the lumber-trade back in Michigan, but out here he has to play second fiddle. Don't you, Nunky-dunk?"

"I'm afraid I do, my dear," the Colonel admitted with his best air of hearty expansiveness. "I'm afraid I do. However, Mr. Cardigan, now that you have—at least, I have been so informed—taken over your father's business, I am hoping we will be enabled to get together on many little details and work them out on a common basis to our mutual advantage. We lumbermen should stand together and not make it hard for each other. For instance, your scale of wages is totally disproportionate to the present high cost of manufacture and the mediocre market; yet just because you pay it, you set a precedent which we are all forced to follow. However," he concluded, "let's not talk shop. I imagine we have enough of that during the day. Besides, here are the cocktails."

With the disposal of the cocktails, the conversation drifted into a discussion of Shirley's adventures with a salmon in Big Lagoon. The Colonel discoursed learnedly on the superior sport of muskellunge-fishing, which prompted Bryce to enter into a description of going after swordfish among the islands of the Santa Barbara channel. "Trout-fishing when the fish gets into white water is good sport; salmon-fishing is fine, and the steel-head in Eel River are hard to beat; muskellunge are a delight, and tarpon are not so bad if you're looking for thrills; but for genuine inspiration give me a sixteen-foot swordfish that will leap out of the water from three to six feet, and do it three or four hundred times—all on a line and rod so light one dares not state the exact weight if he values his reputation for veracity. Once I was fishing at San—"

The butler appeared in the doorway and bowed to Shirley, at the time announcing that dinner was served. The girl rose and gave her arm to Bryce; with her other arm linked through her uncle's she turned toward the dining room.

Just inside the entrance Bryce paused. The soft glow of the candles in the old-fashioned silver candlesticks upon the table was reflected in the polished walls of the room-walls formed of panels of the most exquisitely patterned redwood burl Bryce Cardigan had ever seen. Also the panels were unusually large.

Shirley Sumner's alert glance followed Bryce's as it swept around the room. "This dining room is Uncle Seth's particular delight, Mr. Cardigan," she explained.

"It is very beautiful, Miss Sumner. And your uncle has worked wonders in the matter of having it polished. Those panels are positively the largest and most beautiful specimens of redwood burl ever turned out in this country. The grain is not merely wavy; it is not merely curly; it is actually so contrary that you have here, Colonel Pennington, a room absolutely unique, in that it is formed of bird's-eye burl. Mark the deep shadows in it. And how it does reflect those candles!"

"It is beautiful," the Colonel declared. "And I must confess to a pardonable pride in it, although the task of keeping these walls from being marred by the furniture knocking against them requires the utmost care."

Bryce turned and his brown eyes blazed into the Colonel's. "Where DID you succeed in finding such a marvellous tree?" he queried pointedly. "I know of but one tree in Humboldt County that could have produced such beautiful burl."

For about a second Colonel Pennington met Bryce's glance unwaveringly; then he read something in his guest's eyes, and his glance shifted, while over his benign countenance a flush spread quickly. Bryce noted it, and his quickly roused suspicions were as quickly kindled into certainty. "Where did you find that tree?" he repeated innocently.

"Rondeau, my woods-boss, knew I was on the lookout for something special—something nobody else could get; so he kept his eyes open."

"Indeed!" There was just a trace of irony in Bryce's tones as he drew Shirley's chair and held it for her. "As you say, Colonel, it is difficult to keep such soft wood from being marred by contact with the furniture. And you are fortunate to have such a woods-boss in your employ. Such loyal fellows are usually too good to be true, and quite frequently they put their blankets on their backs and get out of the country when you least expect it. I dare say it would be a shock to you if Rondeau did that."

There was no mistaking the veiled threat behind that apparently innocent observation, and the Colonel, being a man of more than ordinary astuteness, realized that at last he must place his cards on the table. His glance, as he rested it on Bryce now, was baleful, ophidian. "Yes," he said, "I would be rather disappointed. However, I pay Rondeau rather more than it is customary to pay woods-bosses; so I imagine he'll stay—unless, of course, somebody takes a notion to run him out of the county. And when that happens, I want to be on hand to view the spectacle."

Bryce sprinkled a modicum of salt in his soup. "I'm going up into Township Nine to-morrow afternoon," he remarked casually. "I think I shall go over to your camp and pay the incomparable Jules a brief visit. Really, I have heard so much about that woods-boss of yours, Colonel, that I ache to take him apart and see what makes him go."

Again the Colonel assimilated the hint, but preferred to dissemble. "Oh, you can't steal him from me, Cardigan," he laughed. "I warn you in advance—so spare yourself the effort."

"I'll try anything once," Bryce retorted with equal good nature. "However, I don't want to steal him from you. I want to ascertain from him where he procured this burl. There may be more of the same in the neighbourhood where he got this."

"He wouldn't tell you."

"He might. I'm a persuasive little cuss when I choose to exert myself."

"Rondeau is not communicative. He requires lots of persuading."

"What delicious soup!" Bryce murmured blandly. "Miss Sumner, may I have a cracker?"

The dinner passed pleasantly; the challenge and defiance between guest and host had been so skillfully and gracefully exchanged that Shirley hadn't the slightest suspicion that these two well-groomed men had, under her very nose, as it were, agreed to be enemies and then, for the time being, turned their attention to other and more trifling matters. Coffee was served in the living room, and through the fragrant smoke of Pennington's fifty-cent perfectos a sprightly three-cornered conversation continued for an hour. Then the Colonel, secretly enraged at the calm, mocking, contemplative glances which Bryce ever and anon bestowed upon him, and unable longer to convince himself that he was too apprehensive—that this cool young man knew nothing and would do nothing even if he knew something—rose, pleaded the necessity for looking over some papers, and bade Bryce good-night. Foolishly he proffered Bryce a limp hand; and a demon of deviltry taking possession of the latter, this time he squeezed with a simple, hearty earnestness, the while he said:

"Colonel Pennington, I hope I do not have to assure you that my visit here this evening has not only been delightful but—er—instructive. Good-night, sir, and pleasant dreams."

With difficulty the Colonel suppressed a groan. However, he was not the sort of man who suffers in silence; for a minute later the butler, leaning over the banisters as his master climbed the stairs to his library, heard the latter curse with an eloquence that was singularly appealing.

CHAPTER XIV

Colonel Seth Pennington looked up sourly as a clerk entered his private office. "Well?" he demanded brusquely. When addressing his employees, the Colonel seldom bothered to assume his pontifical manner.

"Mr. Bryce Cardigan is waiting to see you, sir."

"Very well. Show him in."

Bryce entered. "Good morning, Colonel," he said pleasantly and brazenly thrust out his hand.

"Not for me, my boy," the Colonel assured him. "I had enough of that last night. We'll just consider the hand-shaking all attended to, if you please. Have a chair; sit down and tell me what I can do to make you happy."

"I'm delighted to find you in such a generous frame of mind, Colonel. You can make me genuinely happy by renewing, for ten years on the same terms as the original contract, your arrangement to freight the logs of the Cardigan Redwood Lumber Company from the woods to tidewater."

Colonel Pennington cleared his throat with a propitiatory "Ahem-m-m!" Then he removed his gold spectacles and carefully wiped them with a silk handkerchief, as carefully replaced them upon his aristocratic nose, and then gazed curiously at Bryce.

"Upon my soul!" he breathed.

"I realized, of course, that this is reopening an issue which you have been pleased to regard as having been settled in the last letter my father had from you, and wherein you named terms that were absolutely prohibitive."

"My dear young friend! My very dear young friend! I must protest at being asked to discuss this matter. Your father and I have been over it in detail; we failed to agree, and that settles it. As a matter of fact, I am not in position to handle your logs with my limited rolling-stock, and that old hauling contract which I took over when I bought the mills, timber-lands, and logging railroad from the late Mr. Henderson and incorporated into the Laguna Grande Lumber Company, has been an embarrassment I have longed to rid myself of. Under those circumstances you could scarcely expect me to saddle myself with it again, at your mere request and solely to oblige you."

"I did not expect you to agree to my request. I am not quite that optimistic," Bryce replied evenly.

"Then why did you ask me?"

"I thought that possibly, if I reopened negotiations, you might have a reasonable counter-proposition to suggest."

"I haven't thought of any."

"I suppose if I agreed to sell you that quarter-section of timber in the little valley over yonder" (he pointed to the east) "and the natural outlet for your Squaw Creek timber, you'd quickly think of one," Bryce suggested pointedly.

"No, I am not in the market for that Valley of the Giants, as your idealistic father prefers to call it. Once I would have purchased it for double its value, but at present I am not interested."

"Nevertheless it would be an advantage for you to possess it."

"My dear boy, the possession of that big timber is an advantage I expect to enjoy before I acquire many more gray hairs. But I do not expect to pay for it."

"Do you expect me to offer it to you as a bonus for renewing our hauling contract?"

The Colonel snapped his fingers. "By George," he declared, "that's a bright idea, and a few months ago I would have been inclined to consider it very seriously. But now—"

"You figure you've got us winging, eh?" Bryce was smiling pleasantly.

"I am making no admissions," Pennington responded enigmatically "—nor any hauling contracts for my neighbour's logs," he added.

"You may change your mind."

"Never."

"I suppose I'll have to abandon logging in Township Nine and go back to the San Hedrin," Bryce sighed resignedly.

"If you do, you'll go broke. You can't afford it. You're on the verge of insolvency this minute."

"I suppose, since you decline to haul our logs, after the expiration of our present contract, and in view of the fact that we are not financially able to build our own logging railroad, that the wisest course my father and I could pursue would be to sell our timber in Township Nine to you. It adjoins your holdings in the same township"

"I had a notion the situation would begin to dawn upon you." The Colonel was smiling now; his handsome face was gradually assuming the expression pontifical. "I'll give you a dollar a thousand feet stumpage for it."

"On whose cruise?"

"Oh, my own cruisers will estimate it."

"I'm afraid I can't accept that offer. We paid a dollar and a half for it, you know, and if we sold it to you at a dollar, the sale would not bring us sufficient money to take up our bonded indebtedness; we'd only have the San Hedrin timber and the Valley of the Giants left, and since we cannot log either of these at present, naturally we'd be out of business."

"That's the way I figured it, my boy."

"Well—we're not going out of business."

"Pardon me for disagreeing with you. I think you are."

"Not much! We can't afford it."

The Colonel smiled benignantly. "My dear boy, my very dear young friend, listen to me. Your paternal ancestor is the only human being who has ever succeeded in making a perfect monkey of me. When I wanted to purchase from him a right of way through his absurd Valley of the Giants, in order that I might log my Squaw Creek timber, he refused me. And to add insult to injury, he spouted a lot of rot about his big trees, how much they meant to him, and the utter artistic horror of running a logging-train through the grove—particularly since he planned to bequeath it to Sequoia as a public park. He expects the city to grow up to it during the next twenty years.

"My boy, that was the first bad break your father made. His second break was his refusal to sell me a mill-site. He was the first man in this county, and he had been shrewd enough to hog all the water-front real estate and hold onto it. I remember he called himself a progressive citizen, and when I asked him why he was so assiduously blocking the wheels of progress, he replied that the railroad would build in from the south some day, but that when it did, its builders would have to be assured of terminal facilities on Humboldt Bay. 'By holding intact the spot where rail and water are bound to meet,' he told me, 'I insure the terminal on tidewater which the railroad must have before consenting to build. But if I sell it to Tom, Dick, and Harry, they will be certain to gouge the railroad when the latter tries to buy it from them. They may scare the railroad away.'"

"Naturally!" Bryce replied. "The average human being is a hog, and merciless when he has the upper hand. He figures that a bird in the hand is worth two in the bush. My father, on the contrary, has always planned for the future. He didn't want that railroad blocked by land-speculators and its building delayed. The country needed rail connection with the outside world, and moreover his San Hedrin timber isn't worth a hoot until that feeder to a transcontinental road shall be built to tap it."

"But he sold Bill Henderson the mill-site on tidewater that he refused to sell me, and later I had to pay Henderson's heirs a whooping price for it. And I haven't half the land I need."

"But he needed Henderson then. They had a deal on together. You must remember, Colonel, that while Bill Henderson held that Squaw Creek timber he later sold you, my father would never sell him a mill-site. Can't you see the sporting point of view involved? My father and Bill Henderson were good-natured rivals; for thirty years they had tried to outgame each other on that Squaw Creek timber. Henderson thought he could force my father to buy at a certain price, and my father thought he could force Henderson to sell at a lesser price; they were perfectly frank about it with each other and held no grudges. Of course, after you bought Henderson out, you foolishly took over his job of trying to outgame my father. That's why you bought Henderson out, isn't it? You had a vision of my father's paying you a nice profit on your investment, but he fooled you, and now you're peeved and won't play."

Bryce hitched his chair farther toward the Colonel. "Why shouldn't my dad be nice to Bill Henderson after the feud ended?" he continued. "They could play the game together then, and they did. Colonel, why can't you be as sporty as Henderson and my father? They fought each other, but they fought fairly and in the open, and they never lost the respect and liking each had for the other."

"I will not renew your logging contract. That is final, young man. No man can ride me with spurs and get away with it."

"Oh, I knew that yesterday."

"Then why have you called on me to-day, taking up my time on a dead issue?"

"I wanted to give you one final chance to repent. I know your plan. You have it in your power to smash the Cardigan Redwood Lumber Company, acquire it at fifty per cent. of its value, and merge its assets with your Laguna Grande Lumber Company. You are an ambitious man. You want to be the greatest redwood manufacturer in California, and in order to achieve your ambitions, you are willing to ruin a competitor: you decline to play the game like a thoroughbred."

"I play the game of business according to the rules of the game; I do nothing illegal, sir."

"And nothing generous or chivalrous. Colonel, you know your plea of a shortage of rolling-stock is that the contract for hauling our logs has been very profitable and will be more profitable in the future if you will accept a fifty-cent-per-thousand increase on the freight-rate and renew the contract for ten years."

"Nothing doing, young man. Remember, you are not in a position to ask favours."

"Then I suppose we'll have to go down fighting?"

"I do not anticipate much of a fight."

"You'll get as much as I can give you."

"I'm not at all apprehensive."

"And I'll begin by running your woods-boss out of the country."

"Ah-h!"

"You know why, of course—those burl panels in your dining room. Rondeau felled a tree in our Valley of the Giants to get that burl for you, Colonel Pennington."

Pennington flushed. "I defy you to prove that," he almost shouted.

"Very well. I'll make Rondeau confess; perhaps he'll even tell me who sent him after the burl. Upon my word, I think you inspired that dastardly raid. At any rate, I know Rondeau is guilty, and you, as his employer and the beneficiary of his crime, must accept the odium."

The Colonel's face went white. "I do not admit anything except that you appear to have lost your head, young man. However, for the sake of argument: granting that Rondeau felled that tree, he did it under the apprehension that your Valley of the Giants is a part of my Squaw Creek timber adjoining."

"I do not believe that. There was malice in the act—brutality even; for my mother's grave identified the land as ours, and Rondeau felled the tree on her tombstone."

"If that is so, and Rondeau felled that tree—I do not believe he did—I am sincerely sorry, Cardigan, Name your price and I will pay you for the tree. I do not desire any trouble to develop over this affair."

"You can't pay for that tree," Bryce burst forth. "No pitiful human being can pay in dollars and cents for the wanton destruction of God's handiwork. You wanted that burl and when my father was blind and could no longer make his Sunday pilgrimage up to that grove, your woods-boss went up and stole that which you knew you could not buy."

"That will be about all from you, young man. Get out of my office. And by the way, forget that you have met my niece."

"It's your office—so I'll get out. As for your second command"—he snapped his fingers in Pennington's face—"fooey!"

When Bryce had gone, the Colonel hurriedly called his logging-camp on the telephone and asked for Jules Rondeau, only to be informed, by the timekeeper who answered the telephone, that Rondeau was up in the green timber with the choppers and could not be gotten to the telephone in less than two hours.

"Do not send for him, then," Pennington commanded. "I'm coming up on the eleven-fifteen train and will talk to him when he comes in for his lunch."

At eleven o'clock, and just as the Colonel was leaving to board the eleven-fifteen logging-train bound empty for the woods, Shirley Sumner made her appearance in his office.

"Uncle Seth," she complained, "I'm lonesome. The bookkeeper tells me you're going up to the logging-camp. May I go with you?"

"By all means. Usually I ride in the cab with the engineer and fireman; but if you're coming, I'll have them hook on the caboose. Step lively, my dear, or they'll be holding the train for us and upsetting our schedule."

CHAPTER XV

By virtue of their logging-contract with Pennington, the Cardigans and their employees were transported free over Pennington's logging railroad; hence, when Bryce Cardigan resolved to wait upon Jules Rondeau in the matter of that murdered Giant, it was characteristic of him to choose the shortest and most direct route to his quarry, and as the long string of empty logging-trucks came crawling off the Laguna Grande Lumber Company's log-dump, he swung over the side, quite ignorant of the fact that Shirley and her precious relative were riding in the little caboose in the rear.

At twelve-ten the train slid in on the log landing of the Laguna Grande Lumber Company's main camp, and Bryce dropped off and approached the engineer of the little donkey-engine used for loading the logs.

"Where's Rondeau?" he asked.

The engineer pointed to a huge, swarthy man approaching across the clearing in which the camp was situated. "That's him," he replied. And without further ado, Bryce strode to meet his man.

"Are you Jules Rondeau?" he demanded as he came up to the woods-boss. The latter nodded. "I'm Bryce Cardigan," his interrogator announced, "and I'm here to thrash you for chopping that big redwood tree over in that little valley where my mother is buried."

"Oh!" Rondeau smiled. "Wiz pleasure, M'sieur." And without a moment's hesitation he rushed. Bryce backed away from him warily, and they circled.

"When I get through with you, Rondeau," Bryce said distinctly, "it'll take a good man to lead you to your meals. This country isn't big enough for both of us, and since you came here last, you've got to go first."

Bryce stepped in, feinted for Rondeau's jaw with his right, and when the woods-boss quickly covered, ripped a sizzling left into the latter's midriff. Rondeau grunted and dropped his guard, with the result that Bryce's great fists played a devil's tattoo on his countenance before he could crouch and cover.

"This is a tough one," thought Bryce. His blows had not, apparently, had the slightest effect on the woods-boss. Crouched low and with his arms wrapped around his head, Rondeau still came on unfalteringly, and Bryce was forced to give way before him; to save his hands, he avoided the risk of battering Rondeau's hard head and sinewy arms.

Already word that the woods-boss was battling with a stranger had been shouted into the camp dining room, and the entire crew of that camp, abandoning their half-finished meal, came pouring forth to view the contest.

Out of the tail of his eye Bryce saw them coming, but he was not apprehensive, for he knew the code of the woodsman: "Let every man roll his own hoop." It would be a fight to a finish, for no man would interfere; striking, kicking, gouging, biting, or choking would not be looked upon as unsportsmanlike; and as Bryce backed cautiously away from the huge, lithe, active, and powerful man before him, he realized that Jules Rondeau was, as his father had stated, "top dog among the lumberjacks."

Rondeau, it was apparent, had no stomach for Bryce's style of combat. He wanted a rough-and-tumble fight and kept rushing, hoping to clinch; if he could but get his great hands on Bryce, he would wrestle him down, climb him, and finish the fight in jig-time. But a rough-and-tumble was exactly what Bryce was striving to avoid; hence when Rondeau rushed, Bryce side-stepped and peppered the woodsman's ribs. But the woods-crew, which by now was ringed around them, began to voice disapproval of this style of battle.

"Clinch with him, dancing-master," a voice roared.

"Tie into him, Rondeau," another shouted.

"It's a fair match," cried another, "and the red one picked on the main push. He was looking for a fight, an' he ought to get it; but these fancy fights don't suit me. Flop him, stranger, flop him."

"Rondeau can't catch him," a fourth man jeered. "He's a foot-racer, not a fighter."

Suddenly two powerful hands were placed between Bryce's shoulders, effectually halting his backward progress; then he was propelled violently forward until he collided with Rondeau. With a bellow of triumph, the woods-boss's gorilla-like arms were around Bryce, swinging him until he faced the man who had forced him into that terrible grip. This was no less a personage than Colonel Seth Pennington, and it was obvious he had taken charge of what he considered the obsequies.

"Stand back, you men, and give them room," he shouted. "Rondeau will take care of him now. Stand back, I say. I'll discharge the man that interferes."

With a heave and a grunt Rondeau lifted his antagonist, and the pair went crashing to the earth together, Bryce underneath. And then something happened. With a howl of pain, Rondeau rolled over on his back and lay clasping his left wrist in his right hand, while Bryce scrambled to his feet.

"The good old wrist-lock does the trick," he announced; and stooping, he grasped the woods-boss by the collar with his left hand, lifted him, and struck him a terrible blow in the face with his right. But for the arm that upheld him, Rondeau would have fallen. To have him fall, however, was not part of Bryce's plan. Jerking the fellow toward him, he passed his arm around

Rondeau's neck, holding the latter's head as in a vise with the crook of his elbow. And then the battering started. When it was finished, Bryce let his man go, and Rondeau, bloody, sobbing, and semi-conscious, sprawled on the ground.

Bryce bent over him. "Now, damn you," he roared, "who felled that tree in Cardigan's Redwoods?"

"I did, M'sieur. Enough—I confess!" The words were a whisper.

"Did Colonel Pennington suggest it to you?"

"He want ze burl. By gar, I do not want to fell zat tree—"

"That's all I want to know." Stooping, Bryce seized Rondeau by the nape of the neck and the slack of his overalls, lifted him shoulder-high and threw him, as one throws a sack of meal, full at Colonel Pennington.

"You threw me at him. Now I throw him at you. You damned, thieving, greedy, hypocritical scoundrel, if it weren't for your years and your gray hair, I'd kill you."

The helpless hulk of the woods-boss descended upon the Colonel's expansive chest and sent him crashing earthward. Then Bryce, war-mad, turned to face the ring of Laguna Grande employees about him.

"Next!" he roared. "Singly, in pairs, or the whole damned pack!"

"Mr. Cardigan!"

He turned. Colonel Pennington's breath had been knocked out of his body by the impact of his semi-conscious woods-boss, and he lay inert, gasping like a hooked fish. Beside him Shirley Sumner was kneeling, her hands clasping her uncle's, but with her violet eyes blazing fiercely on Bryce Cardigan.

"How dare you?" she cried. "You coward! To hurt my uncle!"

He gazed at her a moment, fiercely, defiantly, his chest rising and falling from his recent exertions, his knotted fists gory with the blood of his enemy. Then the light of battle died, and he hung his head. "I'm sorry," he murmured, "not for his sake, but yours. I didn't know you were here. I forgot—myself."

"I'll never speak to you again so long as I live," she burst out passionately.

He advanced a step and stood gazing down upon her. Her angry glance met his unflinchingly; and presently for him the light went out of the world.

"Very well," he murmured. "Good-bye." And with bowed head he turned and made off through the green timber toward his own logging-camp five miles distant.

CHAPTER XVI

With the descent upon his breast of the limp body of his big woods-bully, Colonel Pennington had been struck to earth as effectively as if a fair-sized tree had fallen on him. Indeed, with such force did his proud head collide with terra firma that had it not been for the soft cushion of ferns and tiny redwood twigs, his neck must have been broken by the shock. To complete his withdrawal from active service, the last whiff of breath had been driven from his lungs; and for the space of a minute, during which Jules Rondeau lay heavily across his midriff, the Colonel was quite unable to get it back. Pale, gasping, and jarred from soul to suspenders, he was merely aware that something unexpected and disconcerting had occurred.

While the Colonel fought for his breath, his woodsmen remained in the offing, paralyzed into inactivity by reason of the swiftness and thoroughness of Bryce Cardigan's work; then Shirley motioned to them to remove the wreckage, and they hastened to obey.

Freed from the weight on the geometric centre of his being, Colonel Pennington stretched his legs, rolled his head from side to side, and snorted violently several times like a buck. After the sixth snort he felt so much better that a clear understanding of the exact nature of the catastrophe came to him; he struggled and sat up, looking around a little wildly.

"Where—did—Cardigan—go?" he gasped.

One of his men pointed to the timber into which the enemy had just disappeared.

"Surround him—take him," Pennington ordered. "I'll give—a month's pay—to each of—the six men that bring—that scoundrel to me. Get him—quickly! Understand?"

Not a man moved. Pennington shook with fury. "Get him," he croaked. "There are enough of you to do—the job. Close in on him—everybody. I'll give a month's pay to—everybody."

A man of that indiscriminate mixture of Spaniard and Indian known in California as cholo swept the circle of men with an alert and knowing glance. His name was Flavio Artelan, but his straight black hair, dark russet complexion, beady eyes, and hawk nose gave him such a resemblance to a fowl that he was known among his fellows as the Black Minorca, regardless of the fact that this sobriquet was scarcely fair to a very excellent breed of chicken. "That offer's good enough for me," he remarked in businesslike tones. "Come on—everybody. A month's pay for five minutes' work. I wouldn't tackle the job with six men, but there are twenty of us here."

"Hurry," the Colonel urged them.

Shirley Sumner's flashing glance rested upon the Black Minorca. "Don't you dare!" she cried. "Twenty to one! For shame!"

"For a month's pay," he replied impudently, and grinned evilly. "And I'm takin' orders from my boss." He started on a dog-trot for the timber, and a dozen men trailed after him.

Shirley turned helplessly on her uncle, seized his arm and shook it frantically. "Call them back! Call them back!" she pleaded.

Her uncle got uncertainly to his feet. "Not on your life!" he growled, and in his cold gray eyes there danced the lights of a thousand devils. "I told you the fellow was a ruffian. Now, perhaps, you'll believe me. We'll hold him until Rondeau revives, and then—"

Shirley guessed the rest, and she realized that it was useless to plead—that she was only wasting time. "Bryce! Bryce!" she called. "Run! They're after you. Twenty of them! Run, run—for my sake!"

His voice answered her from the timber: "Run? From those cattle? Not from man or devil." A silence. Then: "So you've changed your mind, have you? You've spoken to me again!" There was triumph, exultation in his voice. "The timber's too thick, Shirley. I couldn't get away anyhow—so I'm coming back."

She saw him burst through a thicket of alder saplings into the clearing, saw half a dozen of her uncle's men close in around him like wolves around a sick steer; and at the shock of their contact, she moaned and hid her face in her trembling hands.

Half man and half tiger that he was, the Black Minorca, as self-appointed leader, reached Bryce first. The cholo was a squat, powerful little man, with more bounce to him than a rubber ball; leading his men by a dozen yards, he hesitated not an instant but dodged under the blow Bryce lashed out at him and came up inside the latter's guard, feeling for Bryce's throat. Instead he met Bryce's knee in his abdomen, and forthwith he folded up like an accordion.

The next instant Bryce had stooped, caught him by the slack of the trousers and the scruff of the neck and thrown him, as he had thrown Rondeau, into the midst of the men advancing to his aid. Three of them went down backward; and Bryce, charging over them, stretched two more with well-placed blows from left and right, and continued on across the clearing, running at top speed, for he realized that for all the desperation of his fight and the losses already inflicted on his assailants, the odds against him were insurmountable.

Seeing him running away, the Laguna Grande woods-men took heart and hope and pursued him. Straight for the loading donkey at the log-landing Bryce ran. Beside the donkey stood a neat tier of firewood; in the chopping block, where the donkey-fireman had driven it prior to abandoning his post to view the contest between Bryce and Jules Rondeau, was a double-bitted axe. Bryce jerked it loose, swung it, whirled on his pursuers, and rushed them. Like turkeys scattering before the raid of a coyote they fled in divers directions and from a safe distance turned to gaze apprehensively upon this demon they had been ordered to bring in.

Bryce lowered the axe, removed his hat, and mopped his moist brow. From the centre of the clearing men were crawling or staggering to safety—with the exception of the Black Minorca, who lay moaning softly. Colonel Pennington, seeing his fondest hopes expire, lost his head completely.

"Get off my property, you savage," he shrilled.

"Don't be a nut, Colonel," Bryce returned soothingly. "I'll get off—when I get good and ready, and not a second sooner. In fact, I was trying to get off as rapidly as I could when you sent your men to bring me back. Prithee why, old thing? Didst crave more conversation with me, or didst want thy camp cleaned out?"

He started toward Pennington, who backed hastily away. Shirley stood her ground, bending upon Bryce, as he approached her, a cold and disapproving glance. "I'll get you yet," the Colonel declared from the shelter of an old stump behind which he had taken refuge.

"Barking dogs never bite, Colonel. And that reminds me: I've heard enough from you. One more cheep out of you, my friend, and I'll go up to my own logging-camp, return here with a crew of bluenoses and wild Irish and run your wops, bohunks, and cholos out of the county. I don't fancy the class of labour you're importing into this county, anyhow."

The Colonel, evidently deciding that discretion was the better part of valour, promptly subsided, although Bryce could see that he was mumbling threats to himself, though not in an audible voice.

The demon Cardigan halted beside Shirley and stood gazing down at her. He was smiling at her whimsically. She met his glance for a few seconds; then her lids were lowered and she bit her lip with vexation.

"Shirley," he said.

"You are presumptuous," she quavered.

"You set me an example in presumption," he retorted good humouredly. "Did you not call ME by MY first name a minute ago?" He glanced toward

Colonel Pennington and observed the latter with his neck craned across his protecting stump. He was all ears. Bryce pointed sternly across the clearing, and the Colonel promptly abandoned his refuge and retreated hastily in the direction indicated.

The heir to Cardigan's Redwoods bent over the girl. "You spoke to me—after your promise not to, Shirley," he said gently. "You will always speak to me."

She commenced to cry softly. "I loathe you," she sobbed.

"For you I have the utmost respect and admiration," he replied.

"No, you haven't. If you had, you wouldn't hurt my uncle—the only human being in all this world who is dear to me."

"Gosh!" he murmured plaintively. "I'm jealous of that man. However, I'm sorry I hurt him. He is no longer young, while I—well, I forgot the chivalry my daddy taught me. I give you my word I came here to fight fairly—"

"He merely tried to stop you from fighting."

"No, he didn't, Shirley. He interfered and fouled me. Still, despite that, if I had known you were a spectator I think I should have controlled myself and refrained from pulling off my vengeance in your presence. I shall never cease to regret that I subjected you to such a distressing spectacle. I do hope, however, that you will believe me when I tell you I am not a bully, although when there is a fight worth while, I never dodge it. And this time I fought for the honour of the House of Cardigan."

"If you want me to believe that, you will beg my uncle's pardon."

"I can't do that. He is my enemy and I shall hate him forever; I shall fight him and his way of doing business until he reforms or I am exhausted."

She looked up at him, showing a face in which resentment, outrage, and wistfulness were mirrored.

"You realize, of course, what your insistence on that plan means, Mr. Cardigan?"

"Call me Bryce," he pleaded. "You're going to call me that some day anyhow, so why not start now?"

"You are altogether insufferable, sir. Please go away and never presume to address me again. You are quite impossible."

He shook his head. "I do not give up that readily, Shirley. I didn't know how dear—what your friendship meant to me, until you sent me away; I didn't think there was any hope until you warned me those dogs were hunting me—

and called me Bryce." He held out his hand. "'God gave us our relations,'" he quoted, "'but thank God, we can choose our friends.' And I'll be a good friend to you, Shirley Sumner, until I have earned the right to be something more. Won't you shake hands with me? Remember, this fight to-day is only the first skirmish in a war to the finish—and I am leading a forlorn hope. If I lose—well, this will be good-bye."

"I hate you," she answered drearily. "All our fine friendship—smashed— and you growing stupidly sentimental. I didn't think it of you. Please go away. You are distressing me."

He smiled at her tenderly, forgivingly, wistfully, but she did not see it. "Then it is really good-by," he murmured with mock dolorousness.

She nodded her bowed head. "Yes," she whispered. "After all, I have some pride, you know. You mustn't presume to be the butterfly preaching contentment to the toad in the dust."

"As you will it, Shirley." He turned away. "I'll send your axe back with the first trainload of logs from my camp, Colonel," he called to Pennington.

Once more he strode away into the timber. Shirley watched him pass out of her life, and gloried in what she conceived to be his agony, for she had both temper and spirit, and Bryce Cardigan calmly, blunderingly, rather stupidly (she thought) had presumed flagrantly on brief acquaintance. Her uncle was right. He was not of their kind of people, and it was well she had discovered this before permitting herself to develop a livelier feeling of friendship for him. It was true he possessed certain manly virtues, but his crudities by far outweighed these.

The Colonel's voice broke in upon her bitter reflections. "That fellow Cardigan is a hard nut to crack—I'll say that for him." He had crossed the clearing to her side and was addressing her with his customary air of expansiveness. "I think, my dear, you had better go back into the caboose, away from the prying eyes of these rough fellows. I'm sorry you came, Shirley. I'll never forgive myself for bringing you. If I had thought—but how could I know that scoundrel was coming here to raise a disturbance? And only last night he was at our house for dinner!"

"That's just what makes it so terrible, Uncle Seth," she quavered.

"It IS hard to believe that a man of young Cardigan's evident intelligence and advantages could be such a boor, Shirley. However, I, for one, am not surprised. You will recall that I warned you he might be his father's son. The best course to pursue now is to forget that you have ever met the fellow."

"I wonder what could have occurred to make such a madman of him?" the girl queried wonderingly. "He acted more like a demon than a human being."

"Just like his old father," the Colonel purred benevolently. "When he can't get what he wants, he sulks. I'll tell you what got on his confounded nerves. I've been freighting logs for the senior Cardigan over my railroad; the contract for hauling them was a heritage from old Bill Henderson, from whom I bought the mill and timber-lands; and of course as his assignee it was incumbent upon me to fulfill Henderson's contract with Cardigan, even though the freight-rate was ruinous.

"Well, this morning young Cardigan came to my office, reminded me that the contract would expire by limitation next year and asked me to renew it, and at the same freight-rate. I offered to renew the contract but at a higher freight-rate, and explained to him that I could not possibly continue to haul his logs at a loss. Well, right away he flew into a rage and called me a robber; whereupon I informed him that since he thought me a robber, perhaps we had better not attempt to have any business dealings with each other—that I really didn't want his contract at any price, having scarcely sufficient rolling-stock to handle my own logs. That made him calm down, but in a little while he lost his head again and grew snarly and abusive—to such an extent, indeed, that finally I was forced to ask him to leave my office."

"Nevertheless, Uncle Seth, I cannot understand why he should make such a furious attack upon your employee."

The Colonel laughed with a fair imitation of sincerity and tolerant amusement. "My dear, that is no mystery to me. There are men who, finding it impossible or inadvisable to make a physical attack upon their enemy, find ample satisfaction in poisoning his favourite dog, burning his house, or beating up one of his faithful employees. Cardigan picked on Rondeau for the reason that a few days ago he tried to hire Rondeau away from me— offered him twenty-five dollars a month more than I was paying him, by George! Of course when Rondeau came to me with Cardigan's proposition, I promptly met Cardigan's bid and retained Rondeau; consequently Cardigan hates us both and took the earliest opportunity to vent his spite on us."

The Colonel sighed and brushed the dirt and leaves from his tweeds. "Thunder," he continued philosophically, "it's all in the game, so why worry over it? And why continue to discuss an unpleasant topic, my dear?"

A groan from the Black Minorca challenged her attention. "I think that man is badly hurt, Uncle," she suggested.

"Serves him right," he returned coldly. "He tackled that cyclone full twenty feet in advance of the others; if they'd all closed in together, they would have pulled him down. I'll have that cholo and Rondeau sent down with the next trainload of logs to the company hospital. They're a poor lot and deserve manhandling—"

They paused, facing toward the timber, from which came a voice, powerful, sweetly resonant, raised in song. Shirley knew that half-trained baritone, for she had heard it the night before when Bryce Cardigan, faking his own accompaniment at the piano, had sung for her a number of carefully expurgated lumberjack ballads, the lunatic humour of which had delighted her exceedingly. She marvelled now at his choice of minstrelsy, for the melody was hauntingly plaintive—the words Eugene Field's poem of childhood, "Little Boy Blue."

> *"The little toy dog is covered with dust,*
>
> *But sturdy and stanch he stands;*
>
> *And the little toy soldier is red with rust,*
>
> *And his musket molds in his hands.*
>
> *Time was when the little toy dog was new,*
>
> *And the soldier was passing fair;*
>
> *And that was the time when our little boy blue,*
>
> *Kissed them and put them there."*

"Light-hearted devil, isn't he?" the Colonel commented approvingly. "And his voice isn't half bad. Just singing to be defiant, I suppose."

Shirley did not answer. But a few minutes previously she had seen the singer a raging fury, brandishing an axe and driving men before him. She could not understand. And presently the song grew faint among the timber and died away entirely.

Her uncle took her gently by the arm and steered her toward the caboose. "Well, what do you think of your company now?" he demanded gayly.

"I think," she answered soberly, "that you have gained an enemy worth while and that it behooves you not to underestimate him."

CHAPTER XVII

Through the green timber Bryce Cardigan strode, and there was a lilt in his heart now. Already he had forgotten the desperate situation from which he had just escaped; he thought only of Shirley Sumner's face, tear-stained with terror; and because he knew that at least some of those tears had been inspired by the gravest apprehensions as to his physical well-being, because in his ears there still resounded her frantic warning, he realized that however stern her decree of banishment had been, she was nevertheless not indifferent to him. And it was this knowledge that had thrilled him into song and which when his song was done had brought to his firm mouth a mobility that presaged his old whimsical smile—to his brown eyes a beaming light of confidence and pride.

The climax had been reached—and passed; and the result had been far from the disaster he had painted in his mind's eye ever since the knowledge had come to him that he was doomed to battle to a knockout with Colonel Pennington, and that one of the earliest fruits of hostilities would doubtless be the loss of Shirley Sumner's prized friendship. Well, he had lost her friendship, but a still small voice whispered to him that the loss was not irreparable—whereat he swung his axe as a bandmaster swings his baton; he was glad that he had started the war and was now free to fight it out unhampered.

Up hill and down dale he went. Because of the tremendous trees he could not see the sun; yet with the instinct of the woodsman, an instinct as infallible as that of a homing pigeon, he was not puzzled as to direction. Within two hours his long, tireless stride brought him out into a clearing in the valley where his own logging-camp stood. He went directly to the log-landing, where in a listless and half-hearted manner the loading crew were piling logs on Pennington's logging-trucks.

Bryce looked at his watch. It was two o'clock; at two-fifteen Pennington's locomotive would appear, to back in and couple to the long line of trucks. And the train was only half loaded.

"Where's McTavish?" Bryce demanded of the donkey-driver.

The man mouthed his quid, spat copiously, wiped his mouth with the back of his hand, and pointed. "Up at his shanty," he made answer, and grinned at Bryce knowingly.

Up through the camp's single short street, flanked on each side with the woodsmen's shanties, Bryce went. Dogs barked at him, for he was a stranger in his own camp; children, playing in the dust, gazed upon him owlishly. At the most pretentious shanty on the street Bryce turned in. He had never seen it before, but he knew it to be the woods-boss's home, for unlike its neighbours the house was painted with the coarse red paint that is used on box-cars, while a fence, made of fancy pointed pickets painted white, inclosed a tiny garden in front of the house. As Bryce came through the gate, a young girl rose from where she knelt in a bed of freshly transplanted pansies.

Bryce lifted his hat. "Is Mr. McTavish at home?" he asked.

She nodded. "He cannot see anybody," she hastened to add. "He's sick."

"I think he'll see me. And I wonder if you're Moira McTavish."

"Yes, I'm Moira."

"I'm Bryce Cardigan."

A look of fright crept into the girl's eyes. "Are you—Bryce Cardigan?" she faltered, and looked at him more closely. "Yes, you're Mr. Bryce. You've changed—but then it's been six years since we saw you last, Mr. Bryce."

He came toward her with outstretched hand. "And you were a little girl when I saw you last. Now—you're a woman." She grasped his hand with the frank heartiness of a man. "I'm mighty glad to meet you again, Moira. I just guessed who you were, for of course I should never have recognized you. When I saw you last, you wore your hair in a braid down your back."

"I'm twenty years old," she informed him.

"Stand right where you are until I have looked at you," he commanded, and backed off a few feet, the better to contemplate her.

He saw a girl slightly above medium height, tanned, robust, simply gowned in a gingham dress. Her hands were soiled from her recent labours in the pansy-bed, and her shoes were heavy and coarse; yet neither hands nor feet were large or ungraceful. Her head was well formed; her hair, jet black and of unusual lustre and abundance, was parted in the middle and held in an old-fashioned coil at the nape of a neck the beauty of which was revealed by the low cut of her simple frock. Moira was a decided brunette, with that wonderful quality of skin to be seen only among brunettes who have roses in their cheeks; her brow was broad and spiritual; in her eyes, large, black, and listrous, there was a brooding tenderness not untouched with sorrow—some such expression, indeed, as da Vinci put in the eyes of his Mona Lisa. Her nose was patrician, her face oval; her lips, full and red, were slightly parted in the adorable Cupid's bow which is the inevitable heritage of a short upper lip; her teeth were white as Parian marble; and her full breast was rising and falling swiftly, as if she laboured under suppressed excitement.

So delightful a picture did Moira McTavish make that Bryce forgot all his troubles in her sweet presence. "By the gods, Moira," he declared earnestly, "you're a peach! When I saw you last, you were awkward and leggy, like a colt. I'm sure you weren't a bit good-looking. And now you're the most ravishing young lady in seventeen counties. By jingo, Moira, you're a stunner and no mistake. Are you married?"

She shook her head, blushing pleasurably at his unpolished but sincere compliments.

"What? Not married. Why, what the deuce can be the matter with the eligible young fellows hereabouts?"

"There aren't any eligible young fellows hereabouts, Mr. Bryce. And I've lived in these woods all my life."

"That's why you haven't been discovered."

"And I don't intend to marry a lumberjack and continue to live in these woods," she went on earnestly, as if she found pleasure in this opportunity to announce her rebellion. Despite her defiance, however, there was a note of sad resignation in her voice.

"You don't know a thing about it, Moira. Some bright day your Prince Charming will come by, riding the log-train, and after that it will always be autumn in the woods for you. Everything will just naturally turn to crimson and gold."

"How do you know, Mr Bryce?"

He laughed. "I read about it in a book."

"I prefer spring in the woods, I think. It seems—It's so foolish of me, I know; I ought to be contented, but it's hard to be contented when it is always winter in one's heart. That frieze of timber on the skyline limits my world, Mr Bryce. Hills and timber, timber and hills, and the thunder of falling redwoods. And when the trees have been logged off so we can see the world, we move back into green timber again." She sighed.

"Are you lonely, Moira?"

She nodded.

"Poor Moira!" he murmured absently.

The thought that he so readily understood touched her; a glint of tears was in her sad eyes. He saw them and placed his arm fraternally around her shoulders. "Tut-tut, Moira! Don't cry," he soothed her. "I understand perfectly, and of course we'll have to do something about it. You're too fine for this." With a sweep of his hand he indicated the camp. He had led her to the low stoop in front of the shanty. "Sit down on the steps, Moira, and we'll talk it over. I really called to see your father, but I guess I don't want to see him after all—if he's sick."

She looked at him bravely. "I didn't know you at first, Mr. Bryce. I fibbed. Father isn't sick. He's drunk."

"I thought so when I saw the loading-crew taking it easy at the log-landing. I'm terribly sorry."

"I loathe it—and I cannot leave it," she burst out vehemently. "I'm chained to my degradation. I dream dreams, and they'll never come true. I—I—oh Mr. Bryce, Mr. Bryce, I'm so unhappy."

"So am I," he retorted. "We all get our dose of it, you know, and just at present I'm having an extra helping, it seems. You're cursed with too much imagination, Moira. I'm sorry about your father. He's been with us a long time, and my father has borne a lot from him for old sake's sake; he told me the other night that he has discharged Mac fourteen times during the past ten years, but to date he hasn't been able to make it stick. For all his sixty years, Moira, your confounded parent can still manhandle any man on the pay-roll, and as fast as Dad put in a new woods-boss old Mac drove him off the job. He simply declines to be fired, and Dad's worn out and too tired to bother about his old woods-boss any more. He's been waiting until I should get back."

"I know," said Moira wearily. "Nobody wants to be Cardigan's woods-boss and have to fight my father to hold his job. I realize what a nuisance he has become."

Bryce chuckled. "I asked Father why he didn't stand pat and let Mac work for nothing; having discharged him, my father was under no obligation to give him his salary just because he insisted on being woods-boss. Dad might have starved your father out of these woods, but the trouble was that old Mac would always come and promise reform and end up by borrowing a couple of hundred dollars, and then Dad had to hire him again to get it back! Of course the matter simmers down to this: Dad is so fond of your father that he just hasn't got the moral courage to work him over—and now that job is up to me. Moira, I'm not going to beat about the bush with you. They tell me your father is a hopeless inebriate."

"I'm afraid he is, Mr. Bryce."

"How long has he been drinking to excess?"

"About ten years, I think. Of course, he would always take a few drinks with the men around pay-day, but after Mother died, he began taking his drinks between pay-days. Then he took to going down to Sequoia on Saturday nights and coming back on the mad-train, the maddest of the lot. I suppose he was lonely, too. He didn't get real bad, however, till about two years ago."

"Just about the time my father's eyes began to fail him and he ceased coming up into the woods to jack Mac up? So he let the brakes go and started to coast, and now he's reached the bottom! I couldn't get him on the telephone to-day or yesterday. I suppose he was down in Arcata, liquoring up."

She nodded miserably.

"Well, we have to get logs to the mill, and we can't get them with old John Barleycorn for a woods-boss, Moira. So we're going to change woods-bosses, and the new woods-boss will not be driven off the job, because I'm going to stay up here a couple of weeks and break him in myself. By the way, is Mac ugly in his cups?"

"Thank God, no," she answered fervently. "Drunk or sober, he has never said an unkind word to me."

"But how do you manage to get money to clothe yourself? Sinclair tells me Mac needs every cent of his two hundred and fifty dollars a month to enjoy himself."

"I used to steal from him," the girl admitted. "Then I grew ashamed of that, and for the past six months I've been earning my own living. Mr. Sinclair was very kind. He gave me a job waiting on table in the camp dining room. You see, I had to have something here. I couldn't leave my father. He had to have somebody to take care of him. Don't you see, Mr. Bryce?"

"Sinclair is a fuzzy old fool," Bryce declared with emphasis. "The idea of our woods-boss's daughter slinging hash to lumberjacks. Poor Moira!"

He took one of her hands in his, noting the callous spots on the plump palm, the thick finger-joints that hinted so of toil, the nails that had never been manicured save by Moira herself. "Do you remember when I was a boy, Moira, how I used to come up to the logging-camps to hunt and fish? I always lived with the McTavishes then. And in September, when the huckleberries were ripe, we used to go out and pick them together. Poor Moira! Why, we're old pals, and I'll be shot if I'm going to see you suffer."

She glanced at him shyly, with beaming eyes. "You haven't changed a bit, Mr. Bryce. Not one little bit!"

"Let's talk about you, Moira. You went to school in Sequoia, didn't you?"

"Yes, I was graduated from the high school there. I used to ride the log-trains into town and back again."

"Good news! Listen, Moira. I'm going to fire your father, as I've said, because he's working for old J.B. now, not the Cardigan Redwood Lumber Company. I really ought to pension him after his long years in the Cardigan service, but I'll be hanged if we can afford pensions any more—particularly to keep a man in booze; so the best our old woods-boss gets from me is this shanty, or another like it when we move to new cuttings, and a perpetual meal-ticket for our camp dining room while the Cardigans remain in business. I'd finance him for a trip to some State institution where they sometimes reclaim such wreckage, if I didn't think he's too old a dog to be taught new tricks."

"Perhaps," she suggested sadly, "you had better talk the matter over with him."

"No, I'd rather not. I'm fond of your father, Moira. He was a man when I saw him last—such a man as these woods will never see again—and I don't want to see him again until he's cold sober. I'll write him a letter. As for you, Moira, you're fired, too. I'll not have you waiting on table in my logging-camp—not by a jugful! You're to come down to Sequoia and go to work in our office. We can use you on the books, helping Sinclair, and relieve him of the task of billing, checking tallies, and looking after the pay-roll. I'll pay you a hundred dollars a month, Moira. Can you get along on that?"

Her hard hand closed over his tightly, but she did not speak.

"All right, Moira. It's a go, then. Hills and timber—timber and hills—and I'm going to set you free. Perhaps in Sequoia you'll find your Prince Charming. There, there, girl, don't cry. We Cardigans had twenty-five years of faithful service from Donald McTavish before he commenced slipping; after all, we owe him something, I think."

She drew his hand suddenly to her lips and kissed it; her hot tears of joy fell on it, but her heart was too full for mere words.

"Fiddle-de-dee, Moira! Buck up," he protested, hugely pleased, but embarrassed withal. "The way you take this, one would think you had expected me to go back on an old pal and had been pleasantly surprised when I didn't. Cheer up, Moira! Cherries are ripe, or at any rate they soon will be; and if you'll just cease shedding the scalding and listen to me, I'll tell you what I'll do. I'll advance you two months' salary for—well, you'll need a lot of clothes and things in Sequoia that you don't need here. And I'm glad I've managed to settle the McTavish hash without kicking up a row and hurting your feelings. Poor old Mac! I'm sorry I can't bear with him, but we simply have to have the logs, you know."

He rose, stooped, and pinched her ear; for had he not known her since childhood, and had they not gathered huckleberries together in the long ago? She was sister to him—just another one of his problems—and nothing more.

"Report on the job as soon as possible, Moira," he called to her from the gate. Then the gate banged behind him, and with a smile and a debonair wave of his hand, he was striding down the little camp street where the dogs and the children played in the dust.

After a while Moira walked to the gate and leaning upon it, looked down the street toward the log-landing where Bryce was ragging the laggard crew into some thing like their old-time speed. Presently the locomotive backed in and coupled to the log tram, and when she saw Bryce leap aboard and seat himself on a top log in such a position that he could not fail to see her at the gate, she waved to him. He threw her a careless kiss, and the train pulled out.

Presently, when Moira lifted her Madonna glance to the frieze of timber on the skyline, there was a new glory in her eyes; and lo, it was autumn in the woods, for over that hill Prince Charming had come to her, and life was all crimson and gold!

When the train loaded with Cardigan logs crawled in on the main track and stopped at the log-landing in Pennington's camp, the locomotive uncoupled and backed in on the siding for the purpose of kicking the caboose, in which Shirley and Colonel Pennington had ridden to the woods, out onto the main line again—where, owing to a slight downhill grade, the caboose, controlled by the brakeman, could coast gently forward and be hooked on to the end of the log-train for the return journey to Sequoia.

Throughout the afternoon Shirley, following the battle royal between Bryce and the Pennington retainers, had sat dismally in the caboose. She was prey to many conflicting emotions; but having had what her sex term "a good cry," she had to a great extent recovered her customary poise—and was busily speculating on the rapidity with which she could leave Sequoia and forget she had ever met Bryce Cardigan—when the log-train rumbled into the landing and the last of the long string of trucks came to a stop directly opposite the caboose.

Shirley happened to be looking through the grimy caboose window at that moment. On the top log of the load the object of her unhappy speculations was seated, apparently quite oblivious of the fact that he was back once more in the haunt of his enemies, although knowledge that the double-bitted axe he had so unceremoniously borrowed of Colonel Pennington was driven deep into the log beside him, with the haft convenient to his hand, probably had much to do with Bryce's air of detached indifference. He was sitting with his elbows on his knees, his chin in his cupped hands, and a pipe thrust aggressively out the corner of his mouth, the while he stared moodily at his feet.

Shirley suspected she knew what he was thinking of; he was less than six feet from her, and a morbid fascination moved her to remain at the window and watch the play of emotions over his strong, stern face. She told herself that should he move, should he show the slightest disposition to raise his head and bring his eyes on a level with hers, she would dodge away from the window in time to escape his scrutiny.

She reckoned without the engine. With a smart bump it struck the caboose and shunted it briskly up the siding; at the sound of the impact Bryce raised his troubled glance just in time to see Shirley's body, yielding to the shock, sway into full view at the window.

With difficulty he suppressed a grin. "I'll bet my immortal soul she was peeking at me," he soliloquized. "Confound the luck! Another meeting this afternoon would be embarrassing." Tactfully he resumed his study of his feet, not even looking up when the caboose, after gaining the main track, slid gently down the slight grade and was coupled to the rear logging-truck. Out of the tail of his eye he caught a glimpse of Colonel Pennington passing alongside the log-train and entering the caboose; he heard the engineer shout to the brakeman—who had ridden down from the head of the train to unlock the siding switch and couple the caboose—to hurry up, lock the switch, and get back aboard the engine.

"Can't get this danged key to turn in the lock," the brakeman shouted presently. "Lock's rusty, and something's gone bust inside."

Minutes passed. Bryce's assumed abstraction became real, for he had many matters to occupy his busy brain, and it was impossible for him to sit idle without adverting to some of them. Presently he was subconsciously aware that the train was moving gently forward; almost immediately, it seemed to him, the long string of trucks had gathered their customary speed; and then suddenly it dawned upon Bryce that the train had started off without a single jerk—and that it was gathering headway rapidly.

He looked ahead—and his hair grew creepy at the roots. There was no locomotive attached to the train! It was running away down a two per cent. grade, and because of the tremendous weight of the train, it was gathering momentum at a fearful rate.

The reason for the runaway dawned on Bryce instantly. The road, being privately owned, was, like most logging-roads, neglected as to roadbed and rolling-stock; also it was undermanned, and the brake-man, who also acted as switchman, had failed to set the hand-brakes on the leading truck after the engineer had locked the air-brakes. As a result, during the five or six minutes required to "spot in" the caboose, and an extra minute or two lost while the brakeman struggled with the recalcitrant lock on the switch, the air had leaked away through the worn valves and rubber tubing, and the brakes had been released—so that the train, without warning, had quietly and almost noiselessly slid out of the log-landing and started on its mad career. Before the engineer could beat it to the other switch with the locomotive, run out on the main track, let the runaway gradually catch up with him and hold it— no matter how or what happened to him or his engine—the first logging-truck had cleared the switch and blocked pursuit. There was nothing to do now save watch the wild runaway and pray, for of all the mad runaways in a mad world, a loaded logging-train is by far the worst.

For an instant after realizing his predicament, Bryce Cardigan was tempted to jump and take his chance on a few broken bones, before the train could reach a greater speed than twenty miles an hour. His impulse was to run forward and set the handbrake on the leading truck, but a glance showed him that even with the train standing still he could not hope to leap from truck to truck and land on the round, freshly peeled surface of the logs without slipping for he had no calks in his boots. And to slip now meant swift and horrible death.

"Too late!" he muttered. "Even if I could get to the head of the train, I couldn't stop her with the hand-brake; should I succeed in locking the wheels, the brute would be doing fifty miles an hour by that time—the front truck would slide and skid, leave the tracks and pile up with me at the bottom of a mess of wrecked rolling-stock and redwood logs."

Then he remembered. In the wildly rolling caboose Shirley Sumner rode with her uncle, while less than two miles ahead, the track swung in a sharp curve high up along the hillside above Mad River. Bryce knew the leading truck would never take that curve at high speed, even if the ancient rolling-stock should hold together until the curve was reached, but would shoot off at a tangent into the canyon, carrying trucks, logs, and caboose with it, rolling over and over down the hillside to the river.

"The caboose must be cut out of this runaway," Bryce soliloquized, "and it must be cut out in a devil of a hurry. Here goes nothing in particular, and may God be good to my dear old man."

He jerked his axe out of the log, drove it deep into the top log toward the end, and by using the haft to cling to, crawled toward the rear of the load and looked down at the caboose coupling. The top log was a sixteen-foot butt; the two bottom logs were eighteen footers. With a silent prayer of thanks to Providence, Bryce slid down to the landing thus formed. He was still five feet above the coupling, however; but by leaning over the swaying, bumping edge and swinging the axe with one hand, he managed to cut through the rubber hose on the air connection. "The blamed thing might hold and drag the caboose along after I've pulled out the coupling-pin," he reflected. "And I can't afford to take chances now."

Nevertheless he took them. Axe in hand, he leaped down to the narrow ledge formed by the bumper in front of the cabooses—driving his face into the front of the caboose; and he only grasped the steel rod leading from the brake-chains to the wheel on the roof in time to avoid falling half stunned between the front of the caboose and the rear of the logging-truck. The caboose had once been a box-car; hence there was no railed front platform to which Bryce might have leaped in safety. Clinging perilously on the bumper, he reached with his foot, got his toe under the lever on the side, jerked it upward, and threw the pin out of the coupling; then with his free hand he swung the axe and drove the great steel jaws of the coupling apart.

The caboose was cut out! But already the deadly curve was in sight; in two minutes the first truck would reach it; and the caboose, though cut loose, had to be stopped, else with the headway it had gathered, it, too, would follow the logging-trucks to glory.

For a moment Bryce clung to the brake-rod, weak and dizzy from the effects of the blow when, leaping down from the loaded truck to the caboose bumper, his face had smashed into the front of the caboose. His chin was bruised, skinned, and bloody; his nose had been broken, and twin rivulets of blood ran from his nostrils. He wiped it away, swung his axe, drove the blade deep into the bumper and left it there with the haft quivering; turning, he climbed swiftly up the narrow iron ladder beside the brake-rod until he reached the roof; then, still standing on the ladder, he reached the brake-wheel and drew it promptly but gradually around until the wheel-blocks began to bite, when he exerted his tremendous strength to the utmost and with his knees braced doggedly against the front of the caboose, held the wheel.

The brake screamed, but the speed of the caboose was not appreciably slackened. "It's had too good a start!" Bryce moaned. "The momentum is more than I can overcome. Oh, Shirley, my love! God help you!"

He cast a sudden despairing look over his shoulder downward at the coupling. He was winning, after all, for a space of six feet now yawned between the end of the logging-truck and the bumper of the caboose. If he could but hold that tremendous strain on the wheel for a quarter of a mile, he might get the demon caboose under control! Again he dug his knees into the front of the car and twisted on the wheel until it seemed that his muscles must crack.

After what seemed an eon of waiting, he ventured another look ahead. The rear logging-truck was a hundred yards in front of him now, and from the wheels of the caboose an odour of something burning drifted up to him. "I've got your wheels locked!" he half sobbed. "I'll hold you yet, you brute. Slide! That's it! Slide, and flatten your infernal wheels. Hah! You're quitting— quitting. I'll have you in control before we reach the curve. Burn, curse you, burn!"

With a shriek of metal scraping metal, the head of the Juggernaut ahead took the curve, clung there an instant, and was catapulted out into space. Logs weighing twenty tons were flung about like kindling; one instant, Bryce could see them in the air; the next they had disappeared down the hillside. A deafening crash, a splash, a cloud of dust—

With a protesting squeal, the caboose came to the point where the logging-train had left the right of way, carrying rails and ties with it. The wheels on the side nearest the bank slid into the dirt first and plowed deep into the soil; the caboose came to an abrupt stop, trembled and rattled, overtopped its centre of gravity, and fell over against the cut-bank, wearily, like a drunken hag.

Bryce, still clinging to the brake, was fully braced for the shock and was not flung off. Calmly he descended the ladder, recovered the axe from the bumper, climbed back to the roof, tiptoed off the roof to the top of the bank and sat calmly down under a manzanita bush to await results, for he was quite confident that none of the occupants of the confounded caboose had been treated to anything worse than a wild ride and a rare fright, and he was curious to see how Shirley Sumner would behave in an emergency.

Colonel Pennington was first to emerge at the rear of the caboose. He leaped lightly down the steps, ran to the front of the car, looked down the track, and swore feelingly. Then he darted back to the rear of the caboose.

"All clear and snug as a bug under a chip, my dear," he called to Shirley. "Thank God, the caboose became uncoupled—guess that fool brakeman forgot to drop the pin; it was the last car, and when it jumped the track and plowed into the dirt, it just naturally quit and toppled over against the bank. Come out, my dear."

Shirley came out, dry-eyed, but white and trembling. The Colonel placed his arm around her, and she hid her face on his shoulder and shuddered. "There, there!" he soothed her affectionately. "It's all over, my dear. All's well that ends well."

"The train," she cried in a choking voice. "Where is it?"

"In little pieces—down in Mad River." He laughed happily. "And the logs weren't even mine! As for the trucks, they were a lot of ratty antiques and only fit to haul Cardigan's logs. About a hundred yards of roadbed ruined—

that's the extent of my loss, for I'd charged off the trucks to profit and loss two years ago."

"Bryce Cardigan," she sobbed. "I saw him—he was riding a top log on the train. He—ah, God help him!"

The Colonel shook her with sudden ferocity. "Young Cardigan," he cried sharply. "Riding the logs? Are you certain?"

She nodded, and her shoulders shook piteously.

"Then Bryce Cardigan is gone!" Pennington's pronouncement was solemn, deadly with its flat finality. "No man could have rolled down into Mad River with a trainload of logs and survived. The devil himself couldn't." He heaved a great sigh, and added: "Well, that clears the atmosphere considerably, although for all his faults, I regret, for his father's sake, that this dreadful affair has happened. Well, it can't be helped, Shirley. Don't cry, my dear. I know it's terrible, but—there, there my love. Do brace up. Poor devil! For all his damnable treatment of me, I wouldn't have had this happen for a million dollars."

Shirley burst into wild weeping. Bryce's heart leaped, for he understood the reason for her grief. She had sent him away in anger, and he had gone to his death; ergo it would be long before Shirley would forgive herself. Bryce had not intended presenting himself before her in his battered and bloody condition, but the sight of her distress now was more than he could bear. He coughed slightly, and the alert Colonel glanced up at him instantly.

"Well, I'll be hanged!" The words fell from Pennington's lips with a heartiness that was almost touching. "I thought you'd gone with the train."

"Sorry to have disappointed you, old top," Bryce replied blithely, "but I'm just naturally stubborn. Too bad about the atmosphere you thought cleared a moment ago! It's clogged worse than ever now."

At the sound of Bryce's voice, Shirley raised her head, whirled and looked up at him. He held his handkerchief over his gory face that the sight might not distress her; he could have whooped with delight at the joy that flashed through her wet lids.

"Bryce Cardigan," she commanded sternly, "come down here this instant."

"I'm not a pretty sight, Shirley. Better let me go about my business."

She stamped her foot. "Come here!"

"Well, since you insist," he replied, and he slid down the bank.

"How did you get up there—and what do you mean by hiding there spying on me, you—you—oh, YOU!"

"Cuss a little, if it will help any," he suggested. "I had to get out of your way—out of your sight—and up there was the best place. I was on the roof of the caboose when it toppled over, so all I had to do was step ashore and sit down."

"Then why didn't you stay there?" she demanded furiously.

"You wouldn't let me," he answered demurely. "And when I saw you weeping because I was supposed to be with the angels, I couldn't help coughing to let you know I was still hanging around, ornery as a book-agent."

"How did you ruin your face, Mr. Cardigan?"

"Tried to take a cast of the front end of the caboose in my classic countenance—that's all."

"But you were riding the top log on the last truck——"

"Certainly, but I wasn't hayseed enough to stay there until we struck this curve. I knew exactly what was going to happen, so I climbed down to the bumper of the caboose, uncoupled it from the truck, climbed up on the roof, and managed to get the old thing under control with the hand-brake; then I skedaddled up into the brush because I knew you were inside, and——By the way, Colonel Pennington, here is your axe, which I borrowed this afternoon. Much obliged for its use. The last up-train is probably waiting on the siding at Freshwater to pass the late lamented; consequently a walk of about a mile will bring you a means of transportation back to Sequoia. Walk leisurely— you have lots of time. As for myself, I'm in a hurry, and my room is more greatly to be desired than my company, so I'll start now."

He lifted his hat, turned, and walked briskly down the ruined track.

Shirley made a little gesture of dissent, half opened her lips to call him back, thought better of it, and let him go. When he was out of sight, it dawned on her that he had risked his life to save hers.

"Uncle Seth," she said soberly, "what would have happened to us if Bryce Cardigan had not come up here to-day to thrash your woods-boss?"

"We'd both be in Kingdom Come now," he answered truthfully.

"Under the circumstances, then," Shirley continued, "suppose we all agree to forget that anything unusual happened to-day——"

"I bear the young man no ill will, Shirley, but before you permit yourself to be carried away by the splendour of his action in cutting out the caboose and getting it under control, it might be well to remember that his own precious hide was at stake also. He would have cut the caboose out even if you and I had not been in it."

"No, he would not," she insisted, for the thought that he had done it for her sake was very sweet to her and would persist. "Cooped up in the caboose, we did not know the train was running away until it was too late for us to jump, while Bryce Cardigan, riding out on the logs, must have known it almost immediately. He would have had time to jump before the runaway gathered too much headway—and he would have jumped, Uncle Seth, for his father's sake."

"Well, he certainly didn't stay for mine, Shirley."

She dried her moist eyes and blushed furiously. "Uncle Seth," she pleaded, taking him lovingly by the arm, "let's be friends with Bryce Cardigan; let's get together and agree on an equitable contract for freighting his logs over our road."

"You are now," he replied severely, "mixing sentiment and business; if you persist, the result will be chaos. Cardigan has in a large measure squared himself for his ruffianly conduct earlier in the day, and I'll forgive him and treat him with courtesy hereafter; but I want you to understand, Shirley, that such treatment by me does not constitute a license for that fellow to crawl up in my lap and be petted. He is practically a pauper now, which makes him a poor business risk, and you'll please me greatly by leaving him severely alone—by making him keep his distance."

"I'll not do that," she answered with a quiet finality that caused her uncle to favour her with a quick, searching glance.

He need not have worried, however, for Bryce Cardigan was too well aware of his own financial condition to risk the humiliation of asking Shirley Sumner to share it with him. Moreover, he had embarked upon a war—a war which he meant to fight to a finish.

CHAPTER XVIII

George Sea Otter, summoned by telephone, came out to Freshwater, the station nearest the wreck, and transported his battered young master back to Sequoia. Here Bryce sought the doctor in the Cardigan Redwood Lumber Company's little hospital and had his wrecked nose reorganized and his cuts bandaged. It was characteristic of his father's son that when this detail had been attended to, he should go to the office and work until the six o'clock whistle blew.

Old Cardigan was waiting for him at the gate when he reached home. George Sea Otter had already given the old man a more or less garbled account of the runaway log-train, and Cardigan eagerly awaited his son's arrival in order to ascertain the details of this new disaster which had come upon them. For disaster it was, in truth. The loss of the logs was trifling—perhaps three or four thousand dollars; the destruction of the rolling-stock was the crowning misfortune. Both Cardigans knew that Pennington would eagerly seize upon this point to stint his competitor still further on logging-equipment, that there would be delays—purposeful but apparently unavoidable—before this lost rolling-stock would be replaced. And in the interim the Cardigan mill, unable to get a sufficient supply of logs to fill orders in hand, would be forced to close down. Full well Pennington knew that anything which, tends to bring about a shortage of raw material for any manufacturing plant will result inevitably in the loss of customers.

"Well, son," said John Cardigan mildly as Bryce unlatched the gate, "another bump, eh?"

"Yes, sir—right on the nose."

"I meant another bump to your heritage, my son."

"I'm worrying more about my nose, partner. In fact, I'm not worrying about my heritage at all. I've come to a decision on that point: We're going to fight and fight to the last; we're going down fighting. And by the way, I started the fight this afternoon. I whaled the wadding out of that bucko woods-boss of Pennington's, and as a special compliment to you, John Cardigan, I did an almighty fine job of cleaning. Even went so far as to muss the Colonel up a little."

"Wow, wow, Bryce! Bully for you! I wanted that man Rondeau taken apart. He has terrorized our woods-men for a long time. He's king of the mad-train, you know."

Bryce was relieved. His father did not know, then, of the act of vandalism in the Valley of the Giants. This fact strengthened Bryce's resolve not to tell him—also to get the fallen monarch sawed up and the stump blasted out before an operation should restore his father's sight and reveal to him the crowning cruelty of his enemy.

Arm in arm they walked up the garden path together.

Just as they entered the house, the telephone in the hall tinkled, and Bryce answered.

"Mr. Cardigan," came Shirley Sumner's voice over the wire.

"Bryce," he corrected her.

She ignored the correction,

"I—I don't know what to say to you," she faltered.

"There is no necessity for saying anything, Shirley."

"But you saved our lives, and at least have a right to expect due and grateful acknowledgment of our debt. I rang up to tell you how splendid and heroic your action was—"

"I had my own life to save, Shirley."

"You did not think of that at the time."

"Well—I didn't think of your uncle's, either," he replied without enthusiasm.

"I'm sure we never can hope to catch even with you, Mr. Cardigan."

"Don't try. Your revered relative will not; so why should you?"

"You are making it somewhat hard for me to—to—rehabilitate our friendship, Mr. Cardigan. We have just passed through a most extraordinary day, and if at evening I can feel as I do now, I think you ought to do your share—and help."

"Bless your heart," he murmured. "The very fact that you bothered to ring me up at all makes me your debtor. Shirley, can you stand some plain speaking—between friends, I mean?"

"I think so, Mr. Cardigan."

"Well, then," said Bryce, "listen to this: I am your uncle's enemy until death do us part. Neither he nor I expect to ask or to give quarter, and I'm going to smash him if I can."

"If you do, you smash me," she warned him.

"Likewise our friendship. I'm sorry, but it's got to be done if I can do it. Shall—shall we say good-bye, Shirley?"

"Yes-s-s!" There was a break in her voice. "Good-bye, Mr Cardigan. I wanted you to know."

"Good-bye! Well, that's cutting the mustard," he murmured sotto voce, "and there goes another bright day-dream." Unknown to himself, he spoke directly into the transmitter, and Shirley, clinging half hopefully to the receiver at the other end of the wire, heard him—caught every inflection of the words, commonplace enough, but freighted with the pathos of Bryce's first real tragedy.

"Oh, Bryce!" she cried sharply. But he did not hear her; he had hung up his receiver now.

The week that ensued was remarkable for the amount of work Bryce accomplished in the investigation of his father's affairs—also for a visit from Donald McTavish, the woods-boss. Bryce found him sitting in the private office one morning at seven o'clock.

"Hello, McTavish," he saluted the woods-boss cheerfully and extended his hand for a cordial greeting. His wayward employee stood up, took the proffered hand in both of his huge and callous ones, and held it rather childishly.

"Weel! 'Tis the wee laddie hissel'," he boomed. "I'm glad to see ye, boy."

"You'd have seen me the day before yesterday—if you had been seeable," Bryce reminded him with a bright smile. "Mac, old man, they tell me you've gotten to be a regular go-to-hell."

"I'll nae deny I take a wee drappie now an' then," the woods-boss admitted frankly, albeit there was a harried, hangdog look in his eyes.

Bryce sat down at his desk, lighted his pipe, and looked McTavish over soberly. The woods-boss was a big, raw-boned Scotsman, with a plentiful sprinkling of silver in his thick mane of red hair, which fell far down on his shoulders. A tremendous nose rose majestically out of a face so strong and rugged one searched in vain for aught of manly beauty in it; his long arms hung gorilla-like, almost to his knees, and he was slightly stooped, as if from bearing heavy burdens. Though in the late fifties, his years had touched him lightly; but John Barleycorn had not been so considerate. Bryce noted that McTavish was carrying some thirty pounds of whiskey fat and that the pupils of his fierce blue eyes were permanently distended, showing that alcohol had begun to affect his brain. His hands trembled as he stood before Bryce, smiling fatuously and plucking at the cuffs of his mackinaw. The latter realized that McTavish was waiting for him to broach the object of the visit; so with an effort he decided to begin the disagreeable task.

"Mac, did Moira give you my message?"

"Aye."

"Well, I guess we understand each other, Mac. Was there something else you wanted to see me about?"

McTavish sidled up to the desk. "Ye'll no be firin' auld Mac oot o' hand?" he pleaded hopefully. "Mon, ha ye the heart to do it—after a' these years?"

Bryce nodded. "If you have the heart—after all these years—to draw pay you do not earn, then I have the heart to put a better man in your place."

"Ye was ever a laddie to hae your bit joke."

"It's no good arguing, Mac. You're off the pay-roll onto the pension-roll—your shanty in the woods, your meals at the camp kitchen, your clothing and tobacco that I send out to you. Neither more nor less!" He reached into his desk and drew forth a check. "Here's your wages to the fifteenth. It's the last Cardigan check you'll ever finger. I'm terribly sorry, but I'm terribly in earnest."

"Who will ye pit in ma place?"

"I don't know. However, it won't be a difficult task to find a better man than you."

"I'll nae let him work." McTavish's voice deepened to a growl. "You worked that racket on my father. Try it on me, and you'll answer to me—personally. Lay the weight of your finger on your successor, Mac, and you'll die in the county poor-farm. No threats, old man! You know the Cardigans; they never bluff."

McTavish's glance met the youthful master's for several seconds; then the woods-boss trembled, and his gaze sought the office floor. Bryce knew he had his man whipped at last, and McTavish realized it, too, for quite suddenly he burst into tears.

"Dinna fire me, lad," he pleaded. "I'll gae back on the job an' leave whusky alone."

"Nothing doing, Mac. Leave whiskey alone for a year and I'll discharge your successor to give you back your job. For the present however, my verdict stands. You're discharged."

"Who kens the Cardigan woods as I ken them?" McTavish blubbered. "Who'll swamp a road into timber sixty per cent. clear when the mill's runnin' on foreign orders an' the owd man's calling for clear logs? Who'll fell trees wi' the least amount o' breakage? Who'll get the work out o' the men? Who'll—"

"Don't plead, Mac," Bryce interrupted gently. "You're quite through, and I can't waste any more time on you."

"Ye dinna mean it, lad. Ye canna mean it."

"On your way, Mac. I loathe arguments. And don't forget your check."

"I maun see yer faither aboot this. He'll nae stand for sic treatment o' an auld employee."

Bryce's temper flared up. "You keep away from my father. You've worried him enough in the past, you drunkard. If you go up to the house to annoy my father with your pleadings, McTavish, I'll manhandle you." He glanced at his watch. "The next train leaves for the woods in twenty minutes. If you do not go back on it and behave yourself, you can never go back to Cardigan woods."

"I will nae take charity from any man," McTavish thundered. "I'll nae bother the owd man, an' I'll nae go back to yon woods to live on yer bounty."

"Well, go somewhere, Mac, and be quick about it. Only—when you've reformed, please come back. You'll be mighty welcome. Until then, however, you're as popular with me—that is, in a business way—as a wet dog."

"Ye're nae the man yer faither was," the woods-boss half sobbed. "Ye hae a heart o' stone."

"You've been drunk for fifteen days—and I'm paying you for it, Mac," Bryce reminded him gently. "Don't leave your check behind. You'll need it."

With a fine show of contempt and rage, McTavish tore the check into strips and threw them at Bryce. "I was never a mon to take charity," he roared furiously, and left the office. Bryce called after him a cheerful good-bye, but he did not answer. And he did not remain in town; neither did he return to his shanty in the woods. For a month his whereabouts remained a mystery; then one day Moira received a letter from him informing her that he had a job knee-bolting in a shingle mill in Mendocino County.

CHAPTER XIX

In the interim Bryce had not been idle. From his woods-crew he picked an old, experienced hand—one Jabez Curtis—to take the place of the vanished McTavish. Colonel Pennington, having repaired in three days the gap in his railroad, wrote a letter to the Cardigan Redwood Lumber Company, informing Bryce that until more equipment could be purchased and delivered to take the place of the rolling-stock destroyed in the wreck, the latter would have to be content with half-deliveries; whereupon Bryce irritated the Colonel profoundly by purchasing a lot of second-hand trucks from a bankrupt sugar-pine mill in Lassen County and delivering them to the Colonel's road via the deck of a steam schooner.

"That will insure delivery of sufficient logs to get out our orders on file," Bryce informed his father. "While we are morally certain our mill will run but one year longer, I intend that it shall run full capacity for that year. In fact, I'm going to saw in that one year remaining to us as much lumber as we would ordinarily saw in two years. To be exact, I'm going to run a night-shift."

The sightless old man raised both hands in deprecation. "The market won't absorb it," he protested.

"Then we'll stack it in piles to air-dry and wait until the market is brisk enough to absorb it," Bryce replied.

"Our finances won't stand the overhead of that night-shift, I tell you," his father warned.

"I know we haven't sufficient cash on hand to attempt it, Dad, but—I'm going to borrow some."

"From whom? No bank in Sequoia will lend us a penny, and long before you came home I had sounded every possible source of a private loan."

"Did you sound the Sequoia Bank of Commerce?"

"Certainly not. Pennington owns the controlling interest in that bank, and I was never a man to waste my time."

Bryce chuckled. "I don't care where the money comes from so long as I get it, partner. Pennington's money may be tainted; in fact, I'd risk a bet that it is; but our employees will accept it for wages nevertheless. Desperate circumstances require desperate measures you know, and the day before yesterday, when I was quite ignorant of the fact that Colonel Pennington controls the Sequoia Bank of Commerce, I drifted in on the president and casually struck him for a loan of one hundred thousand dollars."

"Well, I'll be shot, Bryce! What did he say?"

"Said he'd take the matter under consideration and give me an answer this morning. He asked me, of course, what I wanted that much money for, and I told him I was going to run a night-shift, double my force of men in the woods, and buy some more logging-trucks, which I can get rather cheap. Well, this morning I called for my answer—and got it. The Sequoia Bank of Commerce will loan me up to a hundred thousand, but it won't give me the cash in a lump sum. I can have enough to buy the logging-trucks now, and on the first of each month, when I present my pay-roll, the bank will advance me the money to meet it."

"Bryce, I am amazed."

"I am not—since you tell me Colonel Pennington controls that bank. That the bank should accommodate us is the most natural procedure imaginable. Pennington is only playing safe—which is why the bank declined to give me the money in a lump sum. If we run a night-shift, Pennington knows that we can't dispose of our excess output under present market conditions. The redwood trade is in the doldrums and will remain in them to a greater or less degree until the principal redwood centres secure a rail outlet to the markets of the country. It's a safe bet our lumber is going to pile up on the mill dock; hence, when the smash comes and the Sequoia Bank of Commerce calls our loan and we cannot possibly meet it, the lumber on hand will prove security for the loan, will it not? In fact, it will be worth two or three dollars per thousand more then than it is now, because it will be air-dried. And inasmuch as all the signs point to Pennington's gobbling us anyhow, it strikes me as a rather good business on his part to give us sufficient rope to insure a thorough job of hanging."

"But what idea have you got back of such a procedure, Bryce?"

"Merely a forlorn hope, Dad. Something might turn up. The market may take a sudden spurt and go up three or four dollars."

"Yes—and it may take a sudden spurt and drop three or four dollars," his father reminded him.

Bryce laughed. "That would be Pennington's funeral, Dad. And whether the market goes up or comes down, it costs us nothing to make the experiment."

"Quite true." his father agreed.

"Then, if you'll come down to the office to-morrow morning, Dad, we'll hold a meeting of our board of directors and authorize me, as president of the company, to sign the note to the bank. We're borrowing this without collateral, you know."

John Cardigan sighed. Such daring financial acrobatics were not usual with him, but as Bryce had remarked there was no reason why, in their present predicament, they should not gamble. Hence he entered no further objection, and the following day the agreement was entered into with the bank. Bryce closed by wire for the extra logging-equipment and immediately set about rounding up a crew for the woods and for the night-shift in the mill.

For a month Bryce was as busy as the proverbial one-armed paper-hanger with the itch, and during all that time he did not see Shirley Sumner or hear of her, directly or indirectly. Only at infrequent intervals did he permit himself to think of her, for he was striving to forget, and the memory of his brief glimpse of paradise was always provocative of pain.

Moira McTavish, in the meantime, had come down from the woods and entered upon her duties in the mill office. The change from her dull, drab life, giving her, as it did, an opportunity for companionship with people of greater mentality and refinement than she had been used to, quickly brought about a swift transition in the girl's nature. With the passing of the coarse shoes and calico dresses and the substitution of the kind of clothing all women of Moira's instinctive refinement and natural beauty long for, the girl became cheerful, animated, and imbued with the optimism of her years. At first old Sinclair resented the advent of a woman in the office; then he discovered that Moira's efforts lightened his own labours in exact proportion to the knowledge of the business which she assimilated from day to day.

Moira worked in the general office, and except upon occasions when Bryce desired to look at the books or Moira brought some document into the private office for his perusal, there were days during which his pleasant "Good morning, Moira," constituted the extent of their conversation. To John Cardigan, however, Moira was a ministering angel. Gradually she relieved Bryce of the care of the old man. She made a cushion for his easy-chair in the office; she read the papers to him, and the correspondence, and discussed with him the receipt and delivery of orders, the movements of the lumber-fleet, the comedies and tragedies of his people, which had become to him matters of the utmost importance. She brushed his hair, dusted his hat, and crowned him with it when he left the office at nightfall, and whenever Bryce was absent in the woods or in San Francisco, it fell to her lot to lead the old man to and from the house on the hill. To his starved heart her sweet womanly attentions were tremendously welcome, and gradually he formed the habit of speaking of her, half tenderly, half jokingly, as "my girl."

Bryce had been absent in San Francisco for ten days. He had planned to stay three weeks, but finding his business consummated in less time, he returned to Sequoia unexpectedly. Moira was standing at the tall bookkeeping desk, her beautiful dark head bent over the ledger, when he entered the office and set his suitcase in the corner.

"Is that you, Mr. Bryce?" she queried.

"The identical individual, Moira. How did you guess it was I?"

She looked up at him then, and her wonderful dark eyes lighted with a flame Bryce had not seen in them heretofore. "I knew you were coming," she replied simply.

"But how could you know? I didn't telegraph because I wanted to surprise my father, and the instant the boat touched the dock, I went overside and came directly here. I didn't even wait for the crew to run out the gangplank—so I know nobody could have told you I was due."

"That is quite right, Mr. Bryce. Nobody told me you were coming, but I just knew, when I heard the Noyo whistling as she made the dock, that you were aboard, and I didn't look up when you entered the office because I wanted to verify my—my suspicion."

"You had a hunch, Moira. Do you get those telepathic messages very often?" He was crossing the office to shake her hand.

"I've never noticed particularly—that is, until I came to work here. But I always know when you are returning after a considerable absence." She gave him her hand. "I'm so glad you're back."

"Why?" he demanded bluntly.

She flushed. "I—I really don't know, Mr. Bryce."

"Well, then," he persisted, "what do you think makes you glad?"

"I had been thinking how nice it would be to have you back, Mr. Bryce. When you enter the office, it's like a breeze rustling the tops of the Redwoods. And your father misses you so; he talks to me a great deal about you. Why, of course we miss you; anybody would."

As he held her hand, he glanced down at it and noted how greatly it had changed during the past few months. The skin was no longer rough and brown, and the fingers, formerly stiff and swollen from hard work, were growing more shapely. From her hand his glance roved over the girl, noting the improvements in her dress, and the way the thick, wavy black hair was piled on top of her shapely head.

"It hadn't occurred to me before, Moira," he said with a bright impersonal smile that robbed his remark of all suggestion of masculine flattery, "but it seems to me I'm unusually glad to see you, also. You've been fixing your hair different."

The soft lambent glow leaped again into Moira's eyes. He had noticed her—particularly. "Do you like my hair done that way?" she inquired eagerly.

"I don't know whether I do or not. It's unusual—for you. You look mighty sweetly old-fashioned with it coiled in back—somewhat like an old-fashioned daguerreotype of my mother. Is this new style the latest in hairdressing in Sequoia?"

"I think so, Mr. Bryce. I copied it from Colonel Pennington's niece, Miss Sumner."

"Oh," he replied briefly. "You've met her, have you? I didn't know she was in Sequoia still."

"She's been away, but she came back last week. I went to the Valley of the Giants last Saturday afternoon—"

Bryce interrupted. "You didn't tell my father about the tree that was cut, did you?" he demanded sharply.

"No."

"Good girl! He mustn't know. Go on, Moira. I interrupted you."

"I met Miss Sumner up there. She was lost; she'd followed the old trail into the timber, and when the trees shut out the sun, she lost all sense of direction. She was terribly frightened and crying when I found her and brought her home."

"Well, I swan, Moira! What was she doing in our timber?"

"She told me that once, when she was a little girl, you had taken her for a ride on your pony up to your mother's grave. And it seems she had a great curiosity to see that spot again and started out without saying a word to any one. Poor dear! She was in a sad state when I found her."

"How fortunate you found her! I've met Miss Sumner three or four times. That was when she first came to Sequoia. She's a stunning girl, isn't she?"

"Perfectly, Mr. Bryce. She's the first lady I've ever met. She's different."

"No doubt! Her kind are not a product of homely little communities like Sequoia. And for that matter, neither is her wolf of an uncle. What did Miss Sumner have to say to you, Moira?"

"She told me all about herself—and she said a lot of nice things about you, Mr. Bryce, after I told her I worked for you. And when I showed her the way home, she insisted that I should walk home with her. So I did—and the butler served us with tea and toast and marmalade. Then she showed me all her wonderful things—and gave me some of them. Oh, Mr. Bryce, she's so sweet. She had her maid dress my hair in half a dozen different styles until they could decide on the right style, and—"

"And that's it—eh, Moira?"

She nodded brightly.

"I can see that you and Miss Sumner evidently hit it off just right with each other. Are you going to call on her again?"

"Oh, yes! She begged me to. She says she's lonesome."

"I dare say she is, Moira. Well, her choice of a pal is a tribute to the brains I suspected her of possessing, and I'm glad you've gotten to know each other. I've no doubt you find life a little lonely sometimes."

"Sometimes, Mr. Bryce."

"How's my father?"

"Splendid. I've taken good care of him for you."

"Moira, you're a sweetheart of a girl. I don't know how we ever managed to wiggle along without you." Fraternally—almost paternally—he gave her radiant cheek three light little pats as he strode past her to the private office. He was in a hurry to get to his desk, upon which he could see through the open door a pile of letters and orders, and a moment later he was deep in a perusal of them, oblivious to the fact that ever and anon the girl turned upon him her brooding, Madonna-like glance.

That night Bryce and his father, as was their custom after dinner, repaired to the library, where the bustling and motherly Mrs. Tully served their coffee. This good soul, after the democratic fashion in vogue in many Western communities, had never been regarded as a servant; neither did she so regard herself. She was John Cardigan's housekeeper, and as such she had for a quarter of a century served father and son their meals and then seated herself at the table with them. This arrangement had but one drawback, although this did not present itself until after Bryce's return to Sequoia and his assumption of the direction of the Cardigan destinies. For Mrs. Tully had a failing common to many of her sex: she possessed for other people's business an interest absolutely incapable of satisfaction—and she was, in addition, garrulous beyond belief. The library was the one spot in the house which at the beginning of her employment John Cardigan had indicated to Mrs. Tully as sanctuary for him and his; hence, having served the coffee this evening, the amiable creature withdrew, although not without a pang as she reflected upon the probable nature of their conversation and the void which must inevitably result by reason of the absence of her advice and friendly cooperation and sympathy.

No sooner had Mrs. Tully departed than Bryce rose and closed the door behind her. John Cardigan opened the conversation with a contented grunt:

"Plug the keyhole, son," he continued. "I believe you have something on your mind—and you know how Mrs. Tully resents the closing of that door. Estimable soul that she is, I have known her to eavesdrop. She can't help it, poor thing! She was born that way."

Bryce clipped a cigar and held a lighted match while his father "smoked up." Then he slipped into the easy-chair beside the old man.

"Well, John Cardigan," he began eagerly, "fate ripped a big hole in our dark cloud the other day and showed me some of the silver lining. I've been making bad medicine for Colonel Pennington. Partner, the pill I'm rolling for that scheming scoundrel will surely nauseate him when he swallows it."

"What's in the wind, boy?"

"We're going to parallel Pennington's logging-road."

"Inasmuch as that will cost close to three quarters of a million dollars, I'm of the opinion that we're not going to do anything of the sort."

"Perhaps. Nevertheless, if I can demonstrate to a certain party that it will not cost more than three quarters of a million, he'll loan me the money."

The old man shook his head. "I don't believe it, Bryce. Who's the crazy man?"

"His name is Gregory. He's Scotch."

"Now I know he's crazy. When he hands you the money, you'll find he's talking real money but thinking of Confederate greenbacks. For a sane Scotchman to loan that much money without collateral security would be equivalent to exposing his spinal cord and tickling it with a rat-tail file."

Bryce laughed. "Pal," he declared, "if you and I have any brains, they must roll around in our skulls like buckshot in a tin pan. Here we've been sitting for three months, and twiddling our thumbs, or lying awake nights trying to scheme a way out of our difficulties, when if we'd had the sense that God gives geese we would have solved the problem long ago and ceased worrying. Listen, now, with all your ears. When Bill Henderson wanted to build the logging railroad which he afterward sold to Pennington, and which Pennington is now using as a club to beat our brains out, did he have the money to build it?"

"No."

"Where did he get it?"

"I loaned it to him. He only had about eight miles of road to build then, so I could afford to accommodate him."

"How did he pay you back?"

"Why, he gave me a ten-year contract for hauling our logs at a dollar and a half a thousand feet, and I merely credited his account with the amount of the freight-bills he sent me until he'd squared up the loan, principal and interest."

"Well, if Bill Henderson financed himself on that plan, why didn't we think of using the same time-honoured plan for financing a road to parallel Pennington's?"

John Cardigan sat up with a jerk. "By thunder!" he murmured. That was as close as he ever came to uttering an oath. "By thunder!" he repeated. "I never thought of that! But then," he added, "I'm not so young as I used to be, and there are any number of ideas which would have occurred to me twenty years ago but do not occur to me now."

"All right, John Cardigan. I forgive you. Now, then, continue to listen: to the north of that great block of timber held by you and Pennington lie the redwood holdings of the Trinidad Redwood Timber Company."

"Never heard of them before."

"Well, timber away in there in back of beyond has never been well advertised, because it is regarded as practically inaccessible. By extending his logging-road and adding to his rolling-stock, Pennington could make it accessible, but he will not. He figures on buying all that back timber rather cheap when he gets around to it, for the reason that the Trinidad Redwood Timber Company cannot possibly mill its timber until a railroad connects its holdings with the outside world. They can hold it until their corporation franchise expires, and it will not increase sufficiently in value to pay taxes."

"I wonder why the blamed fools ever bought in there, Bryce."

"When they bought, it looked like a good buy. You will remember that some ten years ago a company was incorporated with the idea of building a railroad from Grant's Pass, Oregon, on the line of the Southern Pacific, down the Oregon and California coast to tap the redwood belt."

"I remember. There was a big whoop and hurrah and then the proposition died abornin'. The engineers found that the cost of construction through that mountainous country was prohibitive."

"Well, before the project died, Gregory and his associates believed that it was going to survive. They decided to climb in on the ground floor—had some advance, inside information that the road was to be built; go they quietly gathered together thirty thousand acres of good stuff and then sat down to wait for the railroad, And they are still waiting. Gregory, by the way, is the president of the Trinidad Redwood Timber Company. He's an Edinburgh man, and the fly American promoters got him to put up the price of the timber and then mortgaged their interests to him as security for the advance. He foreclosed on their notes five years ago."

"And there he is with his useless timber!" John Cardigan murmured thoughtfully. "The poor Scotch sucker!"

"He isn't poor. The purchase of that timber didn't even dent his bank-roll. He's what they call in England a tinned-goods manufacturer—purveyor to His Majesty the King, and all that. But he would like to sell his timber, and being Scotch, naturally he desires to sell it at a profit. In order to create a market for it, however, he has to have an outlet to that market. We supply the outlet—with his help; and what happens? Why, timber that cost him fifty and seventy-five cents per thousand feet stumpage—and the actual timber will overrun the cruiser's estimate every time—will be worth two dollars and fifty cents—perhaps more."

The elder Cardigan turned slowly in his chair and bent his sightless gaze upon his son. "Well, well," he cried impatiently.

"He loans us the money to build our road. We build it—on through our timber and into his. The collateral security which we put up will be a twenty-five-years contract to haul his logs to tidewater on Humboldt Bay, at a base freight-rate of one dollar and fifty cents, with an increase of twenty-five cents per thousand every five years thereafter, and an option for a renewal of the contract upon expiration, at the rate of freight last paid. We also grant him perpetual booming-space for his logs in the slough which we own and where we now store our logs until needed at the mill. In addition we sell him, at a reasonable figure, sufficient land fronting on tidewater to enable him to erect a sawmill, lay out his yards, and build a dock out into the deep water.

"Thus Gregory will have that which he hasn't got now—an outlet to his market by water; and when the railroad to Sequoia builds in from the south, it will connect with the road which we have built from Sequoia up into Township Nine to the north; hence Gregory will also have an outlet to his market by rail. He can easily get a good manager to run his lumber business until he finds a customer for it, and in the meantime we will be charging his account with our freight-bills against him and gradually pay off the loan without pinching ourselves."

"Have you talked with Gregory?"

"Yes. I met him while I was in San Francisco. Somebody brought him up to a meeting of the Redwood Lumber Manufacturers' Association, and I pounced on him like an owl on a mouse."

John Cardigan's old hand came gropingly forth and rested affectionately upon his boy's. "What a wonderful scheme it would have been a year ago," he murmured sadly. "You forget, my son, that we cannot last in business long enough to get that road built though Gregory should agree to finance the building of it. The interest on our bonded indebtedness is payable on the first—"

"We can meet it, sir."

"Aye, but we can't meet the fifty thousand dollars which, under the terms of our deed of trust, we are required to pay in on July first of each year as a sinking fund toward the retirement of our bonds. By super-human efforts—by sacrificing a dozen cargoes, raising hob with the market, and getting ourselves disliked by our neighbours—we managed to meet half of it this year and procure an extension of six months on the balance due.

"That is Pennington's way. He plays with us as a cat does with a mouse, knowing, like the cat, that when he is weary of playing, he will devour us. And now, when we are deeper in debt than ever, when the market is lower and more sluggish than it has been in fifteen years, to hope to meet the interest and the next payment to the sinking fund taxes my optimism. Bryce, it just can't be done. We'd have our road about half completed when we'd bust up in business; indeed, the minute Pennington suspected we were paralleling his line, he'd choke off our wind. I tell you it can't be done."

But Bryce contradicted him earnestly. "It can be done," he said. "Gregory knows nothing of our financial condition. Our rating in the reports of the commercial agencies is as good as it ever was, and a man's never broke till somebody finds it out."

"What do you mean?"

"I mean that if we can start building our road and have it half completed before Pennington jumps on us, GREGORY WILL SIMPLY HAVE TO COME TO OUR AID IN SELF-DEFENSE. Once he ties up with us, he's committed to the task of seeing us through. If we fall, he must pick us up and carry us, whether he wants to or not; and I will so arrange the deal that he will have to. I can do it, I tell you."

John Cardigan raised his hand. "No," he said firmly, "I will not allow you to do this. That way—that is the Pennington method. If we fall, my son, we pass out like gentlemen, not blackguards. We will not take advantage of this man Gregory's faith. If he joins forces with us, we lay our hand on the table and let him look."

"Then he'll never join hands with us, partner. We're done."

"We're not done, my son. We have one alternative, and I'm going to take it. I've got to—for your sake. Moreover, your mother would have wished it so."

"You don't mean—"

"Yes, I do. I'm going to sell Pennington my Valley of the Giants. Thank God, that quarter-section does not belong to the Cardigan Redwood Lumber Company. It is my personal property, and it is not mortgaged. Pennington can never foreclose on it—and until he gets it, twenty-five hundred acres of virgin timber on Squaw Creek are valueless—nay, a source of expense to him. Bryce, he has to have it; and he'll pay the price, when he knows I mean business."

With a sweeping gesture he waved aside the arguments that rose to his son's lips. "Lead me to the telephone," he commanded; and Bryce, recognizing his sire's unalterable determination, obeyed.

"Find Pennington's number in the telephone-book," John Cardigan commanded next.

Bryce found it, and his father proceeded to get the Colonel on the wire. "Pennington," he said hoarsely, "this is John Cardigan speaking. I've decided to sell you that quarter-section that blocks your timber on Squaw Creek."

"Indeed," the Colonel purred. "I had an idea you were going to present it to the city for a natural park."

"I've changed my mind. I've decided to sell at your last offer."

"I've changed my mind, too. I've decided not to buy—at my last offer. Good-night."

Slowly John Cardigan hung the receiver on the hook, turned and groped for his son. When he found him, the old man held him for a moment in his arms. "Lead me upstairs, son," he murmured presently. "I'm tired. I'm going to bed."

When Colonel Seth Pennington turned from the telephone and faced his niece, Shirley read his triumph in his face. "Old Cardigan has capitulated at last," he cried exultingly. "We've played a waiting game and I've won; he just telephoned to say he'd accept my last offer for his Valley of the Giants, as the sentimental old fool calls that quarter-section of huge redwoods that blocks the outlet to our Squaw Creek timber."

"But you're not going to buy it. You told him so, Uncle Seth."

"Of course I'm not going to buy it—at my last offer. It's worth five thousand dollars in the open market, and once I offered him fifty thousand for it. Now I'll give him five."

"I wonder why he wants to sell," Shirley mused. "From what Bryce Cardigan told me once, his father attaches a sentimental value to that strip of woods; his wife is buried there; it's—or rather, it used to be—a sort of shrine to the old gentleman."

"He's selling it because he's desperate. If he wasn't teetering on the verge of bankruptcy, he'd never let me outgame him," Pennington replied gayly. "I'll say this for the old fellow: he's no bluffer. However, since I know his financial condition almost to a dollar, I do not think it would be good business to buy his Valley of the Giants now. I'll wait until he has gone bust—and save twenty-five or thirty thousand dollars."

"I think you're biting off your nose to spite your face, Uncle Seth. The Laguna Grande Lumber Company needs that outlet. In dollars and cents, what is it worth to the Company?"

"If I thought I couldn't get it from Cardigan a few months from now, I'd go as high as a hundred thousand for it to-night," he answered coolly.

"In that event, I advise you to take it for fifty thousand. It's terribly hard on old Mr. Cardigan to have to sell it, even at that price."

"You do not understand these matters, Shirley. Don't try. And don't waste your sympathy on that old humbug. He has to dig up fifty thousand dollars to pay on his bonded indebtedness, and he's finding it a difficult job. He's just sparring for time, but he'll lose out."

As if to indicate that he considered the matter closed, the Colonel drew his chair toward the fire, picked up a magazine, and commenced idly to slit the pages. Shirley studied the back of his head for some time, then got out some fancy work and commenced plying her needle. And as she plied it, a thought, nebulous at first, gradually took form in her head until eventually she murmured loud enough for the Colonel to hear:

"I'll do it."

"Do what?" Pennington queried.

"Something nice for somebody who did something nice for me," she answered.

"That McTavish girl?" he suggested.

"Poor Moira! Isn't she sweet, Uncle Seth? I'm going to give her that black suit of mine. I've scarcely worn it—"

"I thought so," he interrupted with an indulgent yawn. "Well, do whatever makes for your happiness, my dear. That's all money is for."

About two o'clock the following afternoon old Judge Moore, of the Superior Court of Humboldt County, drifted into Bryce Cardigan's office, sat down uninvited, and lifted his long legs to the top of an adjacent chair.

"Well, Bryce, my boy," he began, "a little bird tells me your daddy is considering the sale of Cardigan's Redwoods, or the Valley of the Giants, as your paternal ancestor prefers to refer to that little old quarter-section out yonder on the edge of town. How about it?"

Bryce stared at him a moment questioningly. "Yes, Judge," he replied, "we'll sell, if we get our price."

"Well," his visitor drawled, "I have a client who might be persuaded. I'm here to talk turkey. What's your price?"

"Before we talk price," Bryce parried, "I want you to answer a question."

"Let her fly," said Judge Moore.

"Are you, directly or indirectly, acting for Colonel Pennington?"

"That's none of your business, young man—at least, it would be none of your business if I were, directly or indirectly, acting for that unconvicted thief. To the best of my information and belief, Colonel Pennington doesn't figure in this deal in any way, shape, or manner; and as you know, I've been your daddy's friend for thirty years."

Still Bryce was not convinced, notwithstanding the fact that he would have staked his honour on the Judge's veracity. Nobody knew better than he in what devious ways the Colonel worked, his wonders to perform.

"Well," he said, "your query is rather sudden, Judge, but still I can name you a price. I will state frankly, however, that I believe it to be over your head. We have several times refused to sell to Colonel Pennington for a hundred thousand dollars."

"Naturally that little dab of timber is worth more to Pennington than to anybody else. However, my client has given me instructions to go as high as a hundred thousand if necessary to get the property."

"What!"

"I said it. One hundred thousand dollars of the present standard weight and fineness."

Judge Moore's last statement swept away Bryce's suspicions. He required now no further evidence that, regardless of the identity of the Judge's client, that client could not possibly be Colonel Seth Pennington or any one acting for him, since only the night before Pennington had curtly refused to buy the property for fifty thousand dollars. For a moment Bryce stared stupidly at his visitor. Then he recovered his wits.

"Sold!" he almost shouted, and after the fashion of the West extended his hand to clinch the bargain. The Judge shook it solemnly. "The Lord loveth a quick trader," he declared, and reached into the capacious breast pocket of his Prince Albert coat. "Here's the deed already made out in favour of myself, as trustee." He winked knowingly.

"Client's a bit modest, I take it," Bryce suggested.

"Oh, very. Of course I'm only hazarding a guess, but that guess is that my client can afford the gamble and is figuring on giving Pennington a pain where he never knew it to ache him before. In plain English, I believe the Colonel is in for a razooing at the hands of somebody with a small grouch against him."

"May the Lord strengthen that somebody's arm," Bryce breathed fervently. "If your client can afford to hold out long enough, he'll be able to buy Pennington's Squaw Creek timber at a bargain."

"My understanding is that such is the programme."

Bryce reached for the deed, then reached for his hat. "If you'll be good enough to wait here, Judge Moore, I'll run up to the house and get my father to sign this deed. The Valley of the Giants is his personal property, you know. He didn't include it in his assets when incorporating the Cardigan Redwood Lumber Company."

A quarter of an hour later he returned with the deed duly signed by John Cardigan and witnessed by Bryce; whereupon the Judge carelessly tossed his certified check for a hundred thousand dollars on Bryce's desk and departed whistling "Turkey in the Straw." Bryce reached for the telephone and called up Colonel Pennington.

"Bryce Cardigan speaking," he began, but the Colonel cut him short.

"My dear, impulsive young friend," he interrupted in oleaginous tones, "how often do you have to be told that I am not quite ready to buy that quarter-section?"

"Oh," Bryce retorted, "I merely called up to tell you that every dollar and every asset you have in the world, including your heart's blood, isn't sufficient to buy the Valley of the Giants from us now."

"Eh? What's that? Why?"

"Because, my dear, overcautious, and thoroughly unprincipled enemy, it was sold five minutes ago for the tidy sum of one hundred thousand dollars, and if you don't believe me, come over to my office and I'll let you feast your eyes on the certified check."

He could hear a distinct gasp. After an interval of five seconds, however, the Colonel recovered his poise. "I congratulate you," he purred. "I suppose I'll have to wait a little longer now, won't I? Well—patience is my middle name. Au revoir."

The Colonel hung up. His hard face was ashen with rage, and he stared at a calendar on the wall with his cold, phidian stare. However, he was not without a generous stock of optimism. "Somebody has learned of the low state of the Cardigan fortune," he mused, "and taken advantage of it to induce the old man to sell at last. They're figuring on selling to me at a neat profit. And I certainly did overplay my hand last night. However, there's nothing to do now except sit tight and wait for the new owner's next move."

Meanwhile, in the general office of the Cardigan Redwood Lumber Company, joy was rampant. Bryce Cardigan was doing a buck and wing dance around the room, while Moira McTavish, with her back to her tall desk, watched him, in her eyes a tremendous joy and a sweet, yearning glow of adoration that Bryce was too happy and excited to notice.

Suddenly he paused before her. "Moira, you're a lucky girl," he declared. "I thought this morning you were going back to a kitchen in a logging-camp. It almost broke my heart to think of fate's swindling you like that." He put his arm around her and gave her a brotherly hug. "It's autumn in the woods, Moira, and all the underbrush is golden."

She smiled, though it was winter in her heart.

CHAPTER XX

Not the least of the traits which formed Shirley Sumner's character was pride. Proud people quite usually are fiercely independent and meticulously honest—and Shirley's pride was monumental. Hers was the pride of lineage, of womanhood, of an assured station in life, combined with that other pride which is rather difficult of definition without verbosity and is perhaps better expressed in the terse and illuminating phrase "a dead-game sport." Unlike her precious relative, unlike the majority of her sex, Shirley had a wonderfully balanced sense of the eternal fitness of things; her code of honour resembled that of a very gallant gentleman. She could love well and hate well.

A careful analysis of Shirley's feelings toward Bryce Cardigan immediately following the incident in Pennington's woods, had showed her that under more propitious circumstances she might have fallen in love with that tempestuous young man in sheer recognition of the many lovable and manly qualities she had discerned in him. As an offset to the credit side of Bryce's account with her, however, there appeared certain debits in the consideration of which Shirley always lost her temper and was immediately quite certain she loathed the unfortunate man.

He had been an honoured and (for aught Shirley knew to the contrary) welcome guest in the Penninton home one night, and the following day had assaulted his host, committed great bodily injuries upon the latter's employees for little or no reason save the satisfaction of an abominable temper, made threats of further violence, declared his unfaltering enmity to her nearest and best-loved relative, and in the next breath had had the insolence to prate of his respect and admiration for her. Indeed, in cogitating on this latter incongruity, Shirley recalled that the extraordinary fellow had been forced rather abruptly to check himself in order to avoid a fervid declaration of love! And all of this under the protection of a double-bitted axe, one eye on her and the other on his enemies.

However, all of these grave crimes and misdemeanors were really insignificant compared with his crowning offense. What had infuriated Shirley was the fact that she had been at some pains to inform Bryce Cardigan that she loathed him—whereat he had looked her over coolly, grinned a little, and declined to believe her! Then, seemingly as if fate had decreed that her futility should be impressed upon her still further, Bryce Cardigan had been granted an opportunity to save, in a strikingly calm, heroic, and painful manner, her and her uncle from certain and horrible death, thus placing upon Shirley an obligation that was as irritating to acknowledge as it was futile to attempt to reciprocate.

That was where the shoe pinched. Before that day was over she had been forced to do one of two things—acknowledge in no uncertain terms her indebtedness to him, or remain silent and be convicted of having been, in plain language, a rotter. So she had telephoned him and purposely left ajar the door to their former friendly relations.

Monstrous! He had seen the open door and deliberately slammed it in her face. Luckily for them both she had heard, all unsuspected by him as he slowly hung the receiver on the hook, the soliloquy wherein he gave her a pointed hint of the distress with which he abdicated—which knowledge was all that deterred her from despising him with the fervour of a woman scorned.

Resolutely Shirley set herself to the task of forgetting Bryce when, after the passage of a few weeks, she realized that he was quite sincere in his determination to forget her. Frequent glimpses of him on the streets of Sequoia, the occasional mention of his name in the Sequoia Sentinel, the very whistle of Cardigan's mill, made her task a difficult one; and presently in desperation she packed up and departed for an indefinite stay in the southern part of the State. At the end of six weeks, however, she discovered that absence had had the traditional effect upon her heart and found herself possessed of a great curiosity to study the villain at short range and discover, if possible, what new rascality he might be meditating. About this time, a providential attack of that aristocratic ailment, gout, having laid Colonel Pennington low, she told herself her duty lay in Sequoia, that she had Shirley Sumner in hand at last and that the danger was over. In consequence, she returned to Sequoia.

The fascination which a lighted candle holds for a moth is too well known to require further elucidation here. In yielding one day to a desire to visit the Valley of the Giants, Shirley told herself that she was going there to gather wild blackberries. She had been thinking of a certain blackberry pie, which thought naturally induced reflection on Bryce Cardigan and reminded Shirley of her first visit to the Giants under the escort of a boy in knickerbockers. She had a very vivid remembrance of that little amphitheatre with the sunbeams falling like a halo on the plain tombstone; she wondered if the years had changed it all and decided that there could not possibly be any harm in indulging a very natural curiosity to visit and investigate.

Her meeting with Moira McTavish that day, and the subsequent friendship formed with the woods-boss's daughter, renewed all her old apprehensions. On the assumption that Shirley and Bryce were practically strangers to each other (an assumption which Shirley, for obvious reasons, did not attempt to dissipate), Moira did not hesitate to mention Bryce very frequently. To her he was the one human being in the world utterly worth while, and it is natural for women to discuss, frequently and at great length, the subject nearest their hearts. In the three stock subjects of the admirable sex—man, dress, and the ills that flesh is heir to—man readily holds the ascendancy; and by degrees Moira—discovering that Shirley, having all the dresses she required (several dozen more, in fact) and being neither subnormal mentally nor fragile physically, gave the last two topics scant attention—formed the habit of expatiating at great length on the latter. Moira described Bryce in minute detail and related to her eager auditor little unconscious daily acts of kindness, thoughtfulness, or humour performed by Bryce—his devotion to his father, his idealistic attitude toward the Cardigan employees, his ability, his industry, the wonderful care he bestowed upon his fingernails, his marvellous taste in neckwear, the boyishness of his lighter and the mannishness of his serious moments. And presently, little by little, Shirley's resentment against him faded, and in her heart was born a great wistfulness bred of the hope that some day she would meet Bryce Cardigan on the street and that he would pause, lift his hat, smile at her his compelling smile and, forthwith proceed to bully her into being friendly and forgiving—browbeat her into admitting her change of heart and glorying in it.

To this remarkable state of mind had Shirley Sumner attained at the time old John Cardigan, leading his last little trump in a vain hope that it would enable him to take the odd trick in the huge game he had played for fifty years, decided to sell his Valley of the Giants.

Shortly after joining her uncle in Sequoia, Shirley had learned from the Colonel the history of old man Cardigan and his Valley of the Giants, or as the townspeople called it, Cardigan's Redwoods. Therefore she was familiar with its importance to the assets of the Laguna Grande Lumber Company, since, while that quarter-section remained the property of John Cardigan, two thousand five hundred acres of splendid timber owned by the former were rendered inaccessible. Her uncle had explained to her that ultimately this would mean the tying up of some two million dollars, and inasmuch as the Colonel never figured less than five per cent. return on anything, he was in this instance facing a net loss of one hundred thousand dollars for each year obstinate John Cardigan persisted in retaining that quarter-section.

"I'd gladly give him a hundred thousand for that miserable little dab of timber and let him keep a couple of acres surrounding his wife's grave, if the old fool would only listen to reason," the Colonel had complained bitterly to her. "I've offered him that price a score of times, and he tells me blandly the property isn't for sale. Well, he who laughs last laughs best, and if I can't get that quarter-section by paying more than ten times what it's worth in the open market, I'll get it some other way, if it costs me a million."

"How?" Shirley had queried at the time.

"Never mind, my dear," he had answered darkly. "You wouldn't understand the procedure if I told you. I'll have to run all around Robin Hood's barn and put up a deal of money, one way or another, but in the end I'll get it all back with interest—and Cardigan's Redwoods! The old man can't last forever, and what with his fool methods of doing business, he's about broke, anyhow. I expect to do business with his executor or his receiver within a year."

Shirley, as explained in a preceding chapter, had been present the night John Cardigan, desperate and brought to bay at last, had telephoned Pennington at the latter's home, accepting Pennington's last offer for the Valley of the Giants. The cruel triumph in the Colonel's handsome face as he curtly rebuffed old Cardigan had been too apparent for the girl to mistake; recalling her conversation with him anent the impending possibility of his doing business with John Cardigan's receiver or executor, she realized now that a crisis had come in the affairs of the Cardigans, and across her vision there flashed again the vision of Bryce Cardigan's homecoming—of a tall old man with his trembling arms clasped around his boy, with grizzled cheek laid against his son's, as one who, seeking comfort through bitter years, at length had found it.

Presently another thought came to Shirley. She knew Bryce Cardigan was far from being indifferent to her; she had given him his opportunity to be friendly with her again, and he had chosen to ignore her though sorely against his will. For weeks Shirley had pondered this mysterious action, and now she thought she caught a glimpse of the reason underlying it all. In Sequoia, Bryce Cardigan was regarded as the heir to the throne of Humboldt's first timber-king, but Shirley knew now that as a timber-king, Bryce Cardigan bade fair to wear a tinsel crown. Was it this knowledge that had led him to avoid her?

"I wonder," she mused. "He's proud. Perhaps the realization that he will soon be penniless and shorn of his high estate has made him chary of acquiring new friends in his old circle. Perhaps if he were secure in his business affairs—Ah, yes! Poor boy! He was desperate for fifty thousand dollars!" Her heart swelled. "Oh, Bryce, Bryce," she murmured, "I think I'm beginning to understand some of your fury that day in the woods. It's all a great mystery, but I'm sure you didn't intend to be so—so terrible. Oh, my dear, if we had only continued to be the good friends we started out to be, perhaps you'd let me help you now. For what good is money if one cannot help one's dear friends in distress. Still, I know you wouldn't let me help you, for men of your stamp cannot borrow from a woman, no matter how desperate their need. And yet—you only need a paltry fifty thousand dollars!"

Shirley carried to bed with her that night the woes of the Cardigans, and in the morning she telephoned Moira McTavish and invited the latter to lunch with her at home that noon. It was in her mind to question Moira with a view to acquiring additional information. When Moira came, Shirley saw that she had been weeping.

"My poor Moira!" she said, putting her arms around her visitor. "What has happened to distress you? Has your father come back to Sequoia? Forgive me for asking. You never mentioned him, but I have heard—There, there, dear! Tell me all about it."

Moira laid her head on Shirley's shoulder and sobbed for several minutes. Then, "It's Mr. Bryce," she wailed. "He's so unhappy. Something's happened; they're going to sell Cardigan's Redwoods; and they—don't want to. Old Mr. Cardigan is home—ill; and just before I left the office, Mr. Bryce came in—and stood a moment looking—at me—so tragically I—I asked him what had happened. Then he patted my cheek—oh, I know I'm just one of his responsibilities—and said 'Poor Moira! Never any luck!' and went into his—private office. I waited a little, and then I went in too; and—oh, Miss Sumner, he had his head down on his desk, and when I touched his head, he reached up and took my hand and held it—and laid his cheek against it a little while—and oh, his cheek was wet. It's cruel of God—to make him—unhappy, He's good—too good. And—oh, I love him so, Miss Shirley, I love him so—and he'll never, never know. I'm just one of his—responsibilities, you know; and I shouldn't presume. But nobody—has ever been kind to me but Mr. Bryce—and you. And I can't help loving people who are kind—and gentle to nobodies."

The hysterical outburst over, Shirley led the girl to her cozy sitting-room upstairs and prevailed upon the girl to put on one of her own beautiful negligees. Moira's story—her confession of love, so tragic because so hopeless—had stirred Shirley deeply. She seated herself in front of Moira and cupped her chin in her palm.

"Of course, dear," she said, "you couldn't possibly see anybody you loved suffer so and not feel dreadfully about it. And when a man like Bryce Cardigan is struck down, he's apt to present rather a tragic and helpless figure. He wanted sympathy, Moira—woman's sympathy, and it was dear of you to give it to him."

"I'd gladly die for him," Moira answered simply. "Oh, Miss Shirley, you don't know him the way we who work for him do. If you did, you'd love him, too. You couldn't help it, Miss Shirley."

"Perhaps he loves you, too, Moira." The words came with difficulty.

Moira shook her head hopelessly. "No, Miss Shirley. I'm only one of his many human problems, and he just won't go back on me, for old sake's sake. We played together ten years ago, when he used to spend his vacations at our house in Cardigan's woods, when my father was woods-boss. He's Bryce Cardigan—and I—I used to work in the kitchen of his logging-camp."

"Never mind, Moira. He may love you, even though you do not suspect it. You mustn't be so despairing. Providence has a way of working out these things. Tell me about his trouble, Moira."

"I think it's money. He's been terribly worried for a long time, and I'm afraid things aren't going right with the business. I've felt ever since I've been there that there's something that puts a cloud over Mr. Bryce's smile. It hurts them terribly to have to sell the Valley of the Giants, but they have to; Colonel Pennington is the only one who would consider buying it; they don't want him to have it—and still they have to sell to him."

"I happen to know, Moira, that he isn't going to buy it."

"Yes, he is—but not at a price that will do them any good. They have always thought he would be eager to buy whenever they decided to sell, and now he says he doesn't want it, and old Mr. Cardigan is ill over it all. Mr. Bryce says his father has lost his courage at last; and oh, dear, things are in such a mess. Mr. Bryce started to tell me all about it—and then he stopped suddenly and wouldn't say another word."

Shirley smiled. She thought she understood the reason for that. However, she did not pause to speculate on it, since the crying need of the present was the distribution of a ray of sunshine to broken-hearted Moira.

"Silly," she chided, "how needlessly you are grieving! You say my uncle has declined to buy the Valley of the Giants?"

Moira nodded.

"My uncle doesn't know what he's talking about, Moira. I'll see that he does buy it. What price are the Cardigans asking for it now?"

"Well, Colonel Pennington has offered them a hundred thousand dollars for it time and again, but last night he withdrew that offer. Then they named a price of fifty thousand, and he said he didn't want it at all."

"He needs it, and it's worth every cent of a hundred thousand to him, Moira. Don't worry, dear. He'll buy it, because I'll make him, and he'll buy it immediately; only you must promise me not to mention a single word of what I'm telling you to Bryce Cardigan, or in fact, to anybody. Do you promise?"

Moira seized Shirley's hand and kissed it impulsively. "Very well, then," Shirley continued. "That matter is adjusted, and now we'll all be happy. Here comes Thelma with luncheon. Cheer up, dear, and remember that sometime this afternoon you're going to see Mr. Bryce smile again, and perhaps there won't be so much of a cloud over his smile this time."

When Moira returned to the office of the Cardigan Redwood Lumber Company, Shirley rang for her maid. "Bring me my motor-coat and hat, Thelma," she ordered, "and telephone for the limousine." She seated herself before the mirror at her dressing-table and dusted her adorable nose with a powder-puff. "Mr. Smarty Cardigan," she murmured happily, "you walked rough-shod over my pride, didn't you! Placed me under an obligation I could never hope to meet—and then ignored me—didn't you? Very well, old boy. We all have our innings sooner or later, you know, and I'm going to make a substantial payment on that huge obligation as sure as my name is Shirley Sumner. Then, some day when the sun is shining for you again, you'll come to me and be very, very humble. You're entirely too independent, Mr. Cardigan, but, oh, my dear, I do hope you will not need so much money. I'll be put to my wit's end to get it to you without letting you know, because if your affairs go to smash, you'll be perfectly intolerable. And yet you deserve it. You're such an idiot for not loving Moira. She's an angel, and I gravely fear I'm just an interfering, mischievous, resentful little devil seeking vengeance on—"

She paused suddenly. "No, I'll not do that, either," she soliloquized. "I'll keep it myself—for an investment. I'll show Uncle Seth I'm a business woman, after all. He has had his fair chance at the Valley of the Giants, after waiting years for it, and now he has deliberately sacrificed that chance to be mean and vindictive. I'm afraid Uncle Seth isn't very sporty—after what Bryce Cardigan did for us that day the log-train ran away. I'll have to teach him not to hit an old man when he's down and begging for mercy. I'LL buy the Valley but keep my identity secret from everybody; then, when Uncle Seth finds a stranger in possession, he'll have a fit, and perhaps, before he recovers, he'll sell me all his Squaw Creek timber—only he'll never know I'm the buyer. And when I control the outlet—well, I think that Squaw Creek timber will make an excellent investment if it's held for a few years. Shirley, my dear, I'm pleased with you. Really, I never knew until now why men could be so devoted to business. Won't it be jolly to step in between Uncle Seth and Bryce Cardigan, hold up my hand like a policeman, and say: 'Stop it, boys. No fighting, IF you please. And if anybody wants to know who's boss around here, start something.'"

And Shirley laid her head upon the dressing-table and laughed heartily. She had suddenly bethought herself of Aesop's fable of the lion and the mouse!

When her uncle came home that night, Shirley observed that he was preoccupied and disinclined to conversation.

"I noticed in this evening's paper," she remarked presently, "that Mr. Cardigan has sold his Valley of the Giants. So you bought it, after all?"

"No such luck!" he almost barked. "I'm an idiot. I should be placed in charge of a keeper. Now, for heaven's sake, Shirley, don't discuss that timber with me, for if you do, I'll go plain, lunatic crazy. I've had a very trying day."

"Poor Uncle Seth!" she purred sweetly. Her apparent sympathy soothed his rasped soul. He continued:

"Oh, I'll get the infernal property, and it will be worth what I have to pay for it, only it certainly does gravel me to realize that I am about to be held up, with no help in sight. I'll see Judge Moore to-morrow and offer him a quick profit for his client. That's the game, you know."

"I do hope the new owner exhibits some common sense, Uncle dear," she replied, and turned back to the piano. "But I greatly fear," she added to herself, "that the new owner is going to prove a most obstinate creature and frightfully hard to discover."

True to his promise, the Colonel called on Judge Moore bright and early the following morning. "Act Three of that little business drama entitled 'The Valley of the Giants,' my dear Judge," he announced pleasantly. "I play the lead in this act. You remember me, I hope. I played a bit in Act Two."

"In so far as my information goes, sir, you've been cut out of the cast in Act Three. I don't seem to find any lines for you to speak."

"One line, Judge, one little line. What profit does your client want on that quarter-section?"

"That quarter-section is not in the market, Colonel. When it is, I'll send for you, since you're the only logical prospect should my client decide to sell. And remembering how you butted in on politics in this county last fall and provided a slush-fund to beat me and place a crook on the Superior Court bench, in order to give you an edge in the many suits you are always filing or having filed against you, I rise to remark that you have about ten split seconds in which to disappear from my office. If you linger longer, I'll start throwing paper-weights." And as if to emphasize his remark, the Judge's hand closed over one of the articles in question.

The Colonel withdrew with what dignity he could muster.

CHAPTER XXI

Upon his return from the office that night, Bryce Cardigan found his father had left his bed and was seated before the library fire.

"Feeling a whole lot better to-day, eh, pal?" his son queried.

John Cardigan smiled. "Yes, son," he replied plaintively. "I guess I'll manage to live till next spring."

"Oh, I knew there was nothing wrong with you, John Cardigan, that a healthy check wouldn't cure. Pennington rather jolted you, though, didn't he?"

"He did, Bryce. It was jolt enough to be forced to sell that quarter—I never expected we'd have to do it; but when I realize that it was a case of sacrificing you or my Giants, of course you won. And I didn't feel so badly about it as I used to think I would. I suppose that's because there is a certain morbid pleasure in a real sacrifice for those we love. And I never doubted but that Pennington would snap up the property the instant I offered to sell. Hence his refusal—in the face of our desperate need for money to carry on until conditions improve—almost floored your old man."

"Well, we can afford to draw our breath now, and that gives us a fighting chance, partner. And right after dinner you and I will sit down and start brewing a pot of powerful bad medicine for the Colonel."

"Son, I've been sitting here simmering all day." There was a note of the old dominant fighting John Cardigan in his voice now. "And it has occurred to me that even if I must sit on the bench and root, I've not reached the point where my years have begun to affect my thinking ability." He touched his leonine head. "I'm as right as a fox upstairs, Bryce."

"Right-o, Johnny. We'll buck the line together. After dinner you trot out your plan of campaign and I'll trot out mine; then we'll tear them apart, select the best pieces of each and weld them into a perfect whole."

Accordingly, dinner disposed of, father and son sat down together to prepare the plan of campaign. For the space of several minutes a silence settled between them, the while they puffed meditatively upon their cigars. Then the old man spoke.

"We'll have to fight him in the dark."

"Why?"

"Because if Pennington knows, or even suspects the identity of the man who is going to parallel his logging railroad, he will throw all the weight of his truly capable mind, his wealth and his ruthlessness against you—and you will be smashed. To beat that man, you must do more than spend money. You will have to outthink him, outwork him, outgame him, and when eventually you have won, you'll know you've been in the fight of your career. You have one advantage starting out. The Colonel doesn't think you have the courage to parallel his road in the first place; in the second place, he knows you haven't the money; and in the third place he is morally certain you cannot borrow it, because you haven't any collateral to secure your note.

"We are mortgaged now to the limit, and our floating indebtedness is very large; on the face of things and according to the Colonel's very correct inside information, we're helpless; and unless the lumber-market stiffens very materially this year, by the time our hauling-contract with Pennington's road expires, we'll be back where we were yesterday before we sold the Giants. Pennington regards that hundred thousand as get-away money for us. So, all things considered, the Colonel, will be slow to suspect us of having an ace in the hole; but by jinks we have it, and we're going to play it."

"No," said Bryce, "we're going to let somebody else play it for us. The point you make—to wit, that we must remain absolutely in the background—is well taken."

"Very well," agreed the old man. "Now let us proceed to the next point. You must engage some reliable engineer to look over the proposed route of the road and give us an estimate of the cost of construction."

"For the sake of argument we will consider that done, and that the estimate comes within the scope of the sum Gregory is willing to advance us."

"Your third step, then, will be to incorporate a railroad company under the laws of the State of California."

"I think I'll favour the fair State of New Jersey with our trade," Bryce suggested dryly. "I notice that when Pennington bought out the Henderson interests and reorganized that property, he incorporated the Laguna Grande Lumber Company under the laws of the State of New Jersey, home of the trusts. There must be some advantage connected with such a course."

"Have it your own way, boy. What's good enough for the Colonel is good enough for us. Now, then, you are going to incorporate a company to build a road twelve miles long—and a private road, at that. That would be a fatal step. Pennington would know somebody was going to build a logging-road, and regardless of who the builders were, he would have to fight them in self-protection. How are you going to cover your trail, my son?"

Bryce pondered. "I will, to begin, have a dummy board of directors. Also, my road cannot be private; it must be a common carrier, and that's where the shoe pinches. Common carriers are subject to the rules and regulations of the Railroad Commission."

"They are wise and just rules," commented the old man, "expensive to obey at times, but quite necessary. We can obey and still be happy. Objection overruled."

"Well, then, since we must be a common carrier, we might as well carry our deception still further and incorporate for the purpose of building a road from Sequoia to Grant's Pass, Oregon, there to connect with the Southern Pacific."

John Cardigan smiled. "The old dream revived, eh? Well, the old jokes always bring a hearty laugh. People will laugh at your company, because folks up this way realize that the construction cost of such a road is prohibitive, not to mention the cost of maintenance, which would be tremendous and out of all proportion to the freight area tapped."

"Well, since we're not going to build more than twelve miles of our road during the next year, and probably not more than ten miles additional during the present century, we won't worry over it. It doesn't cost a cent more to procure a franchise to build a road from here to the moon. If we fail to build to Grant's Pass, our franchise to build the uncompleted portion of the road merely lapses and we hold only that portion which we have constructed. That's all we want to hold."

"How about rights of way?"

"They will cost us very little, if anything. Most or the landowners along the proposed route will give us rights of way free gratis and for nothing, just to encourage the lunatics. Without a railroad the land is valueless; and as a common carrier they know we can condemn rights of way capriciously withheld—something we cannot do as a private road. Moreover, deeds to rights of way can be drawn with a time-limit, after which they revert to the original owners."

"Good strategy, my son! And certainly as a common carrier we will be welcomed by the farmers and cattlemen along our short line. We can handle their freight without much annoyance and perhaps at a slight profit."

"Well, that about completes the rough outline of our plan. The next thing to do is to start and keep right on moving, for as old Omar has it, 'The bird of time hath but a little way to flutter,' and the birdshot is catching up with him. We have a year in which to build our road; if we do not hurry, the mill will have to shut down for lack of logs, when our contract with Pennington expires."

"You forget the manager for our new corporation—the vice-president and general manager. The man we engage must be the fastest and most convincing talker in California; not only must he be able to tell a lie with a straight face, but he must be able to believe his own lies. And he must talk in millions, look millions, and act as if a million dollars were equivalent in value to a redwood stump. In addition, he must be a man of real ability and a person you can trust implicitly."

"I have the very man you mention. His name is Buck Ogilvy and only this very day I received a letter from him begging me for a small loan. I have Buck on ice in a fifth-class San Francisco hotel."

"Tell me about him, Bryce."

"Don't have to. You've just told me about him, However, I'll read you his letter. I claim there is more character in a letter than in a face."

Here Bryce read aloud:

Golden Gate Hotel—Rooms fifty cents—and up. San Francisco, California, August fifteenth, 1916.

MY DEAR CARDIGAN: Hark to the voice of one crying in the wilderness; then picture to yourself the unlovely spectacle of a strong man crying.

Let us assume that you have duly considered. Now wind up your wrist and send me a rectangular piece of white, blue, green, or pink paper bearing in the lower right-hand corner, in your clear, bold chirography, the magic words "Bryce Cardigan"—with the little up-and-down hook and flourish which identifies your signature given in your serious moods and lends value to otherwise worthless paper. Five dollars would make me chirk up; ten would start a slight smile; twenty would put a beam in mine eye; fifty would cause me to utter shrill cries of unadulterated joys and a hundred would inspire me to actions like unto those of a whirling dervish.

I am so flat busted my arches make hollow sounds as I tread the hard pavements of a great city, seeking a job. Pausing on the brink of despair, that destiny which shapes our ends inspired me to think of old times and happier days and particularly of that pink-and-white midget of a girl who tended the soda-fountain just back of the railroad station at Princeton. You stole that damsel from me, and I never thanked you. Then I remembered you were a timber-king with a kind heart and that you lived somewhere in California; so I looked in the telephone book and found the address of the San Francisco office of the Cardigan Redwood Lumber Company. You have a mean man in charge there. I called on him, told him I was an old college pal of yours, and tried to borrow a dollar. He spurned me with contumely—so much of it, in fact, that I imagine you have a number of such friends. While he was abusing me, I stole from his desk the stamped envelope which bears to you these tidings of great woe; and while awaiting your reply, be advised that I subsist on the bitter cud of reflection, fresh air, and water, all of which, thank God, cost nothing.

My tale is soon told. When you knew me last, I was a prosperous young contractor. Alas! I put all my eggs in one basket and produced an omelet. Took a contract to build a railroad in Honduras. Honduras got to fighting with Nicaragua; the government I had done business with went out of business; and the Nicaraguan army recruited all my labourers and mounted them on my mules and horses, swiped all my grub, and told me to go home. I went. Why stay? Moreover, I had an incentive consisting of about an inch of bayonet—fortunately not applied in a vital spot—which accelerated rather than decreased my speed.

Hurry, my dear Cardigan. Tempest fidgets; remember Moriarity—which, if you still remember your Latin, means: "Time flies. Remember to-morrow!" I finished eating my overcoat the day before yesterday.

Make it a hundred, and God will bless you. When I get it, I'll come to Sequoia and kiss you. I'll pay you back sometime—of course.

Wistfully thine—Buck Ogilvy

P.S.—Delays are dangerous, and procrastination is the thief of time.—B.

John Cardigan chuckled. "I'd take Buck Ogilvy, Bryce. He'll do. Is he honest?"

"I don't know. He was, the last time I saw him."

"Then wire him a hundred. Don't wait for the mail. The steamer that carries your letter might be wrecked and your friend Ogilvy forced to steal."

"I have already wired him the hundred. In all probability he is now out whirling like a dervish."

"Good boy! Well, I think we've planned sufficient for the present, Bryce. You'd better leave for San Francisco to-morrow and close your deal with Gregory. Arrange with him to leave his own representative with Ogilvy to keep tab on the job, check the bills, and pay them as they fall due; and above all things, insist that Gregory shall place the money in a San Francisco bank, subject to the joint check of his representative and ours. Hire a good lawyer to draw up the agreement between you; be sure you're right, and then go ahead—full speed. When you return to Sequoia, I'll have a few more points to give you. I'll mull them over in the meantime."

CHAPTER XXII

When Bryce Cardigan walked down the gang-plank at the steamship-dock in San Francisco, the first face he saw among the waiting crowd was Buck Ogilvy's. Mr. Ogilvy wore his over-coat and a joyous smile, proving that in so far as he was concerned all was well with the world; he pressed forward and thrust forth a great speckled paw for Bryce to shake. Bryce ignored it.

"Why, don't you remember me?" Ogilvy demanded. "I'm Buck Ogilvy."

Bryce looked him fairly in the eye and favoured him with a lightning wink. "I have never heard of you, Mr. Ogilvy. You are mistaking me for someone else."

"Sorry," Ogilvy murmured. "My mistake! Thought you were Bill Kerrick, who used to be a partner of mine. I'm expecting him on this boat, and he's the speaking image of you."

Bryce nodded and passed on, hailed a taxicab, and was driven to the San Francisco office of his company. Five minutes later the door opened and Buck Ogilvy entered.

"I was a bit puzzled at the dock, Bryce," he explained as they shook hands, "but decided to play safe and then follow you to your office. What's up? Have you killed somebody, and are the detectives on your trail? If so, 'fess up and I'll assume the responsibility for your crime, just to show you how grateful I am for that hundred."

"No, I wasn't being shadowed, Buck, but my principal enemy was coming down the gangplank right behind me, and—"

"So was my principal enemy," Ogilvy interrupted. "What does our enemy look like?"

"Like ready money. And if he had seen me shaking hands with you, he'd have suspected a connection between us later on. Buck, you have a good job— about five hundred a month."

"Thanks, old man. I'd work for you for nothing. What are we going to do?"

"Build twelve miles of logging railroad and parallel the line of the old wolf I spoke of a moment ago."

"Good news! We'll do it. How soon do you want it done?"

"As soon as possible. You're the vice-president and general manager."

"I accept the nomination. What do I do first?"

"Listen carefully to my story, analyze my plan for possible weak spots, and then get busy, because after I have provided the funds and given the word 'Go!' the rest is up to you. I must not be known in the transaction at all, because that would be fatal. And I miss my guess if, once we start building or advertising the building of the road, you and I and everybody connected with the enterprise will not be shadowed day and night by an army of Pinkertons."

"I listen," said Buck Ogilvy, and he inclined a large speckled ear in Bryce's direction, the while his large speckled hand drew a scratch-pad toward him.

Three hours later Ogilvy was in possession of the most minute details of the situation in Sequoia, had tabulated, indexed, and cross-indexed them in his ingenious brain and was ready for business—and so announced himself. "And inasmuch as that hundred you sent me has been pretty well shattered," he concluded, "suppose you call in your cold-hearted manager who refused me alms on your credit, and give him orders to honour my sight-drafts. If I'm to light in Sequoia looking like ready money, I've got to have some high-class, tailor-made clothes, and a shine and a shave and a shampoo and a trunk and a private secretary. If there was a railroad running into Sequoia, I'd insist on a private car."

This final detail having been attended to, Mr. Ogilvy promptly proceeded to forget business and launched forth into a recital of his manifold adventures since leaving Princeton; and when at length all of their classmates had been accounted for and listed as dead, married, prosperous, or pauperized, the amiable and highly entertaining Buck took his departure with the announcement that he would look around a little and try to buy some good second-hand grading equipment and a locomotive, in addition to casting an eye over the labour situation and sending a few wires East for the purpose of sounding the market on steel rails. Always an enthusiast in all things, in his mind's eye Mr. Ogilvy could already see a long trainload of logs coming down the Northern California & Oregon Railroad, as he and Bryce had decided to christen the venture.

"N. C. & O.," Mr. Ogilvy murmured. "Sounds brisk and snappy. I like it. Hope that old hunks Pennington likes it, too. He'll probably feel that N. C. & O. stands for Northern California Outrage."

When Bryce Cardigan returned to Sequoia, his labours, insofar as the building of the road were concerned, had been completed. His agreement with Gregory of the Trinidad Redwood Timber Company had been signed, sealed, and delivered; the money to build the road had been deposited in bank; and Buck Ogilvy was already spending it like a drunken sailor. From now on, Bryce could only watch, wait, and pray.

On the next steamer a surveying party with complete camping-equipment arrived in Sequoia, purchased a wagon and two horses, piled their dunnage into the wagon, and disappeared up-country. Hard on their heels came Mr. Buck Ogilvy, and occupied the bridal suite in the Hotel Sequoia, arrangements for which had previously been made by wire. In the sitting room of the suite Mr. Ogilvy installed a new desk, a filing-cabinet, and a brisk young male secretary.

He had been in town less than an hour when the editor of the Sequoia Sentinel sent up his card. The announcement of the incorporation of the Northern California Outrage (for so had Mr. Ogilvy, in huge enjoyment of the misery he was about to create, dubbed the road) had previously been flashed to the Sentinel by the United Press Association, as a local feature story, and already speculation was rife in Sequoia as to the identity of the harebrained individuals who dared to back an enterprise as nebulous as the millennium. Mr. Ogilvy was expecting the visit—in fact, impatiently awaiting it; and since the easiest thing he did was to speak for publication, naturally the editor of the Sentinel got a story which, to that individual's simple soul, seemed to warrant a seven-column head—which it received. Having boned up on the literature of the Redwood Manufacturers' Association, what Buck Ogilvy didn't know about redwood timber, redwood lumber, the remaining redwood acreage and market conditions, past and present, might have been secreted in the editorial eye without seriously hampering the editorial sight. He stated that the capital behind the project was foreign, that he believed in the success of the project and that his entire fortune was dependent upon the completion of it. In glowing terms he spoke of the billions of tons of timber-products to be hauled out of this wonderfully fertile and little-known country, and confidently predicted for the county a future commercial supremacy that would be simply staggering to contemplate.

When Colonel Seth Pennington read this outburst he smiled. "That's a bright scheme on the part of that Trinidad Redwood Timber Company gang to start a railroad excitement and unload their white elephant," he declared. "A scheme like that stuck them with their timber, and I suppose they figure there's a sucker born every minute and that the same old gag might work again. Chances are they have a prospect in tow already."

When Bryce Cardigan read it, he laughed. The interview was so like Buck Ogilvy! In the morning the latter's automobile was brought up from the steamship-dock, and accompanied by his secretary, Mr. Ogilvy disappeared into the north following the bright new stakes of his surveying-gang, and for three weeks was seen no more. As for Bryce Cardigan, that young man buckled down to business, and whenever questioned about the new railroad was careful to hoot at the idea.

On a day when Bryce's mind happened to be occupied with thoughts of Shirley Sumner, he bumped into her on the main street of Sequoia, and to her great relief but profound surprise, he paused in his tracks, lifted his hat, smiled, and opened his mouth to say something—thought better of it, changed his mind, and continued on about his business. As Shirley passed him, she looked him squarely in the face, and in her glance there was neither coldness nor malice.

Bryce felt himself afire from heels to hair one instant, and cold and clammy the next, for Shirley spoke to him.

"Good morning, Mr. Cardigan."

He paused, turned, and approached her. "Good morning, Shirley," he replied. "How have you been?"

"I might have been dead, for all the interest you took in me," she replied sharply. "As matters stand, I'm exceedingly well—thank you. By the way, are you still belligerent?"

He nodded. "I have to be."

"Still peeved at my uncle?"

Again he nodded.

"I think you're a great big grouch, Bryce Cardigan," she flared at him suddenly. "You make me unutterably weary."

"I'm sorry," he answered, "but just at present I am forced to subject you to the strain. Say a year from now, when things are different with me, I'll strive not to offend."

"I'll not be here a year from now," she warned him. He bowed. "Then I'll go wherever you are—and bring you back." And with a mocking little grin, he lifted his hat and passed on.

CHAPTER XXIII

Though Buck Ogilvy was gone from Sequoia for a period of three weeks, he was by no means forgotten. His secretary proved to be an industrious press-agent who by mail, telegraph, and long-distance telephone managed daily to keep the editor of the Sequoia Sentinel fully apprised of all developments in the matter of the Northern California Oregon Railroad Company—including some that had not as yet developed! The result was copious and persistent publicity for the new railroad company, and the arousing in the public mind of a genuine interest in this railroad which was to do so much for the town of Sequoia.

Colonel Seth Pennington was among those who, skeptical at first and inclined to ridicule the project into an early grave, eventually found himself swayed by the publicity and gradually coerced into serious consideration of the results attendant upon the building of the road. The Colonel was naturally as suspicious as a rattlesnake in August; hence he had no sooner emerged from the ranks of the frank scoffers than his alert mind framed the question:

"How is this new road—improbable as I know it to be—going to affect the interests of the Laguna Grande Lumber Company, if the unexpected should happen and those bunco-steerers should actually build a road from Sequoia to Grant's Pass, Oregon, and thus construct a feeder to a transcontinental line?"

Five minutes of serious reflection sufficed to bring the Colonel to the verge of panic, notwithstanding the fact that he was ashamed of himself for yielding to fright despite his firm belief that there was no reason why he should be frightened. Similar considerations occur to a small boy who is walking home in the dark past a cemetery.

The vital aspects of his predicament dawned on the Colonel one night at dinner, midway between the soup and the fish. So forcibly did they occur to him, in fact, that for the nonce he forgot that his niece was seated opposite him.

"Confound them," the Colonel murmured distinctly, "I must look into this immediately."

"Look into what, Uncle dear?" Shirley asked innocently.

"This new railroad that man Ogilvy talks of building—which means, Shirley, that with Sequoia as his starting point, he is going to build a hundred and fifty miles north to connect with the main line of the Southern Pacific in Oregon."

"But wouldn't that be the finest thing that could possibly happen to Humboldt County?" she demanded of him.

"Undoubtedly it would—to Humboldt County; but to the Laguna Grande Lumber Company, in which you have something more than a sentimental interest, my dear, it would be a blow. A large part of the estate left by your father is invested in Laguna Grande stock, and as you know, all of my efforts are devoted to appreciating that stock and to fighting against anything that has a tendency to depreciate it."

"Which reminds me, Uncle Seth, that you never discuss with me any of the matters pertaining to my business interests," she suggested.

He beamed upon her with his patronizing and indulgent smile. "There is no reason why you should puzzle that pretty head of yours with business affairs while I am alive and on the job," he answered. "However, since you have expressed a desire to have this railroad situation explained to you, I will do so. I am not interested in seeing a feeder built from Sequoia north to Grant's Pass, and connecting with the Southern Pacific, but I am tremendously interested in seeing a feeder built south from Sequoia toward San Francisco, to connect with the Northwestern Pacific."

"Why?"

"For cold, calculating business reasons, my dear." He hesitated a moment and then resumed: "A few months ago I would not have told you the things I am about to tell you, Shirley, for the reason that a few months ago it seemed to me you were destined to become rather friendly with young Cardigan. When that fellow desires to be agreeable, he can be rather a likable boy— lovable, even. You are both young; with young people who have many things in common and are thrown together in a community like Sequoia, a lively friendship may develop into an ardent love; and it has been my experience that ardent love not infrequently leads to the altar."

Shirley blushed, and her uncle chuckled good-naturedly. "Fortunately," he continued, "Bryce Cardigan had the misfortune to show himself to you in his true colours, and you had the good sense to dismiss him. Consequently I see no reason why I should not explain to you now what I considered it the part of wisdom to withhold from you at that time—provided, of course, that all this does not bore you to extinction."

"Do go on, Uncle Seth. I'm tremendously interested," averred Shirley.

"Shortly after I launched the Laguna Grande Lumber Company—in which, as your guardian and executor of your father's estate, I deemed it wise to invest part of your inheritance—I found myself forced to seek further for sound investments for your surplus funds. Now, good timber, bought cheap, inevitably will be sold dear. At least, such has been my observation during a quarter of a century—and old John Cardigan had some twenty thousand acres of the finest redwood timber in the State—timber which had cost him an average price of less than fifty cents per thousand.

"Well, in this instance the old man had overreached himself, and finding it necessary to increase his working capital, he incorporated his holdings into the Cardigan Redwood Lumber Company and floated a bond-issue of a million dollars. They were twenty-year six per cent. certificates; the security was ample, and I invested for you three hundred thousand dollars in Cardigan bonds. I bought them at eighty, and they were worth two hundred; at least, they would have been worth two hundred under my management—"

"How did you manage to buy them so cheap?" she interrupted.

"Old Cardigan had had a long run of bad luck—due to bad management and bad judgment, my dear—and when a corporation is bonded, the bondholders have access to its financial statements. From time to time I discovered bondholders who needed money and hence unloaded at a sacrifice; but by far the majority of the bonds I purchased for your account were owned by local people who had lost confidence in John Cardigan and the future of the redwood lumber industry hereabouts. You understand, do you not?"

"I do not understand what all this has to do with a railroad."

"Very well—I shall proceed to explain." He held up his index finger. "Item one: For years old John Cardigan has rendered valueless, because inaccessible, twenty-five hundred acres of Laguna Grande timber on Squaw Creek. His absurd Valley of the Giants blocks the outlet, and of course he persisted in refusing me a right of way through that little dab of timber in order to discourage me and force me to sell him that Squaw Creek timber at his price."

"Yes," Shirley agreed, "I dare say that was his object. Was it reprehensible of him, Uncle Seth?"

"Not a bit, my dear. He was simply playing the cold game of business. I would have done the same thing to Cardigan had the situation been reversed. We played a game together—and I admit that he won, fairly and squarely."

"Then why is it that you feel such resentment against him?"

"Oh, I don't resent the old fool, Shirley. He merely annoys me. I suppose I feel a certain natural chagrin at having been beaten, and in consequence cherish an equally natural desire to pay the old schemer back in his own coin.

Under the rules as we play the game, such action on my part is perfectly permissible, is it not?"

"Yes," she agreed frankly, "I think it is, Uncle Seth. Certainly, if he blocked you and rendered your timber valueless, there is no reason why, if you have the opportunity, you should not block him—and render his timber valueless."

The Colonel banged the table with his fist so heartily that the silver fairly leaped. "Spoken like a man!" he declared. "I HAVE the opportunity and am proceeding to impress the Cardigans with the truth of the old saying that every dog must have his day. When Cardigan's contract with our road for the hauling of his logs expires by limitation next year, I am not going to renew it—at least not until I have forced him to make me the concessions I desire, and certainly not at the present ruinous freight-rate."

"Then," said Shirley eagerly, "if you got a right of way through his Valley of the Giants, you would renew the contract he has with you for the hauling of his logs, would you not?"

"I would have, before young Cardigan raised such Hades that day in the logging-camp, before old Cardigan sold his Valley of the Giants to another burglar—and before I had gathered indubitable evidence that neither of the Cardigans knows enough about managing a sawmill and selling lumber to guarantee a reasonable profit on the capital they have invested and still pay the interest on their bonded and floating indebtedness. Shirley, I bought those Cardigan bonds for you because I thought old Cardigan knew his business and would make the bonds valuable—make them worth par. Instead, the Cardigan Redwood Lumber Company is tottering on the verge of bankruptcy; the bonds I purchased for you are now worth less than I paid for them, and by next year the Cardigans will default on the interest.

"So I'm going to sit tight and decline to have any more business dealings with the Cardigans. When their hauling contract expires, I shall not renew it under any circumstances; that will prevent them from getting logs, and so they will automatically go out of the lumber business and into the hands of a receiver; and since you are the largest individual stockholder, I, representing you and a number of minor bondholders, will dominate the executive committee of the bondholders when they meet to consider what shall be done when the Cardigans default on their interest and the payment due the sinking fund. I shall then have myself appointed receiver for the Cardigan Redwood Lumber Company, investigate its affairs thoroughly, and see for myself whether or no there is a possibility of working it out of the jam it is in and saving you a loss on your bonds.

"I MUST pursue this course, my dear, in justice to you and the other bondholders. If, on the other hand, I find the situation hopeless or conclude that a period of several years must ensue before the Cardigans work out of debt, I shall recommend to the bank which holds the deed of trust and acts as trustee, that the property be sold at public auction to the highest bidder to reimburse the bondholders. Of course," he hastened to add, "if the property sells for more than the corporation owes such excess will then in due course be turned over to the Cardigans."

"Is it likely to sell at a price in excess of the indebtedness?" Shirley queried anxiously.

"It is possible, but scarcely probable," he answered dryly. "I have in mind, under those circumstances, bidding the property in for the Laguna Grande Lumber Company and merging it with our holdings, paying part of the purchase-price of the Cardigan property in Cardigan bonds, and the remainder in cash."

"But what will the Cardigans do then, Uncle Seth?"

"Well, long before the necessity for such a contingency arises, the old man will have been gathered to the bosom of Abraham; and after the Cardigan Redwood Lumber Company has ceased to exist, young Cardigan can go to work for a living."

"Would you give him employment, Uncle Seth?"

"I would not. Do you think I'm crazy, Shirley? Remember, my dear, there is no sentiment in business. If there was, we wouldn't have any business."

"I think I understand, Uncle Seth—with the exception of what effect the building of the N. C. O. has upon your plans."

"Item two," he challenged, and ticked it off on his middle finger. "The Cardigan Redwood Lumber Company owns two fine bodies of redwood timber widely separated—one to the south of Sequoia in the San Hedrin watershed and at present practically valueless because inaccessible, and the other to the north of Sequoia, immediately adjoining our holdings in Township Nine and valuable because of its accessibility." He paused a moment and looked at her smilingly, "The logging railroad of our corporation, the Laguna Grande Lumber Company, makes it accessible. Now, while the building of the N.C.O. would be a grand thing for the county in general, we can get along without it because it doesn't help us out particularly. We already have a railroad running from our timber to tidewater, and we can reach the markets of the world with our ships."

"I think I understand, Uncle Seth. When Cardigan's hauling contract with our road expires, his timber in Township Nine will depreciate in value because it will no longer be accessible, while our timber, being still accessible, retains its value."

"Exactly. And to be perfectly frank with you, Shirley, I do not want Cardigan's timber in Township Nine given back its value through accessibility provided by the N.C.O. If that road is not built, Cardigan's timber in Township Nine will be valuable to us, but not to another living soul. Moreover, the Trinidad Redwood Timber Company has a raft of fine timber still farther north and adjoining the holdings of our company and Cardigan's, and if this infernal N.C.O. isn't built, we'll be enabled to buy that Trinidad timber pretty cheap one of these bright days, too."

"All of which appears to me to constitute sound business logic, Uncle Seth."

He nodded. "Item three," he continued, and ticked it off on his third finger: "I want to see the feeder for a transcontinental line built into Sequoia from the south, for the reason that it will tap the Cardigan holdings in the San Hedrin watershed and give a tremendous value to timber which at the present time is rather a negative asset; consequently I would prefer to have that value created after Cardigan's San Hedrin timber has been merged with the assets of the Laguna Grande Lumber Company."

"And so—"

"I must investigate this N.C.O. outfit and block it if possible—and it should be possible."

"How, for instance?"

"I haven't considered the means, my dear. Those come later. For the present I am convinced that the N.C.O. is a corporate joke, sprung on the dear public by the Trinidad Redwood Timber Company to get the said dear public excited, create a real-estate boom, and boost timber-values. Before the boom collapses—a condition which will follow the collapse of the N.C.O.—the Trinidad people hope to sell their holdings and get from under."

"Really," said Shirley, demurely, "the more I see of business, the more fascinating I find it."

"Shirley, it's the grandest game in the world."

"And yet," she added musingly, "old Mr. Cardigan is so blind and helpless."

"They'll be saying that about me some day if I live to be as old as John Cardigan."

"Nevertheless, I feel sorry for him, Uncle Seth."

"Well, if you'll continue to waste your sympathy on him rather than on his son, I'll not object," he retorted laughingly.

"Oh, Bryce Cardigan is able to take care of himself."

"Yes, and mean enough."

"He saved our lives, Uncle Seth."

"He had to—in order to save his own. Don't forget that, my dear." Carefully he dissected a sand-dab and removed the backbone. "I'd give a ripe peach to learn the identity of the scheming buttinsky who bought old Cardigan's Valley of the Giants," he said presently. "I'll be hanged if that doesn't complicate matters a little."

"You should have bought it when the opportunity offered," she reminded him. "You could have had it then for fifty thousand dollars less than you would have paid for it a year ago—and I'm sure that should have been sufficient indication to you that the game you and the Cardigans had been playing so long had come to an end. He was beaten and acknowledged it, and I think you might have been a little more generous to your fallen enemy, Uncle Seth."

"I dare say," he admitted lightly. "However, I wasn't, and now I'm going to be punished for it, my dear: so don't roast me any more. By the way, that speckled hot-air fellow Ogilvy, who is promoting the Northern California Oregon Railroad, is back in town again. Somehow, I haven't much confidence in that fellow. I think I'll wire the San Francisco office to look him up in Dun's and Bradstreet's. Folks up this way are taking too much for granted on that fellow's mere say—so, but I for one intend to delve for facts—particularly with regard to the N.C.O. bank-roll and Ogilvy's associates. I'd sleep a whole lot more soundly to-night if I knew the answer to two very important questions."

"What are they, Uncle Seth?"

"Well, I'd like to know whether the N.C.O. is genuine or a screen to hide the operations of the Trinidad Redwood Timber Company."

"It might," said Shirley, with one of those sudden flashes of intuition peculiar to women, "be a screen to hide the operations of Bryce Cardigan. Now that he knows you aren't going to renew his hauling contract, he may have decided to build his own logging railroad."

After a pause the Colonel made answer: "No, I have no fear of that. It would cost five hundred thousand dollars to build that twelve-mile line and bridge Mad River, and the Cardigans haven't got that amount of money. What's more, they can't get it."

"But suppose," she persisted, "that the real builder of the road should prove to be Bryce Cardigan, after all. What would you do?"

Colonel Pennington's eyes twinkled. "I greatly fear, my dear, I should make a noise like something doing."

"Suppose you lost the battle."

"In that event the Laguna Grande Lumber Company wouldn't be any worse off than it is at present. The principal loser, as I view the situation, would be Miss Shirley Sumner, who has the misfortune to be loaded up with Cardigan bonds. And as for Bryce Cardigan—well, that young man would certainly know he'd been through a fight."

"I wonder if he'll fight to the last, Uncle Seth."

"Why, I believe he will," Pennington replied soberly.

"I'd love to see you beat him."

"Shirley! Why, my dear, you're growing ferocious." Her uncle's tones were laden with banter, but his countenance could not conceal the pleasure her last remark had given him.

"Why not? I have something at stake, have I not?"

"Then you really want me to smash him?" The Colonel's voice proclaimed his incredulity.

"You got me into this fight by buying Cardigan bonds for me," she replied meaningly, "and I look to you to save the investment or as much of it as possible; for certainly, if it should develop that the Cardigans are the real promoters of the N.C.O., to permit them to go another half-million dollars into debt in a forlorn hope of saving a company already top-heavy with indebtedness wouldn't savor of common business sense. Would it?"

The Colonel rose hastily, came around the table, and kissed her paternally. "My dear," he murmured, "you're such a comfort to me. Upon my word, you are."

"I'm so glad you have explained the situation to me, Uncle Seth."

"I would have explained it long ago had I not cherished a sneaking suspicion that—er—well, that despite everything, young Cardigan might—er—influence you against your better judgment and—er—mine."

"You silly man!"

He shrugged. "One must figure every angle of a possible situation, my dear, and I should hesitate to start something with the Cardigans, and have you, because of foolish sentiment, call off my dogs."

Shirley thrust out her adorable chin aggressively. "Sick 'em. Tige!" she answered. "Shake 'em up, boy!"

"You bet I'll shake 'em up," the Colonel declared joyously. He paused with a morsel of food on his fork and waved the fork at her aggressively. "You stimulate me into activity, Shirley. My mind has been singularly dull of late; I have worried unnecessarily, but now that I know you are with me, I am inspired. I'll tell you how we'll fix this new railroad, if it exhibits signs of being dangerous." Again he smote the table. "We'll sew 'em up tighter than a new buttonhole."

"Do tell me how," she pleaded eagerly.

"I'll block them on their franchise to run over the city streets of Sequoia."

"How?"

"By making the mayor and the city council see things my way," he answered dryly. "Furthermore, in order to enter Sequoia, the N. C. O. will have to cross the tracks of the Laguna Grande Lumber Company's line on Water Street—make a jump-crossing—and I'll enjoin them and hold them up in the courts till the cows come home."

"Uncle Seth, you're a wizard."

"Well, at least I'm no slouch at looking after my own interests—and yours, Shirley. In the midst of peace we should be prepared for war. You've met Mayor Poundstone and his lady, haven't you?"

"I had tea at her house last week."

"Good news. Suppose you invite her and Poundstone here for dinner some night this week. Just a quiet little family dinner, Shirley, and after dinner you can take Mrs. Poundstone upstairs, on some pretext or other, while I sound Poundstone out on his attitude toward the N. C. O. They haven't asked for a franchise yet; at least, the Sentinel hasn't printed a word about it;—but when they do, of course the franchise will be advertised for sale to the highest bidder. Naturally, I don't want to bid against them; they might run the price up on me and leave me with a franchise on my hands—something I do not want, because I have no use for the blamed thing myself. I feel certain, however, I can find some less expensive means of keeping them out of it— say by convincing Poundstone and a majority of the city council that the N. C. O. is not such a public asset as its promoters claim for it. Hence I think it wise to sound the situation out in advance, don't you, my dear?"

She nodded. "I shall attend to the matter, Uncle Seth."

Five minutes after dinner was over, Shirley joined her uncle in the library and announced that His Honor, the Mayor, and Mrs. Poundstone, would be delighted to dine with them on the following Thursday night.

CHAPTER XXIV

To return to Bryce Cardigan: Having completed his preliminary plans to build the N. C. O., Bryce had returned to Sequoia, prepared to sit quietly on the side-lines and watch his peppery henchman Buck Ogilvy go into action. The more Bryce considered that young man's fitness for the position he occupied, the more satisfied did he become with his decision. While he had not been in touch with Ogilvy for several years, he had known him intimately at Princeton.

In his last year at college Ogilvy's father, a well-known railroad magnate, had come a disastrous cropper in the stock market, thus throwing Buck upon his own resources and cutting short his college career—which was probably the very best thing that could happen to his father's son. For a brief period—perhaps five minutes—Buck had staggered under the blow; then his tremendous optimism had asserted itself, and while he packed his trunk, he had planned for the future. As to how that future had developed, the reader will have gleaned some slight idea from the information imparted in his letter to Bryce Cardigan, already quoted. In a word, Mr. Ogilvy had had his ups and downs.

Ogilvy's return to Sequoia following his three-weeks tour in search of rights of way for the N. C. O. was heralded by a visit from him to Bryce Cardigan at the latter's office. As he breasted the counter in the general office, Moira McTavish left her desk and came over to see what the visitor desired.

"I should like to see Mr. Bryce Cardigan," Buck began in crisp businesslike accents. He was fumbling in his card-case and did not look up until about to hand his card to Moira—when his mouth flew half open, the while he stared at her with consummate frankness. The girl's glance met his momentarily, then was lowered modestly; she took the card and carried it to Bryce.

"Hum-m-m!" Bryce grunted. "That noisy fellow Ogilvy, eh?"

"His clothes are simply wonderful—and so is his voice. He's very refined. But he's carroty red and has freckled hands, Mr. Bryce."

Bryce rose and sauntered into the general office.

"Mr. Bryce Cardigan?" Buck queried politely, with an interrogative lift of his blond eyebrows.

"At your service, Mr. Ogilvy. Please come in."

"Thank you so much, sir." He followed Bryce to the latter's private office, closed the door carefully behind him, and stood with his broad back against it.

"Buck, are you losing your mind?" Bryce demanded.

"Losing it? I should say not. I've just lost it."

"I believe you. If you were quite sane, you wouldn't run the risk of being seen entering my office."

"Tut-tut, old dear! None of that! Am I not the main-spring of the Northern California Oregon Railroad and privileged to run the destinies of that soulless corporation as I see fit?" He sat down, crossed his long legs, and jerked a speckled thumb toward the outer office. "I was sane when I came in here, but the eyes of the girl outside—oh, yow, them eyes! I must be introduced to her. And you're scolding me for coming around here in broad daylight. Why, you duffer, if I come at night, d'ye suppose I'd have met her? Be sensible."

"You like Moira's eyes, eh?"

"I've never seen anything like them. Zounds, I'm afire. I have little prickly sensations, like ants running over me. How can you be insensate enough to descend to labour with an houri like that around? Oh, man! To think of an angel like that WORKING—to think of a brute like you making her work!"

"Love at first sight, eh, Buck?"

"I don't know what it is, but it's nice. Who is she?"

"She's Moira McTavish, and you're not to make love to her. Understand? I can't have you snooping around this office after to-day."

Mr. Ogilvy's eyes popped with interest. "Oh," he breathed. "You have an eye to the main chance yourself have you? Have you proposed to the lady as yet?"

"No, you idiot."

"Then I'll match you for her—or rather for the chance to propose first." Buck produced a dollar and spun it in the air.

"Nothing doing, Buck. Spare yourself these agonizing suspicions. The fact of the matter is that you give me a wonderful inspiration. I've always been afraid Moira would fall in love with some ordinary fellow around Sequoia—propinquity, you know—"

"You bet. Propinquity's the stuff. I'll stick around."

"—and I we been on the lookout for a fine man to marry her off to. She's too wonderful for you, Buck, but in time you might learn to live up to her."

"Duck! I'm liable to kiss you."

"Don't be too precipitate. Her father used to be our woods-boss. I fired him for boozing."

"I wouldn't care two hoots if her dad was old Nick himself. I'm going to marry her—if she'll have me. Ah, the glorious creature!" He waved his long arms despairingly. "O Lord, send me a cure for freckles. Bryce, you'll speak a kind word for me, won't you—sort of boom my stock, eh? Be a good fellow."

"Certainly. Now come down to earth and render a report on your stewardship."

"I'll try. To begin, I've secured rights of way, at a total cost of twelve thousand, one hundred and three dollars and nine cents, from the city limits of Sequoia to the southern boundary of your timber in Township Nine. I've got my line surveyed, and so far as the building of the road is concerned, I know exactly what I'm going to do, and how and when I'm going to do it, once I get my material on the ground."

"What steps have you taken toward securing your material?"

"Well, I can close a favourable contract for steel rails with the Colorado Steel Products Company. Their schedule of deliveries is O. K. as far as San Francisco, but it's up to you to provide water transportation from there to Sequoia."

"We can handle the rails on our steam schooners. Next?"

"I have an option of a rattling good second-hand locomotive down at the Santa Fe shops, and the Hawkins & Barnes Construction Company have offered me a steam shovel, half a dozen flat-cars, and a lot of fresnos and scrapers at ruinous prices. This equipment is pretty well worn, and they want to get rid of it before buying new stuff for their contract to build the Arizona and Sonora Central. However, it is first-rate equipment for us, because it will last until we're through with it; then we can scrap it for junk. We can buy or rent teams from local citizens and get half of our labour locally. San Francisco employment bureaus will readily supply the remainder, and I have half a dozen fine boys on tap to boss the steam shovel, pile-driver, bridge-building gang, track-layer and construction gang. And as soon as you tell me how I'm to get my material ashore and out on the job, I'll order it and get busy."

"That's exactly where the shoe begins to pinch, Pennington's main-line tracks enter the city along Water Street, with one spur into his log-dump and another out on his mill-dock. From the main-line tracks we also have built a spur through our drying-yard out to our log-dump and a switch-line out on to our milldock. We can unload our locomotive, steam shovel, and flat-cars on our own wharf, but unless Pennington gives us permission to use his main-line tracks out to a point beyond the city limits—where a Y will lead off to the point where our construction begins—we're up a stump."

"Suppose he refuses, Bryce. What then?"

"Why, we'll simply have to enter the city down Front Street, paralleling Pennington's tracks on Water Street, turning down B Street, make a jump-crossing of Pennington's line on Water Street, and connecting with the spur into our yard."

"Can't have an elbow turn at Front and B streets?"

"Don't have to. We own a square block on that corner, and we'll build across it, making a gradual turn."

"See here, my son," Buck said solemnly, "is this your first adventure in railroad building?"

Bryce nodded.

"I thought so; otherwise you wouldn't talk so confidently of running your line over city streets and making jump-crossings on your competitor's road. If your competitor regards you as a menace to his pocketbook, he can give you a nice little run for your money and delay you indefinitely."

"I realize that, Buck. That's why I'm not appearing in this railroad deal at all. If Pennington suspected I was back of it, he'd fight me before the city council and move heaven and earth to keep me out of a franchise to use the city streets and cross his line. Of course, since his main line runs on city property, under a franchise granted by the city, the city has a perfect right to grant me the privilege of making a jump-crossing of his line——"

"Will they do it? That's the problem. If they will not, you're licked, my son, and I'm out of a job."

"We can sue and condemn a right of way."

"Yes, but if the city council puts up a plea that it is against the best interests of the city to grant the franchise, you'll find that except in most extraordinary cases, the courts regard it as against public policy to give judgment against a municipality, the State or the Government of the United States. At any rate, they'll hang you up in the courts till you die of old age; and as I understand the matter, you have to have this line running in less than a year, or go out of business."

Bryce hung his head thoughtfully. "I've been too cocksure," he muttered presently. "I shouldn't have spent that twelve thousand for rights of way until I had settled the matter of the franchise."

"Oh, I didn't buy any rights of way—yet," Ogilvy hastened to assure him. "I've only signed the land-owners up on an agreement to give or sell me a right of way at the stipulated figures any time within one year from date. The cost of the surveying gang and my salary and expenses are all that you are out to date."

"Buck, you're a wonder."

"Not at all. I've merely been through all this before and have profited by my experience. Now, then, to get back to our muttons. Will the city council grant you a franchise to enter the city and jump Pennington's tracks?"

"I'm sure I don't know, Buck. You'll have to ask them—sound them out. The city council meets Saturday morning."

"They'll meet this evening—in the private diningroom of the Hotel Sequoia, if I can arrange it," Buck Ogilvy declared emphatically. "I'm going to have them all up for dinner and talk the matter over. I'm not exactly aged, Bryce, but I've handled about fifteen city councils and county boards of supervisors, not to mention Mexican and Central American governors and presidents, in my day, and I know the breed from cover to cover. Following a preliminary conference, I'll let you know whether you're going to get that franchise without difficulty or whether somebody's itchy palm will have to be crossed with silver first. Honest men never temporize. You know where they stand, but a grafter temporizes and plays a waiting game, hoping to wear your patience down to the point where you'll ask him bluntly to name his figure. By the way, what do you know about your blighted old city council, anyway?"

"Two of the five councilmen are for sale; two are honest men—and one is an uncertain quantity. The mayor is a politician. I've known them all since boyhood, and if I dared come out in the open, I think that even the crooks have sentiment enough for what the Cardigans stand for in this county to decline to hold me up."

"Then why not come out in the open and save trouble and expense?"

"I am not ready to have a lot of notes called on me," Bryce replied dryly. "Neither am I desirous of having the Laguna Grande Lumber Company start a riot in the redwood lumber market by cutting prices to a point where I would have to sell my lumber at a loss in order to get hold of a little ready money. Neither do I desire to have trees felled across the right of way of Pennington's road after his trainloads of logs have gone through and before mine have started from the woods. I don't want my log-landings jammed until I can't move, and I don't want Pennington's engineer to take a curve in such a hurry that he'll whip my loaded logging-trucks off into a canon and leave me hung up for lack of rolling-stock. I tell you, the man has me under his thumb, and the only way I can escape is to slip out when he isn't looking.

He can do too many things to block the delivery of my logs and then dub them acts of God, in order to avoid a judgment against him on suit for non-performance of his hauling contract with this company."

"Hum-m-m! Slimy old beggar, isn't he? I dare say he wouldn't hesitate to buy the city council to block you, would he?"

"I know he'll lie and steal. I dare say he'd corrupt a public official."

Buck Ogilvy rose and stretched himself. "I've got my work cut out for me, haven't I?" he declared with a yawn. "However, it'll be a fight worth while, and that at least will make it interesting. Well?"

Bryce pressed the buzzer on his desk, and a moment later Moira entered. "Permit me, Moira, to present Mr. Ogilvy. Mr. Ogilvy, Miss McTavish." The introduction having been acknowledged by both parties, Bryce continued: "Mr. Ogilvy will have frequent need to interview me at this office, Moira, but it is our joint desire that his visits here shall remain a profound secret to everybody with the exception of ourselves. To that end he will hereafter call at night, when this portion of the town is absolutely deserted. You have an extra key to the office, Moira. I wish you would give it to Mr. Ogilvy."

The girl nodded. "Mr. Ogilvy will have to take pains to avoid our watchman," she suggested.

"That is a point well taken, Moira. Buck, when you call, make it a point to arrive here promptly on the hour. The watchman will be down in the mill then, punching the time-clock."

Again Moira inclined her dark head and withdrew. Mr. Buck Ogilvy groaned. "God speed the day when you can come out from under and I'll be permitted to call during office hours," he murmured. He picked up his hat and withdrew, via the general office. Half an hour later, Bryce looked out and saw him draped over the counter, engaged in animated conversation with Moira McTavish. Before Ogilvy left, he had managed to impress Moira with a sense of the disadvantage under which he laboured through being forced, because of circumstances Mr. Cardigan would doubtless relate to her in due course, to abandon all hope of seeing her at the office—at least for some time to come. Then he spoke feelingly of the unmitigated horror of being a stranger in a strange town, forced to sit around hotel lobbies with drummers and other lost souls, and drew from Moira the assurance that it wasn't more distressing than having to sit around a boardinghouse night after night watching old women tat and tattle.

This was the opening Buck Ogilvy had sparred for. Fixing Moira with his bright blue eyes, he grinned boldly and said: "Suppose, Miss McTavish, we start a league for the dispersion of gloom. You be the president, and I'll be the financial secretary."

"How would the league operate?" Moira demanded cautiously.

"Well, it might begin by giving a dinner to all the members, followed by a little motor-trip into the country next Saturday afternoon," Buck suggested.

Moira's Madonna glance appraised him steadily. "I haven't known you very long, Mr. Ogilvy," she reminded him.

"Oh, I'm easy to get acquainted with," he retorted lightly. "Besides, don't I come well recommended?" He pondered for a moment. Then: "I'll tell you what, Miss McTavish. Suppose we put it up to Bryce Cardigan. If he says it's all right we'll pull off the party. If he says it's all wrong, I'll go out and drown myself—and fairer words than them has no man spoke."

"I'll think it over," said Moira.

"By all means. Never decide such an important matter in a hurry. Just tell me your home telephone number, and I'll ring up at seven this evening for your decision."

Reluctantly Moira gave him the number. She was not at all prejudiced against this carroty stranger—in fact, she had a vague suspicion that he was a sure cure for the blues, an ailment which she suffered from all too frequently; and, moreover, his voice, his respectful manner, his alert eyes, and his wonderful clothing were all rather alluring. Womanlike, she was flattered at being noticed—particularly by a man like Ogilvy, whom it was plain to be seen was vastly superior to any male even in Sequoia, with the sole exception of Bryce Cardigan. The flutter of a great adventure was in Moira's heart, and the flush of a thousand roses in her cheeks when, Buck Ogilvy having at length departed, she went into Bryce's private office to get his opinion as to the propriety of accepting the invitation.

Bryce listened to her gravely as with all the sweet innocence of her years and unworldliness she laid the Ogilvy proposition before him.

"By all means, accept," he counselled her. "Buck Ogilvy is one of the finest gentlemen you'll ever meet. I'll stake my reputation on him. You'll find him vastly amusing, Moira. He'd make Niobe forget her troubles, and he DOES know how to order a dinner."

"Don't you think I ought to have a chaperon?"

"Well, it isn't necessary, although it's good form in a small town like Sequoia, where everybody knows everybody else."

"I thought so," Moira murmured thoughtfully. "I'll ask Miss Sumner to come with us. Mr. Ogilvy won't mind the extra expense, I'm sure."

"He'll be delighted," Bryce assured her maliciously. "Ask Miss Sumner, by all means."

When Moira had left him, Bryce sighed. "Gosh!" he murmured. "I wish I could go, too."

He was roused from his bitter introspections presently by the ringing of the telephone. To his amazement Shirley Sumner was calling him!

"You're a wee bit surprised, aren't you, Mr. Cardigan?" she said teasingly.

"I am," he answered honestly. "I had a notion I was quite persona non grata with you."

"Are you relieved to find you are not? You aren't, you know."

"Thank you. I am relieved."

"I suppose you're wondering why I have telephoned to you?"

"No, I haven't had time. The suddenness of it all has left me more or less dumb. Why did you ring up?"

"I wanted some advice. Suppose you wanted very, very much to know what two people were talking about, but found yourself in a position where you couldn't eavesdrop. What would you do?"

"I wouldn't eavesdrop," he told her severely. "That isn't a nice thing to do, and I didn't think you would contemplate anything that isn't nice."

"I wouldn't ordinarily. But I have every moral, ethical, and financial right to be a party to that conversation, only—well—"

"With you present there would be no conversation—is that it?"

"Exactly, Mr. Cardigan."

"And it is of the utmost importance that you should know what is said?"

"Yes."

"And you do not intend to use your knowledge of this conversation, when gained, for an illegal or unethical purpose?"

"I do not. On the contrary, if I am aware of what is being planned, I can prevent others from doing something illegal and unethical."

"In that event, Shirley, I should say you are quite justified in eavesdropping."

"But how can I do it? I can't hide in a closet and listen."

"Buy a dictograph and have it hidden in the room where the conversation takes place. It will record every word of it."

"Where can I buy one?"

"In San Francisco."

"Will you telephone to your San Francisco office and have them buy one for me and ship it to you, together with directions for using. George Sea Otter can bring it over to me when it arrives."

"Shirley, this is most extraordinary."

"I quite realize that. May I depend upon you to oblige me in this matter?"

"Certainly. But why pick on me, of all persons, to perform such a mission for you?"

"I can trust you to forget that you have performed it."

"Thank you. I think you may safely trust me. And I shall attend to the matter immediately."

"You are very kind, Mr. Cardigan. How is your dear old father? Moira told me sometime ago that he was ill."

"He's quite well again, thank you. By the way, Moira doesn't know that you and I have ever met. Why don't you tell her?"

"I can't answer that question—now. Perhaps some day I may be in a position to do so."

"It's too bad the circumstances are such that we, who started out to be such agreeable friends, see so little of each other, Shirley."

"Indeed, it is. However, it's all your fault. I have told you once how you can obviate that distressing situation. But you're so stubborn, Mr. Cardigan."

"I haven't got to the point where I like crawling on my hands and knees," he flared back at her.

"Even for your sake, I decline to simulate friendship or tolerance for your uncle; hence I must be content to let matters stand as they are between us."

She laughed lightly. "So you are still uncompromisingly belligerent—still after Uncle Seth's scalp?"

"Yes; and I think I'm going to get it. At any rate, he isn't going to get mine."

"Don't you think you're rather unjust to make me suffer for the sins of my relative, Bryce?" she demanded.

She had called him by his first name. He thrilled. "I'm lost in a quagmire of debts—I'm helpless now," he murmured. "I'm not fighting for myself alone, but for a thousand dependents—for a principle—for an ancient sentiment that was my father's and is now mine. You do not understand."

"I understand more than you give me credit for, and some day you'll realize it. I understand just enough to make me feel sorry for you. I understand what even my uncle doesn't suspect at present, and that is that you're the directing genius of the Northern California Oregon Railroad and hiding behind your friend Ogilvy. Now, listen to me, Bryce Cardigan: You're never going to build that road. Do you understand?"

The suddenness of her attack amazed him to such an extent that he did not take the trouble to contradict her. Instead he blurted out, angrily and defiantly: "I'll build that road if it costs me my life—if it costs me you. Understand! I'm in this fight to win."

"You will not build that road," she reiterated.

"Why?"

"Because I shall not permit you to. I have some financial interest in the Laguna Grande Lumber Company, and it is not to that financial interest that you should build the N.C.O."

"How did you find out I was behind Ogilvy?"

"Intuition. Then I accused you of it, and you admitted it."

"I suppose you're going to tell your uncle now," he retorted witheringly.

"On the contrary, I am not. I greatly fear I was born with a touch of sporting blood, Mr. Cardigan, so I'm going to let you two fight until you're exhausted, and then I'm going to step in and decide the issue. You can save money by surrendering now. I hold the whip hand."

"I prefer to fight. With your permission this bout will go to a knockout."

"I'm not so certain I do not like you all the more for that decision. And if it will comfort you the least bit, you have my word of honour that I shall not reveal to my uncle the identity of the man behind the N. C. O. I'm not a tattletale, you know, and moreover I have a great curiosity to get to the end of the story. The fact is, both you and Uncle Seth annoy me exceedingly. How lovely everything would have been if you two hadn't started this feud and forced upon me the task of trying to be fair and impartial to you both."

"Can you remain fair and impartial?"

"I think I can—even up to the point of deciding whether or not you are going to build that road. Then I shall act independently of you both. Forgive my slang, but—I'm going to hand you each a poke then."

"Shirley," he told her earnestly, "listen carefully to what I am about to say: I love you. I've loved you from the day I first met you. I shall always love you; and when I get around to it, I'm going to ask you to marry me. At present, however, that is a right I do not possess. However, the day I acquire the right I shall exercise it."

"And when will that day be?" Very softly, in awesome tones!

"The day I drive the last spike in the N. C. O."

Fell a silence. Then: "I'm glad, Bryce Cardigan, you're not a quitter. Good-bye, good luck—and don't forget my errand." She hung up and sat at the telephone for a moment, dimpled chin in dimpled hand, her glance wandering through the window and far away across the roofs of the town to where the smoke-stack of Cardigan's mill cut the sky-line. "How I'd hate you if I could handle you!" she murmured.

Following this exasperating but illuminating conversation with Shirley Sumner over the telephone, Bryce Cardigan was a distressed and badly worried man. However, Bryce was a communicant of a very simple faith—to wit, that one is never whipped till one is counted out, and the first shock of Shirley's discovery having passed, he wasted no time in vain repinings but straightway set himself to scheme a way out of his dilemma.

For an hour he sat slouched in his chair, chin on breast, the while he reviewed every angle of the situation.

He found it impossible, however, to dissociate the business from the personal aspects of his relations with Shirley, and he recalled that she had the very best of reasons for placing their relations on a business basis rather than a sentimental one. He had played a part in their little drama which he knew must have baffled and infuriated her. More, had she, in those delightful few days of their early acquaintance, formed for him a sentiment somewhat stronger than friendship (he did not flatter himself that this was so), he could understand her attitude toward him as that of the woman scorned. For the present, however, it was all a profound and disturbing mystery, and after an hour of futile concentration there came to Bryce the old childish impulse to go to his father with his troubles. That sturdy old soul, freed from the hot passions of youth, its impetuosity and its proneness to consider cause rather than effect, had weathered too many storms in his day to permit the present one to benumb his brain as it had his son's.

"He will be able to think without having his thoughts blotted out by a woman's face," Bryce soliloquized. "He's like one of his own big redwood trees; his head is always above the storm."

Straightway Bryce left the office and went home to the old house on the knoll. John Cardigan was sitting on the veranda, and from a stand beside him George Sea Otter entertained him with a phonograph selection—"The Suwanee River," sung by a male quartet. As the gate clicked, John raised his head; then as Bryce's quick step spurned the cement walk up the little old-fashioned garden, he rose and stood with one hand outstretched and trembling a little. He could not see, but with the intuition of the blind, he knew.

"What is it, son?" he demanded gently as Bryce came up the low steps. "George, choke that contraption off."

Bryce took his father's hand. "I'm in trouble, John Cardigan," he said simply, "and I'm not big enough to handle it alone."

The leonine old man smiled, and his smile had all the sweetness of a benediction. His boy was in trouble and had come to him. Good! Then he would not fail him. "Sit down, son, and tell the old man all about it. Begin at the beginning and let me have all the angles of the angle."

Bryce obeyed, and for the first time John Cardigan learned of his son's acquaintance with Shirley Sumner and the fact that she had been present in Pennington's woods the day Bryce had gone there to settle the score with Jules Rondeau. In the wonderful first flush of his love a sense of embarrassment, following his discovery of the fact that his father and Colonel Pennington were implacable enemies, had decided Bryce not to mention the matter of the girl to John Cardigan until the ENTENTE CORDIALE between Pennington and his father could be reestablished, for Bryce had, with the optimism of his years, entertained for a few days a thought that he could bring about this desirable condition of affairs. The discovery that he could not, together with his renunciation of his love until he should succeed in protecting his heritage and eliminating the despair that had come upon his father in the latter's old age, had further operated to render unnecessary any discussion of the girl with the old man.

With the patience and gentleness of a confessor John Cardigan heard the story now, and though Bryce gave no hint in words that his affections were involved in the fight for the Cardigan acres, yet did his father know It, for he was a parent. And his great heart went out in sympathy for his boy.

"I understand, sonny, I understand. This young lady is only one additional reason why you must win, for of course you understand she is not indifferent to you."

"I do not know that she feels for me anything stronger than a vagrant sympathy, Dad, for while she is eternally feminine, nevertheless she has a masculine way of looking at many things. She is a good comrade with a bully sense of sportsmanship, and unlike her skunk of an uncle, she fights in the open. Under the circumstances, however, her first loyalty is to him; in fact, she owes none to me. And I dare say he has given her some extremely plausible reason why we should be eliminated; while I think she is sorry that it must be done, nevertheless, in a mistaken impulse of self-protection she is likely to let him do it."

"Perhaps, perhaps. One never knows why a woman does things, although it is a safe bet that if they're with you at all, they're with you all the way. Eliminate the girl, my boy. She's trying to play fair to you and her relative. Let us concentrate on Pennington."

"The entire situation hinges on that jump-crossing of his tracks on Water Street."

"He doesn't know you plan to cross them, does he?"

"No."

"Then, lad, your job is to get your crossing in before he finds out, isn't it?"

"Yes, but it is an impossible task, partner. I'm not Aladdin, you know. I have to have a franchise from the city council, and I have to have rails."

"Both are procurable, my son. Induce the city council to grant you a temporary franchise to-morrow, and buy your rails from Pennington. He has a mile of track running up Laurel Creek, and Laurel Creek was logged out three years ago. I believe that spur is useless to Pennington, and the ninety-pound rails are rusting there."

"But will he sell them to me?"

"Not if you tell him why you want them."

"But he hates me, old pal."

"The Colonel never permits sentiment to interfere with business, my son. He doesn't need the rails, and he does desire your money. Consider the rail-problem settled."

"How do you stand with the Mayor and the council?"

"I do not stand at all. I opposed Poundstone for the office; Dobbs, who was appointed to fill a vacancy caused by the death of a regularly elected councilman, was once a bookkeeper in our office, you will remember. I discharged him for looting the petty-cash drawer. Andrews and Mullin are professional politicians and not to be trusted. In fact, Poundstone, Dobbs,

Andrews, and Mullin are known as the Solid Four. Yates and Thatcher, the remaining members of the city council, are the result of the reform ticket last fall, but since they are in the minority, they are helpless."

"That makes it bad."

"Not at all. The Cardigans are not known to be connected with the N. C. O. Send your bright friend Ogilvy after that franchise. He's the only man who can land it. Give him a free hand and tell him to deliver the goods by any means short of bribery. I imagine he's had experience with city councils and will know exactly how to proceed. I KNOW you can procure the rails and have them at the intersection of B and Water streets Thursday night. If Ogilvy can procure the temporary franchise and have it in his pocket by six o'clock Thursday night, you should have that crossing in by sunup Friday morning. Then let Pennington rave. He cannot procure an injunction to restrain us from cutting his tracks, thus throwing the matter into the courts and holding us up indefinitely, because by the time he wakes up, the tracks will have been cut. The best he can do then will be to fight us before the city council when we apply for our permanent franchise. Thank God, however, the name of Cardigan carries weight in this county, and with the pressure of public sympathy and opinion back of us, we may venture, my boy, to break a lance with the Solid Four, should they stand with Pennington."

"Partner, it looks like a forlorn hope," said Bryce.

"Well, you're the boy to lead it. And it will cost but little to put in the crossing and take a chance. Remember, Bryce, once we have that crossing in, it stands like a spite-fence between Pennington and the law which he knows so well how to pervert to suit his ignoble purposes." He turned earnestly to Bryce and waved a trembling admonitory finger. "Your job is to keep out of court. Once Pennington gets the law on us, the issue will not be settled in our favour for years; and in the meantime—you perish. Run along now and hunt up Ogilvy. George, play that 'Suwannee River' quartet again. It sort o' soothes me."

CHAPTER XXV

It was with a considerably lighter heart that Bryce returned to the mill-office, from which he lost no time in summoning Buck Ogilvy by telephone.

"Thanks so much for the invitation," Ogilvy murmured gratefully. "I'll be down in a pig's whisper." And he was. "Bryce, you look like the devil," he declared the moment he entered the latter's private office.

"I ought to, Buck. I've just raised the devil and spilled the beans on the N. C. O."

"To whom, when, and where?"

"To Pennington's niece, over the telephone about two hours ago."

Buck Ogilvy smote his left palm with his right fist. "And you've waited two hours to confess your crime? Zounds, man, this is bad."

"I know. Curse me, Buck. I've probably talked you out of a good job."

"Oh, say not so, old settler. We may still have an out. How did you let the cat out of the bag?"

"That remarkable girl called me up, and accused you of being a mere screen for me and amazed me so I admitted it."

Ogilvy dropped his red head in simulated agony and moaned. Presently he raised it and said: "Well, it might have been worse. Think of what might have happened had she called in person. She would have picked your pocket for the corporate seal, the combination of the safe, and the list of stockholders, and probably ended up by gagging you and binding you in your own swivel-chair."

"Don't, Buck. Comfort and not abuse is what I need now."

"All right. I'll conclude my remarks by stating that I regard you as a lovable fat-head devoid of sufficient mental energy to pound the proverbial sand into the proverbial rat-hole. Now, then, what do you want me to do to save the day?"

"Deliver to me by six o'clock Thursday night a temporary franchise from the city council, granting the N. C. O. the right to run a railroad from our drying-yard across Water Street at its intersection with B Street and out Front Street."

"Certainly. By all means! Easiest thing I do! Sure you don't want me to arrange to borrow a star or two to make a ta-ra-ra for the lady that's made a monkey out of you? No? All right, old dear! I'm on my way to do my damnedest, which angels can't do no more. Nevertheless, for your sins, you shall do me a favour before my heart breaks after falling down on this contract you've just given me."

"Granted, Buck. Name it."

"I'm giving a nice little private, specially cooked dinner to Miss McTavish to-night. We're going to pull it off in one of those private screened corrals in that highly decorated Chink restauraw on Third Street. Moira—that is, Miss McTavish—is bringing a chaperon, one Miss Shirley Sumner. Your job is to be my chaperon and entertain Miss Sumner, who from all accounts is most brilliant and fascinating."

"Nothing doing!" Bryce almost roared. "Why, she's the girl that bluffed the secret of the N. C. O. out of me!"

"Do you hate her for it?"

"No, I hate myself."

"Then you'll come. You promised in advance, and no excuses go now. The news will be all over town by Friday morning; so why bother to keep up appearances any longer. Meet me at the Canton at seven and check dull care at the entrance."

And before Bryce could protest, Ogilvy had thrown open the office door and called the glad tidings to Moira, who was working in the next room; whereupon Moira's wonderful eyes shone with that strange lambent flame. She clasped her hands joyously. "Oh, how wonderful!" she exclaimed "I've always wanted Miss Shirley to meet Mr. Bryce."

Again Bryce was moved to protest, but Buck Ogilvy reached around the half-opened door and kicked him in the shins. "Don't crab my game, you miserable snarley-yow. Detract one speck from that girl's pleasure, and you'll never see that temporary franchise," he threatened. "I will not work for a quitter—so, there!" And with his bright smile he set out immediately upon the trail of the city council, leaving Bryce Cardigan a prey to many conflicting emotions, the chief of which, for all that he strove to suppress it, was riotous joy in the knowledge that while he had fought against it, fate had decreed that he should bask once more in the radiance of Shirley Sumner's adorable presence. Presently, for the first time in many weeks, Moira heard him whistling "Turkey in the Straw."

CHAPTER XXVI

Fortunately for the situation which had so suddenly confronted him, Bryce Cardigan had Mr. Buck Ogilvy; and out of the experiences gained in other railroad-building enterprises, the said Ogilvy, while startled, was not stunned by the suddenness and immensity of the order so casually given him by his youthful employer, for he had already devoted to the matter of that crossing the better part of the preceding night. Also he had investigated, indexed, and cross-indexed the city council with a view to ascertaining how great or how little would be the effort he must devote to obtaining from it the coveted franchise.

"Got to run a sandy on the Mayor," Buck soliloquized as he walked rapidly uptown. "And I'll have to be mighty slick about it, too, or I'll get my fingers in the jam. If I get the Mayor on my side—if I get him to the point where he thinks well of me and would like to oblige me without prejudicing himself financially or politically—I can get that temporary franchise. Now, how shall I proceed to sneak up on that oily old cuss's blind side?"

Two blocks farther on, Mr. Ogilvy paused and snapped his fingers vigorously. "Eureka!" he murmured. "I've got Poundstone by the tail on a downhill haul. Is it a cinch? Well, I just guess I should tell a man!"

He hurried to the telephone building and put in a long-distance call for the San Francisco office of the Cardigan Redwood Lumber Company. When the manager came on the line, Ogilvy dictated to him a message which he instructed the manager to telegraph back to him at the Hotel Sequoia one hour later; this mysterious detail attended to, he continued on to the Mayor's office in the city hall.

Mayor Poundstone's bushy eyebrows arched with interest when his secretary laid upon his desk the card of Mr. Buchanan Ogilvy, vice-president and general manager of the Northern California Oregon Railroad. "Ah-h-h!" he breathed with an unpleasant resemblance to a bon vivant who sees before him his favourite vintage. "I have been expecting Mr. Ogilvy to call for quite a while. At last we shall see what we shall see. Show him in."

The visitor was accordingly admitted to the great man's presence and favoured with an official handshake of great heartiness. "I've been hoping to have this pleasure for quite some time, Mr. Poundstone," Buck announced easily as he disposed of his hat and overcoat on an adjacent chair. "But unfortunately I have had so much preliminary detail to attend to before making an official call that at last I grew discouraged and concluded I'd just drop in informally and get acquainted." Buck's alert blue eyes opened wide in sympathy with his genial mouth, to deluge Mayor Poundstone with a smile that was friendly, guileless, confidential, and singularly delightful. Mr. Ogilvy was a man possessed of tremendous personal magnetism when he chose to exert it, and that smile was ever the opening gun of his magnetic bombardment, for it was a smile that always had the effect of making the observer desire to behold it again—of disarming suspicion and establishing confidence.

"Glad you did—mighty glad," the Mayor cried heartily. "We have all, of course, heard of your great plans and are naturally anxious to hear more of them, in the hope that we can do all that anybody reasonably and legally can to promote your enterprise and incidentally our own, since we are not insensible to the advantages which will accrue to this county when it is connected by rail with the outside world."

"That extremely broad view is most encouraging," Buck chirped, and he showered the Mayor with another smile. "Reciprocity is the watchword of progress. I might state, however, that while you Humboldters are fully alive to the benefits to be derived from a feeder to a transcontinental road, my associates and myself are not insensible of the fact that the success of our enterprise depends to a great extent upon the enthusiasm with which the city of Sequoia shall cooperate with us; and since you are the chief executive of the city, naturally I have come to you to explain our plans fully."

"I have read your articles of incorporation, Mr. Ogilvy," Mayor Poundstone boomed paternally. "You will recall that they were published in the Sequoia SENTINEL. It strikes me——"

"Then you know exactly what we purpose doing, and any further explanation would be superfluous," Buck interrupted amiably, glad to dispose of the matter so promptly. Again he favoured the Mayor with his bright smile, and the latter, now fully convinced that here was a young man of vast emprise whom it behooved him to receive in a whole-hearted and public-spirited manner, nodded vigorous approval.

"Well, that being the case, Mr. Ogilvy," he continued, "what can we Sequoians do to make you happy?"

"Why, to begin with, Mr. Poundstone, you might accept my solemn assurances that despite the skepticism which, for some unknown reason, appears to shroud our enterprise in the minds of some people, we have incorporated a railroad company for the purpose of building a railroad. We purpose commencing grading operations in the very near future, and the only thing that can possibly interfere with the project will be the declination of the city council to grant us a franchise to run our line through the city to tidewater."

He handed his cigar-case to Mayor Poundstone and continued lightly: "And I am glad to have your assurance that the city council will not drop a cold chisel in the cogs of the wheels of progress."

Mr. Poundstone had given no such assurance, but for some reason he did not feel equal to the task of contradicting this pleasant fellow. Ogilvy continued: "At the proper time we shall apply for the franchise. It will then be time enough to discuss it. In the meantime the N. C. O. plans a public dedicatory ceremony at the first breaking of ground, and I would be greatly honoured, Mr. Mayor, if you would consent to turn the first shovelful of earth and deliver the address of welcome upon that occasion."

The Mayor swelled like a Thanksgiving turkey. "The honour will be mine," he corrected his visitor.

"Thank you so much, sir. Well, that's another worry off my mind." With the tact of a prime minister Buck then proceeded deliberately to shift the conversation to the weather and asked a number of questions anent the annual rainfall. Then he turned to crops, finance, and national politics and gradually veered around to an artistic word-picture of the vast expansion of the redwood-lumber industry when the redwood-belt should be connected by rail with the markets of the entire country. He spoke of the magic effect the building of such a line would have upon the growth of Sequoia. Sequoia, he felt convinced, was destined to become a city of at least a hundred thousand inhabitants; he rhapsodized over the progressive spirit of the community and with a wave of his hand studded the waters of Humboldt Bay with the masts of the world's shipping. Suddenly he checked himself, glanced at his watch, apologized for consuming so much of His Honour's valuable time, expressed himself felicitated at knowing the Mayor, gracefully expressed his appreciation for the encouragement given his enterprise, and departed. When he had gone, Mayor Poundstone declared to his secretary that without doubt Ogilvy was the livest, keenest fellow that had struck Sequoia since the advent of old John Cardigan.

Half an hour later the Mayor's telephone-bell rang. Buck Ogilvy was on the line. "I beg your pardon for bothering you with my affairs twice in the same day, Mr. Mayor," he announced deprecatingly, "but the fact is, a condition has just arisen which necessitates the immediate employment of an attorney. The job is not a very important one and almost any lawyer would do, but in view of the fact that we must, sooner or later, employ an attorney to look after our interests locally, it occurred to me that I might as well make the selection of a permanent attorney now. I am a stranger in this city Mr. Poundstone. Would it be imposing on your consideration if I asked you to recommend such a person?"

"Why, not at all, not at all! Delighted to help you, Mr. Ogilvy. Let me see, now. There are several attorneys in Sequoia, all men of excellent ability and unimpeachable integrity, whom I can recommend with the utmost pleasure. Cadman look up the relatives of a public official! Well! Forward, men, follow me—to Henry's office."

Henry Poundstone, Junior, proved to be the sole inhabitant of one rather bare office in the Cardigan Block. Buck had fully resolved to give him a retainer of a thousand dollars, or even more, if he asked for it, but after one look at Henry he cut the appropriation to two hundred and fifty dollars. Young Mr. Poundstone was blonde and frail, with large round spectacles, rabbit teeth, and the swiftly receding chin of the terrapin. Moreover, he was in such a flutter of anticipation over the arrival of his client that Buck deduced two things—to wit, that the Mayor had telephoned Henry he was apt to have a client, and that as a result of this miracle, Henry was in no fit state to discuss the sordid subject of fees and retainers. Ergo, Mr. Ogilvy decided to obviate such discussion now or in the future. He handed Henry a check for two hundred and fifty dollars, which he wrote out on the spot, and with his bright winning smile remarked: "Now, Mr. Poundstone, we will proceed to business. That retainer isn't a large one, I admit, but neither is the job I have for you to-day. Later, if need of your services on a larger scale should develop, we shall of course expect to make a new arrangement whereby you will receive the customary retainer of all of our corporation attorneys I trust that is quite satisfactory."

"Eminently so," gasped the young disciple of Blackstone.

"Very well, then; let us proceed to business." Buck removed from a small leather bag a bale of legal-looking documents. "I have here," he announced, "agreements from landowners along the proposed right of way of the N. C. O. to give to that company, on demand, within one year from date, satisfactory deeds covering rights of way which are minutely described in the said agreements. I wish these deeds prepared for signing and recording at the earliest possible moment."

"You shall have them at this time to-morrow," Henry promised.

The head of Henry Poundstone, Junior, was held high for the first time since he had flung forth his modest shingle to the breezes of Sequoia six months before, and there was an unaccustomed gleam of importance in his pale eyes as he rushed into big father's office in the city hall.

"By jinks, Dad!" he exulted. "I've hooked a fish at last—and he's a whopper."

"Omit the cheers, my boy. Remember I sent that fish to you," his father answered with a bland and indulgent smile. "What are you doing for Ogilvy, and how large a retainer did he give you?"

"I'm making out deeds to his rights of way. Ordinarily it's about a fifty-dollar job, but without waiting to discuss finances he handed me out two hundred and fifty dollars. Why, Dad, that's more than you make in a month from your job as Mayor."

"Well, that isn't a bad retainer. It's an opening wedge. However, it would be mere chicken-feed in San Francisco."

"Read this," Henry urged, and thrust a yellow telegraph-form under the Mayor's nose. The latter adjusted his glasses and read:

Imperative building operations commence immediately. Local skepticism injurious and delays dangerous. We must show good faith to our New York friends. J. P. M. insists upon knowing promptly where we stand with Sequoia city council. See them immediately and secure temporary franchise, if possible, to enable us to cross Water Street at B Street and build out Front Street. Your arrangement with Cardigan for use of his mill-dock and spur for unloading material from steamer ratified by board but regarded as hold-up. If your judgment indicates no hold-up on permanent franchise, commence active operations immediately upon acquisition of permanent franchise. Engage local labour as far as possible. Cannot impress upon you too fully necessity for getting busy, as road must be completed in three years if our plans are to bear fruit and time is all too short. Impress this upon city council and wire answer to-morrow.

HOCKLEY.

This telegram, as the Mayor observed, was dated that day and addressed to Mr. Buchanan Ogilvy, Hotel Sequoia, Sequoia, Calif. Also, with a keen eye to minor details, lie noted that it had been filed at San Francisco SUBSEQUENT to Ogilvy's visit to him that afternoon.

"Ah-h-h!" breathed His Honour. "That accounts for his failure to bring the matter up at our interview. Upon his return to the hotel he found this telegram and got busy at once. By Jupiter, this looks like business. Henry, how did you come into possession of this telegram?"

"It must have been mixed up in the documents Ogilvy left with me. I found it on my desk when I was sorting out the papers, and in my capacity of attorney for the N.C.O. I had no hesitancy in reading it."

"Well, I do declare! Wonder who Hockley is. Never heard of that fellow in connection with the N.C.O."

"Hockley doesn't matter," young Henry declared triumphantly, "although I'd bet a hat he's one of those heavy-weight Wall Street fellows and one of J.P.M's vice-presidents, probably. J.P.M., of course, is the man behind."

"Who the devil is J.P.M.?"

Henry smiled tolerantly upon his ignorant and guileless parent. "Well, how would J. Pierpont Morgan do for a guess?" he queried.

"Hell's bells and panther-tracks!" Mayor Poundstone started as if snake-bitten. "I should say you have hooked a big fish. Boy, you've landed a whale!" And the Mayor whistled softly in his amazement and delight. "By golly, to think of you getting in with that bunch! Tremendyous! Per-fect-ly tree-mend-yous! Did Ogilvy say anything about future business?"

"He did. Said if I proved satisfactory, he would probably take me on and pay the customary retainer given all of their corporation attorneys."

"Well, by golly, he'd better take you on! I had a notion that chap Ogilvy was smart enough to know which side his bread is buttered on and who does the buttering."

"If I could guarantee Mr. Ogilvy that temporary franchise mentioned in his telegram, it might help me to get in right with J.P.M, at the start," his hopeful suggested. "I guess it would be kind of poor to be taken on as one of the regular staff of attorneys for a Morgan corporation, eh? Say, they pay those chaps as high as fifty thousand dollars a year retainer!"

"Guarantee it!" his father shouted. "Guarantee it! Well, I should snicker! We'll just show J. P. M. and his crowd that they made no mistake when they picked you as their Sequoia legal representative. I'll call a special meeting of that little old city council of mine and jam that temporary franchise through while you'd be saying 'Jack Robinson!'"

"I'll tell you what let's do," Henry suggested. "I'll draw up the temporary franchise to-night, and we'll put it through to-morrow at, say, ten o'clock without saying a word to Mr. Ogilvy about it. Then when the city clerk has signed and attested it and put the seal of the city on it, I'll just casually take it over to Mr. Ogilvy. Of course he'll be surprised and ask me how I came to get it, and—"

"And you LOOK surprised," his father cautioned, "—sort of as if you failed to comprehend what he's driving at. Make him repeat. Then you say: 'Oh, that! Why, that's nothing, Mr. Ogilvy. I found the telegram in those papers you left with me, read it, and concluded you'd left it there to give me the dope so I could go ahead and get the franchise for you. Up here, whenever anybody wants a franchise from the city, they always hire an attorney to get it for them, so I didn't think anything about this but just naturally went and got it for you. If it ain't right, why, say so and I'll have it made right.'" Old Poundstone nudged his son in the short ribs and winked drolly. "Let him get the idea you're a fly bird and on to your job."

"Leave it to yours truly," said Henry.

His father carefully made a copy of the telegram.

"H'm!" he grunted. "Wants to cross Water Street at B and build out Front Street. Well, I dare say nobody will kick over the traces at that. Nothing but warehouses and lumber-drying yards along there, anyhow. Still, come to think of it, Pennington will probably raise a howl about sparks from the engines of the N. C. O. setting his lumber piles afire. And he won't relish the idea of that crossing, because that means a watchman and safety-gates, and he'll have to stand half the cost of that."

"He'll be dead against it," Henry declared. "I know, because at the Wednesday meeting of the Lumber Manufacturers' Association the subject of the N. C. O. came up, and Pennington made a talk against it. He said the N. C. O. ought to be discouraged, if it was a legitimate enterprise, which he doubted, because the most feasible and natural route for a road would be from Willits, Mendocino County, north to Sequoia. He said the N. C. O. didn't tap the main body of the redwood-belt and that his own road could be extended to act as a feeder to a line that would build in from the south. I tell you he's dead set against it."

"Then we won't tell him anything about it, Henry. We'll just pull off this special session of the council and forget to invite the reporters; after the job has been put over, Pennington can come around and howl all he wants. We're not letting a chance like this slip by us without grabbing a handful of the tail-feathers, Henry. No, sir—not if we know it."

"You bet!" said Henry earnestly.

And it was even so. The entire council was present with the exception of Thatcher, who was home ill. His running mate Yates was heartily in favour of doing all and sundry of those things which would aid and encourage the building of the much-to-be-desired railroad and offered no objection to the motion to grant a sixty-day temporary franchise. However, he always played ball with the absent Thatcher and he was fairly well acquainted with his other colleagues on the council; where they were concerned he was as suspicious as a rattlesnake in August—in consequence of which he considered it policy to play safe pending Thatcher's recovery. Rising in his place, he pointed out to the board the fact that many prominent citizens who yearned for such a road as the N. C. O. had warned him of the danger of lending official aid and comfort to a passel of professional promoters and fly-by-nights; that after all, the N. C. O. might merely be the stalking-horse to a real-estate boom planned to unload the undesirable timber holdings of the Trinidad Redwood Lumber Company, in which event it might be well for the council to proceed with caution. It was Mr. Yates' opinion that for the present a temporary franchise for thirty days only should be given; if during that thirty days the N. C. O. exhibited indubitable signs of activity, he would gladly vote for a thirty-day extension to enable the matter of a permanent franchise to be taken up in regular order.

This amendment to the original motion met with the unqualified approval of the Mayor, as he was careful to announce for the benefit of the other members of the Solid Four. The fact of the matter was, however, that he was afraid to oppose Yates in such a simple matter through fear that Yates might grow cantankerous and carry his troubles to the Sequoia Sentinel—a base trick he had been known to do in the past. After explaining the advisability of keeping secret for the present the fact that a thirty-day franchise had been granted, His Honour, with the consent of the maker of the original motion and the second thereof, submitted the amended motion to a vote, which was carried unanimously.

At eleven-thirty Thursday morning, therefore, young Henry Poundstone, having worked the greater part of the previous night preparing the deeds, delivered both deeds and franchise to Buck Ogilvy at the latter's hotel. It was with difficulty that the latter could conceal his tremendous amazement when Henry casually handed him the franchise. True, he had slipped that fake telegram among the contracts as bait for Henry and his father, but in his wildest flights of fancy had not looked for them to swallow hook, line, and sinker. His fondest hope, at the time he conceived the brilliant idea, was that Henry would show the telegram to his father and thus inculcate in the old gentleman a friendly feeling toward the N. C. O. not unmixed with pleasurable anticipations of the day when Henry Poundstone, Junior, should be one of the most highly prized members of the legal staff of a public-service corporation.

When he could control his emotions, Mr. Ogilvy gazed approvingly upon Henry Poundstone. "Mr. Poundstone," he said solemnly, "I have met some meteoric young attorneys in my day, but you're the first genuine comet I have seen in the legal firmament. Do you mind telling me exactly how you procured this franchise—and why you procured it without explicit orders from me?"

Henry did his best to look puzzled. "Why," he said, "you left that telegram with me, and I concluded that you regarded it as self-explanatory or else had forgotten to mention it. I knew you were busy, and I didn't want to bother you with details, so I just went ahead and filled the order for you. Anything wrong about that?"

"Certainly not. It's perfectly wonderful. But how did you put it over?"

Henry smirked. "My dad's the engineer," he said bluntly. "If thirty days ain't enough time, see me and I'll get you thirty days more. And in the meantime nobody knows a thing about this little deal. What's more, they won't know. I figured Colonel Pennington might try to block you at that crossing so I—"

Buck Ogilvy extended his hand in benediction and let it drop lightly on Henry Poundstone's thin shoulder. Henry quivered with anticipation under that gentle accolade and swallowed his heart while the great Ogilvy made a portentous announcement.

"My dear Poundstone," he said earnestly, "I am not a man to forget clever work. At the proper time I shall—" He smiled his radiant smile. "You understand, of course, that I am speaking for and can make you no firm promises. However—" He smiled again. "All I have to say is that you'll do!"

"Thank you," said Henry Poundstone, Junior. "Thank you ever so much."

CHAPTER XVII

An experience extending over a very active business career of thirty years had convinced Colonel Seth Pennington of the futility of wracking his brains in vain speculation over mysteries. In his day he had been interested in some small public-service corporations, which is tantamount to saying that he knew peanut politics and had learned that the very best way to fight the devil is with fire. Frequently he had found it of great interest and profit to him to know exactly how certain men spent their time and his money, and since he was a very busy man himself, naturally he had to delegate somebody else, to procure this information for him. When, therefore, the Northern California Oregon Railroad commenced to encroach on the Colonel's time-appropriation for sleep, he realized that there was but one way in which to conserve his rest and that was by engaging to fathom the mystery for him a specialist in the unravelling of mysteries. In times gone by, the Colonel had found a certain national detective-agency an extremely efficient aid to well-known commercial agencies, and to these tried and true subordinates he turned now for explicit and satisfying information anent the Northern California Outrage!

The information forthcoming from Dun's and Bradstreet's was vague and unsatisfying. Neither of these two commercial agencies could ascertain anything of interest regarding the finances of the N. C. O. For the present the corporation had no office, its destinies in San Francisco being guarded by a well-known attorney who had declined to make any statement regarding the company but promised one at an early date. The board of directors consisted of this attorney, his two assistants, his stenographer, and Mr. Buchanan Ogilvy. The company had been incorporated for five million dollars, divided into five million shares of par value of one dollar each, and five shares had been subscribed! Both agencies forwarded copies of the articles of incorporation, but since the Colonel had already read this document in the Sequoia Sentinel, he was not further interested.

"It looks fishy to me," the Colonel commented to his manager, "and I'm more than ever convinced it's a scheme of that Trinidad Redwood Timber Company to start a timber-boom and unload. And that is something the Laguna Grande Lumber Company does not view with favour, for the reason that one of these bright days those Trinidad people will come to their senses and sell cheap to us. A slight extension of our logging-road will make that Trinidad timber accessible; hence we are the only logical customers and should control the situation. However, to be sure is to be satisfied. Telephone the San Francisco office to have the detective-agency that handled the longshoremen's strike job for us send a couple of their best operatives up on the next steamer, with instructions to report to me on arrival."

When the operatives reported, the Colonel's orders were brief and explicit. "I want to know all about a man named Buchanan Ogilvy, who is up north somewhere procuring rights of way for the Northern California Oregon Railroad. Find him. Get up with him in the morning and put him to bed at night. Report to me daily."

Buck was readily located in the country north of Arcata, and one of the operatives actually procured a job as chainman with his surveying gang, while the other kept Ogilvy and his secretary under surveillance. Their reports, however, yielded the Colonel nothing until the first day of Buck's return to Sequoia, when the following written report caused the Colonel to sit up and take notice. It was headed: "Report of Operative No. 41," and it read:

Ogilvy in his room until 12 o'clock noon. At 12:05 entered dining room, leaving at 1 P. M. and proceeding direct to office of Cardigan Redwood Lumber Company. Operative took post behind a lumber-pile at side of office so as to command view of interior of office. From manner of greeting accorded Ogilvy by Bryce Cardigan, operative is of opinion they had not met before. Ogilvy remained in Cardigan's private office half an hour, spent another half-hour conversing with young lady in general office. Young lady a brunette. O. then returned to Hotel Sequoia, where he wrote several letters in writing-room. At 3 p. M. called to telephone. At 3:02 p. M. left hurriedly for Cardigan Redwood Lumber Company's office. Entered private office without waiting to be announced. Emerged at 3:12, walking slowly and in deep thought. At B and Cedar streets stopped suddenly, snapped his fingers and started walking rapidly, in the manner of one who has arrived at a decision. At 3:24 entered the telephone building and placed a long-distance call. Operative standing at counter close by heard him place call with the girl on duty. He asked for the Cardigan Redwood Lumber Company in San Francisco.

Concluded his conversation at 3:32 and proceeded to the city hall, entering the Mayor's office at 3:43 and emerging at 4:10. He then returned to the Hotel Sequoia and sat in the lobby until handed a telegram at 4:40; whereupon he entered the telephone-booth and talked to someone, emerging at 4:43 to go to his room. He returned at 4:46 and hurried to the law-office of Henry Poundstone, Junior, in the Cardigan Block. He was with Poundstone until 4:59, when he returned leisurely to the Hotel Sequoia, carrying a small leather grip. He also had this grip when he entered Poundstone's office.

Arrived at the hotel at 5:03 and went to his room. At 6:45 he entered a public automobile in front of the hotel and was driven to No. 846 Elm Street. The brunette young lady who works m the Cardigan Redwood Lumber Company's office emerged presently and entered the car, which then proceeded to No. 38 Redwood Boulevard, where the brunette young lady alighted and entered the house. She returned at 7 sharp, accompanied by a young lady whom she introduced to O. All three were then driven to the Canyon restaurant at 432 Third Street and escorted to a reserved table in one of the screened-off semi-private rooms along the right side of the dining room. At 7:15 Bryce Cardigan entered the restaurant and was escorted by the waiter to the table occupied by O. and party.

At 9:30 entire party left restaurant and entered a Napier car driven by a half-breed Indian whom the second young lady hailed as George. O. and the brunette young lady were dropped at 846 Elm Street while Cardigan and the other young lady proceeded directly to No. 38 Redwood Boulevard. After aiding the lady to alight, Cardigan talked with her a few minutes at the gate, then bade her good-night and after waiting until she had disappeared inside the front door, returned to the automobile and was driven to his home, while the chauffeur George ran the car into the Cardigan garage.

Upon returning to Hotel Sequoia, found O. in hotel bar. Saw him to bed at 10 sharp.

Needless to relate, this report had a most amazing effect upon Colonel Pennington, and when at length he could recover his mental equilibrium, he set about quite calmly to analyze the report, word by word and sentence by sentence, with the result that he promptly arrived at the following conclusion:

(1) His niece Shirley Sumner was not to be trusted in so far as young Bryce Cardigan was concerned. Despite her assumption of hostility toward the fellow since that memorable day in Pennington's woods, the Colonel was now fully convinced that she had made her peace with him and had been the recipient of his secret attentions right along. The Colonel was on the verge of calling his niece up to demand an explanation, but on second thought decided to wait a few days and see what his gum-shoe men might have to report further.

(2) The N. C. O. was still a mystery, but a mystery in which Bryce Cardigan was interested. Moreover, he was anxious to aid the N. C. O. in every way possible. However, the Colonel could understand this. Cardigan would aid anything that might possibly tend to lift the Cardigan lumber interests out from under the iron heel of Colonel Pennington and he was just young enough and unsophisticated enough to be fooled by that Trinidad Redwood Timber gang.

(3) The N. C. O. was going to make a mighty bluff, even to the extent of applying for a franchise to run over the city streets of Sequoia. Hence Ogilvy's visit to Mayor Poundstone—doubtless on the advice of Bryce Cardigan. Hence, also, his visit to young Henry Poundstone, whom he had doubtless engaged as his legal representative in order to ingratiate himself with the young man's father. Coarse work!

(4) Ogilvy had carried a small leather bag to and from Henry Poundstone's office. That bag was readily explained. It had contained a bribe in gold coin and young Henry had been selected as the go-between. That meant that Mayor Poundstone had agreed to deliver the franchise—for a consideration; and like the smooth scoundrel he was, he wanted his bit in gold coin, which could not be marked without the marks being discovered! Ogilvy had called first on the Mayor to arrange the details; then he had called on the Mayor's son to complete the transaction.

(5) If a franchise had been arranged for and the bribe already delivered, that meant the prompt and unadvertised commencement of operations. Where (the Colonel asked himself) would these operations begin? Why, close to the waterfront, where materials could be landed from the steamer that brought them to Sequoia. At whose mill-dock would those materials be discharged? Why, Cardigan's dock, of course. Ogilvy had probably called first on Cardigan to arrange that detail. Yes, the N. C. O. was going to carry its monumental bluff to the point of building a mile of track through town. ... No—no, they wouldn't spend that much money on a bluff; they wouldn't bribe Poundstone unless the road was meant. And was it a common carrier, after all? Had Cardigan in some mysterious manner managed to borrow enough money to parallel the Laguna Grande Lumber Company's logging-road, and was he disguising it as a common carrier?

The trail was growing hot; the Colonel mopped his brow and concentrated further. If the N. C. O. was really going to start operations, in order to move its material from the Cardigan dock to the scene of operations it would have to cut his (the Colonel's) tracks somewhere on Water Street. Damnation! That was it. They were trying to slip one over on him. They were planning to get a jump-crossing in before he should awake to the situation; they were planning, too, to have the city council slip through the franchise when nobody was looking, and once the crossing should be in, they could laugh at Colonel Pennington!

"The scoundrels!" he murmured. "I'm on to them! Cardigan is playing the game with them. That's why he bought those rails from the old Laurel Creek spur! Oh, the sly young fox—quoting that portion of our hauling contract which stipulates that all spurs and extensions of my road, once it enters Cardigan's lands, must be made at Cardigan's expense! And all to fool me into thinking he wanted those rails for an extension of his logging-system. Oh, what a blithering idiot I have been! However, it's not too late yet. Poundstone is coming over to dinner Thursday night, and I'll wring the swine dry before he leaves the house. And as for those rails Cardigan managed to hornswoggle me out of—"

He seized the telephone and fairly shouted to his exchange operator to get his woods-foreman Jules Rondeau on the line.

"That you, Rondeau?" he shouted when the big French Canadian responded. "Pennington talking. What has young Cardigan done about those rails I sold him from the abandoned spur up Laurel Creek?"

"He have two flat-cars upon ze spur now. Dose woods-gang of hees she tear up dose rails from ze head of ze spur and load in ze flat-cars."

"The ears haven't left the Laurel Creek spur, then?"

"No, she don't leave yet."

"See to it, Rondeau, that they do not leave until I give the word. Understand? Cardigan's woods-boss will call you up and ask you to send a switch-engine tip to snake them out late this afternoon or to-morrow afternoon. Tell him the switch-engine is in the shop for repairs or is busy at other work—anything that will stall him off and delay delivery."

"Suppose Bryce Cardigan, he comes around and say 'Why?'" Rondeau queried cautiously.

"Kill him," the Colonel retorted coolly. "It strikes me you and the Black Minorca are rather slow playing even with young Cardigan."

Rondeau grunted. "I theenk mebbe so you kill heem yourself, boss," he replied enigmatically, and hung up.

CHAPTER XVIII

The dictograph which Shirley had asked Bryce to obtain for her in San Francisco arrived on the regular passenger-steamer on Thursday morning and Bryce called her up to ask when she desired it sent over.

"Good morning, Mr. Cardigan," she greeted him cheerily. "How do you feel this morning? Any the worse for having permitted yourself to be a human being last night?"

"Why, I feel pretty fine, Shirley. I think it did me a lot of good to crawl out of my shell last night."

"You feel encouraged to go on living, eh?"

"Yes."

"And fighting?"

"By all means."

"Then, something has occurred of late to give you new courage?"

"Oh, many things. Didn't I give an exhibition of my courage in accepting Ogilvy's invitation to dinner, knowing you were going to be there?"

She did not like that. "You carry your frankness to extremes, my friend," she retorted. "I'm sure I've always been much nicer to you than you deserve."

"Nevertheless there wasn't any valid reason why I should tantalize myself last night."

"Then why did you come?" He had a suspicion that she was laughing silently at him.

"Partly to please Ogilvy, who has fallen head over heels in love with Moira; partly to please Moira, who wanted me to meet you, but mostly to please myself, because, while I dreaded it, nevertheless I wanted to see you again. I comforted myself with the thought that for the sake of appearances we dared not quarrel in the presence of Moira and my friend Ogilvy, and I dare say you felt the same way. At any rate, I have seldom had more enjoyment when partaking of a meal with an enemy."

"Please do not say that," she answered. "I am your opponent, but not your enemy."

"That's nice of you. By the way, Shirley, you may inform your uncle at breakfast Friday morning about my connection with the N. C. O. In fact, I think it would be far better for you if you made it a point to do so."

"Why?"

"Because both Ogilvy and myself have a very strong suspicion that your uncle has a detective or two on our trails. There was a strange man rather prevalent around him all day yesterday and I noticed a fellow following my car last night. He was on a bicycle and followed me home. I communicated my suspicions to Ogilvy, and this morning he spent two hours trying to shake the same man off his trail—and couldn't. So I judge your uncle will learn to-day that you dined with Ogilvy, Moira, and me last night."

"Oh, dear! That's terrible." He could sense her distress.

"Ashamed of having been seen in my company, eh?"

"Please don't. Are you quite serious in this matter?"

"Quite."

"Uncle Seth will think it so—so strange."

"He'll probably tell you about it. Better beat him to the issue by 'fessing up, Shirley. Doubtless his suspicions are already aroused, and if you inform him that you know I am the real builder of the N. C. O., he'll think you're a smart woman and that you've been doing a little private gum-shoe work of your own on behalf of the Laguna Grande Lumber Company."

"Which is exactly what I have been doing," she reminded him.

"I know. But then, I'm not afraid of you, Shirley—that is, any more. And after Friday morning I'll not be afraid of your uncle. Do tell him at breakfast. Then watch to see if it affects his appetite."

"Oh, dear! I feel as if I were a conspirator."

"I believe you are one. Your dictograph has arrived. Shall I send George Sea Otter over with it? And have you somebody to install it?"

"Oh, bother! Does it have to be installed?"

"It does. You place the contraption—hide it, rather—in the room where the conspirators conspire; then you run wires from it into another room where the detectives listen in on the receivers."

"Could George Sea Otter install it?"

"I think he could. There is a printed card of instructions, and I dare say George would find the job no more baffling than the ignition-system on the Napier."

"Will he tell anybody?"

"Not if you ask him not to."

"Not even you?"

"Not even a whisper to himself, Shirley."

"Very well, then. Please send him over. Thank you so much, Bryce Cardigan. You're an awful good old sort, after all. Really, it hurts me to have to oppose you. It would be so much nicer if we didn't have all those redwood trees to protect, wouldn't it?"

"Let us not argue the question, Shirley. I think I have my redwood trees protected. Good-bye."

He had scarcely finished telephoning his home to instruct George Sea Otter to report with the express package to Shirley when Buck Ogilvy strolled into the office and tossed a document on his desk. "There's your little old temporary franchise, old thing," he announced; and with many a hearty laugh he related to Bryce the ingenious means by which he had obtained it. "And now if you will phone up to your logging-camp and instruct the woods-boss to lay off about fifty men to rest for the day, pending a hard night's work, and arrange to send them down on the last log-train to-day, I'll drop around after dinner and we'll fly to that jump-crossing. Here's a list of the tools we'll need."

"I'll telephone Colonel Pennington's manager and ask him to kick a switch-engine in on the Laurel Creek spur and snake those flat-cars with my rails aboard out to the junction with the main line," Bryce replied. And he called up the Laguna Grande Lumber Company—only to be informed by no less a person than Colonel Pennington himself that it would be impossible to send the switch-engine in until the following afternoon. The Colonel was sorry, but the switch-engine was in the shop having the brick in her fire-box renewed, while the mogul that hauled the log trams would not have time to attend to the matter, since the flats would have to be spotted on the sidetrack at Cardigan's log-landing in the woods, and this could not be done until the last loaded log-train for the day had been hauled out to make room.

"Why not switch back with the mogul after the logtrain has been hauled out on the main line?" Bryce demanded pointedly.

Pennington, however, was not trapped. "My dear fellow," he replied patronizingly, "quite impossible, I assure you. That old trestle across the creek, my boy—it hasn't been looked at for years. While I'd send the light switch-engine over it and have no fears—"

"I happen to know, Colonel, that the big mogul kicked those flats in to load the rails!"

"I know it. And what happened? Why, that old trestle squeaked and shook and gave every evidence of being about to buckle in the centre. My engineer threatened to quit if I sent him in again."

"Very well. I suppose I'll have to wait until the switch-engine comes out of the shop," Bryce replied resignedly, and hung up. He turned a troubled face to Ogilvy. "Checkmated!" he announced. "Whipped to a frazzle. The Colonel is lying, Buck, and I've caught him at it. As a matter of fact, the mogul didn't kick those flats in at all. The switch-engine did—and I know it. Now I'm going to send a man over to snoop around Pennington's roundhouse and verify his report about the switch-engine being in the shop."

He did so. Half an hour later the messenger returned with the information that not only was the switch-engine not in the shop but her fire-box had been overhauled the week before and was reported to be in excellent condition.

"That settles it," Buck Ogilvy mourned. "He had gum-shoe men on my trail, after all; they have reported, and the Colonel is as suspicious as a rhino. He doesn't know anything, but he smells danger just the same."

"Exactly, Buck. So he is delaying the game until he can learn something definite." He drummed idly on his desk for several minutes. Then:

"Buck, can you run a locomotive?"

"With one hand, old man."

"Fine business! Well, I guess we'll put in that crossing to-morrow night. The switch-engine will be in the roundhouse at Pennington's mill to-morrow night so we can't steal that; but we can steal the mogul. I'll just send word up to my woods-boss not to have his train loaded when the mogul comes up late to-morrow afternoon to haul it down to our log-landing. He will explain to the engineer and fireman that our big bull donkey went out and we couldn't get our logs down to the landing in time to get them loaded that day. Of course, the engine-crew won't bother to run down to Sequoia for the night—that is, they won't run the mogul down. They'll just leave her at our log-landing all night and put up for the night at our camp. However, if they should be forced, because of their private affairs, to return to Sequoia, they'll borrow my trackwalker's velocipede. I have one that is driven with a small gasolene engine—I use it in running back and forth to the logging-camp in case I fail to connect with a log-train."

"But how do you know they will put up at your camp all night, Bryce?"

"My men will make them comfortable, and it means they can lie abed until seven o'clock instead of having to roll out at five o'clock, which would be the case if they spent the night at this end of the line. If they do not stay at our logging-camp, the mogul will stay there, provided my woods-foreman lends them my velocipede. The fireman would prefer that to firing that big mogul all the way back to Sequoia."

"Yes," Buck agreed, "I think he would."

"There is a slight grade at our log-landing. I know that, because the air leaked out of the brakes on a log-train I was on a short time ago, and the train ran away with me. Now, the engine-crew will set the airbrakes on the mogul and leave her with steam up to throb all night; they'll not blow her down, for that would mean work firing her in the morning. Our task, Buck, will be to throw off the airbrakes and let her glide silently out of our log-landing. About a mile down the road we'll stop, get up steam, run down to the junction with the main line, back in on the Laurel Creek spur, couple on to those flat-cars and breeze merrily down to Sequoia with them. They'll be loaded waiting for us; our men will be congregated in our dry-yard just off Water Street near B, waiting for us to arrive with the rails—and bingo—we go to it. After we drop the flats, we'll run the engine back to the woods, leave it where we found it, return a-flying on the velocipede, if it's there, or in my automobile, if it isn't there. You can get back in ample time to superintend the cutting of the crossing!"

"Spoken like a man!" quoth Buck Ogilvy. "You're the one man in this world for whom I'd steal a locomotive. 'At-a boy!"

Had either of the conspirators known of Pennington's plans to entertain Mayor Poundstone at dinner on Thursday night, it is probable they would not have cheered until those flat-cars were out of the woods.

CHAPTER XXIX

Mayor Poundstone and his wife arrived at the Pennington home in Redwood Boulevard at six forty-five Thursday evening. It was with a profound feeling of relief that His Honour lifted the lady from their modest little "flivver," for once inside the Pennington house, he felt, he would be free from a peculiarly devilish brand of persecution inaugurated by his wife about three months previously. Mrs. Poundstone wanted a new automobile. And she had entered upon a campaign of nagging and complaint; hoping to wear Poundstone's resistance down to the point where he would be willing to barter his hope of salvation in return for a guarantee of peace on earth.

"I feel like a perfect fool, calling upon these people in this filthy little rattletrap," Mrs. Poundstone protested as they passed up the cement walk toward the Pennington portal.

Mayor Poundstone paused. Had he been Medusa, the glance he bent upon his spouse would have transformed her instantly into a not particularly symmetrical statue of concrete. He had reached the breaking-point.

"In pity's name, woman," he growled, "talk about something else. Give me one night of peace. Let me enjoy my dinner and this visit."

"I can't help it," Mrs. P. retorted with asperity. She pointed to Shirley Sumner's car parked under the porte-cochere. "If I had a sedan like that, I could die happy. And it only cost thirty-two hundred and fifty dollars."

"I paid six hundred and fifty for the rattletrap, and I couldn't afford that," he almost whimpered. "You were happy with it until I was elected mayor."

"You forget our social position, my dear," she purred sweetly.

He could have struck her. "Hang your social position," he gritted savagely. "Shut up, will you? Social position in a sawmill town! Rats!"

"Sh—sh! Control yourself, Henry!" She plucked gently at his arm; with her other hand she lifted the huge knocker on the front door.

"Dammit, you'll drive me crazy yet," Poundstone gurgled, and subsided.

The Pennington butler, a very superior person, opened the door and swept them with a faintly disapproving glance. It is possible that he found Mayor Poundstone, who was adorned with a white string tie, a soft slouch hat, a Prince Albert coat, and horseshoe cut vest, mildly amusing.

The Poundstones entered. At the entrance to the living room the butler announced sonorously: "Mayor Poundstone and Mrs. Poundstone."

"Glad to see you aboard the ship," Colonel Pennington boomed with his best air of hearty expansiveness. "Well, well," he continued, leading Mrs. Poundstone to a divan in front of the fire, "this is certainly delightful. My niece will be down in two shakes of a lamb's tail. Have a cigarette, Mr. Poundstone."

In the midst of the commonplace chatter incident to such occasions, Shirley entered the room; and the Colonel, leaving her to entertain the guests, went to a small sideboard in one corner and brought forth the "materials," as he jocularly termed them. James appeared like magic with a tray, glasses, and tiny serviettes, and the Colonel's elixir was passed to the company.

"To your beautiful eyes, Mrs. Poundstone," was Pennington's debonair toast as he fixed Mrs. P.'s green orbs with his own. "Poundstone, your very good health, sir."

"Dee-licious," murmured Mrs. Poundstone. "Perfectly dee-licious. And not a bit strong!"

"Have another," her hospitable host suggested, and he poured it, quite oblivious of the frightened wink which the mayor telegraphed his wife.

"I will, if Miss Sumner will join me," Mrs. P. acquiesced.

"Thanks. I seldom drink a cocktail, and one is always my limit," Shirley replied smilingly.

"Oh, well," the Colonel retorted agreeably, "we'll make it a three-cornered festival. Poundstone, smoke up."

They "smoked up," and Poundstone prayed to his rather nebulous gods that Mrs. P. would not discuss automobiles during the dinner.

Alas! The Colonel's cocktails were not unduly fortified, but for all that, the two which Mrs. Poundstone had assimilated contained just sufficient "kick" to loosen the lady's tongue without thickening it. Consequently, about the time the piece de resistance made its appearance, she threw caution to the winds and adverted to the subject closest to her heart.

"I was telling Henry as we came up the walk how greatly I envied you that beautiful sedan, Miss Sumner," she gushed. "Isn't it a perfectly stunning car?"

Poundstone made one futile attempt to head her off. "And I was telling Mrs. Poundstone," he struck in with a pathetic attempt to appear humorous and condescending, "that a little jitney was our gait, and that she might as well abandon her passionate yearning for a closed car. Angelina, my dear, something tells me I'm going to enjoy this dinner a whole lot more if you'll just make up your mind to be real nice and resign yourself to the inevitable."

"Never, my dear, never." She shook a coy finger at him. "You dear old tightie," she cooed, "you don't realize what a closed car means to a woman." She turned to Shirley. "How an open car does blow one around, my dear!"

"Yes, indeed," said Shirley innocently.

"Heard the McKinnon people had a man killed up in their woods yesterday, Colonel," Poundstone remarked, hoping against hope to divert the conversation.

"Yes. The fellow's own fault," Pennington replied. "He was one of those employees who held to the opinion that every man is the captain of his own soul and the sole proprietor of his own body—hence that it behooved him to look after both, in view of the high cost of safety-appliances. He was warned that the logging-cable was weak at that old splice and liable to pull out of the becket—and sure enough it did. The free end of the cable snapped back like a whip, and—"

"I hold to the opinion," Mrs. Poundstone interrupted, "that if one wishes for a thing hard enough and just keeps on wishing, one is bound to get it."

"My dear," said Mr. Poundstone impressively, "if you would only confine yourself to wishing, I assure you your chances for success would be infinitely brighter."

There was no mistaking this rebuke; even two cocktails were powerless to render Mrs. Poundstone oblivious to it. Shirley and her uncle saw the Mayor's lady flush slightly; they caught the glint of murder in His Honour's eye; and the keen intelligence of each warned them that closed cars should be a closed topic of conversation with the Poundstones. With the nicest tact in the world, Shirley adroitly changed the subject to some tailored shirt-waists she had observed in the window of a local dry-goods emporium that day, and Mrs. Poundstone subsided.

About nine o'clock, Shirley, in response to a meaning glance from her relative, tactfully convoyed Mrs. Poundstone upstairs, leaving her uncle alone with his prey. Instantly Pennington got down to business.

"Well," he queried, apropos of nothing, "what do you hear with reference to the Northern-California-Gregon Railroad?"

"Oh, the usual amount of wind, Colonel. Nobody knows what to make of that outfit."

Pennington studied the end of his cigar a moment. "Well, I don't know what to think of that project either," he admitted presently, "But while it looks like a fake, I have a suspicion that where there's so much smoke, one is likely to discover a little fire. I've been waiting to see whether or not they will apply for a franchise to enter the city, but they seem to be taking their time about it."

"They certainly are a deliberate crowd," the Mayor murmured.

"Have they made any move to get a franchise?" Pennington asked bluntly. "If they have, I suppose you would be the first man to hear about it. I don't mean to be impertinent," he added with a gracious smile, "but the fact is I noticed that windbag Ogilvy entering your office in the city hall the other afternoon, and I couldn't help wondering whether his visit was social or official."

"Social—so far as I could observe," Poundstone replied truthfully, wondering just how much Pennington knew, and rather apprehensive that he might get caught in a lie before the evening was over.

"Preliminary to the official visit, I dare say."

The Colonel puffed thoughtfully for a while—for which the Mayor was grateful, since it provided time in which to organize himself. Suddenly, however, Pennington turned toward his guest and fixed the latter with a serious glance.

"I hadn't anticipated discussing this matter with you, Poundstone, and you must forgive me for it; but the fact is—I might as well be frank with you—I am very greatly interested in the operation of this proposed railroad."

"Indeed! Financially?"

"Yes, but not in the financial way you think. If that railroad is built, it will have a very distinct effect on my finances."

"In just what way?"

"Disastrous."

"I am amazed, Colonel."

"You wouldn't if you had given the subject very close consideration. The logical route for this railroad is from Willits north to Sequoia, not from Sequoia north to Grant's Pass, Oregon. Such a road as the N.C.O. contemplates will tap about one third of the redwood belt only, while a line built in from the south will tap two thirds of it. The remaining third can be tapped by an extension of my own logging-road; when my own timber is logged out, I will want other business for my road, and if the N.C.O. parallels it, I will be left with two streaks of rust on my hands."

"Ah, I perceive. So it will, so it will!"

"You agree with me, then, Poundstone, that the N.C.O. is not designed to foster the best interests of the community. Of course you do."

"Well, I hadn't given the subject very mature thought, Colonel, but in the light of your observations it would appear that you are quite right."

"Of course I am right. I take it, therefore, that when the N.C.O. applies for its franchise to run through Sequoia, neither you nor your city council will consider the proposition at all."

"I cannot, of course, speak for the city council—" Poundstone began, but Pennington's cold, amused smile froze further utterance.

"Be frank with me, Poundstone. I am not a child. What I would like to know is this: will you exert every effort to block that franchise in the firm conviction that by so doing you will accomplish a laudable public service?"

Poundstone squirmed. "I should not care, at this time, to go on record," he replied evasively. "When I have had time to look into the matter more thoroughly—"

"Tut-tut, my dear man! Let us not straddle the fence. Business is a game, and so is politics. Neither knows any sentiment. Suppose you should favour this N.C.O. crowd in a mistaken idea that you were doing the right thing, and that subsequently numberless fellow-citizens developed the idea that you had not done your public duty? Would some of them not be likely to invoke a recall election and retire you and your city council—in disgrace?"

"I doubt if they could defeat me, Colonel."

"I have no such doubt," Pennington replied pointedly.

Poundstone looked up at him from under lowered lids. "Is that a threat?" he demanded tremulously.

"My dear fellow! Threaten my guest!" Pennington laughed patronizingly. "I am giving you advice, Poundstone—and rather good advice, it strikes me. However, while we're on the subject, I have no hesitancy in telling you that in the event of a disastrous decision on your part, I should not feel justified in supporting you."

He might, with equal frankness, have said: "I would smash you." To his guest his meaning was not obscure. Poundstone studied the pattern of the rug, and Pennington, watching him sharply, saw that the man was distressed. Then suddenly one of those brilliant inspirations, or flashes of rare intuition, which had helped so materially to fashion Pennington into a captain of industry, came to him. He resolved on a bold stroke.

"Let's not beat about the bush, Poundstone," he said with the air of a father patiently striving to induce his child to recant a lie, tell the truth, and save himself from the parental wrath. "You've been doing business with Ogilvy; I know it for a fact, and you might as well admit it."

Poundstone looked up, red and embarrassed. "If I had known—" he began.

"Certainly, certainly! I realize you acted in perfect good faith. You're like the majority of people in Sequoia. You're all so crazy for rail-connection with the outside world that you jump at the first plan that seems to promise you one. Now, I'm as eager as the others, but if we are going to have a railroad, I, for one, desire the right kind of railroad; and the N.C.O. isn't the right kind—that is, not for the interests I represent. Have you promised Ogilvy a franchise?"

There was no dodging that question. A denial, under the present circumstances, would be tantamount to an admission; Poundstone could not guess just how much the Colonel really knew, and it would not do to lie to him, since eventually the lie must be discovered. Caught between the horns of a dilemma, Poundstone only knew that Ogilvy could never be to him such a powerful enemy as Colonel Seth Pennington; so, after the fashion of his kind, he chose the lesser of two evils. He resolved to "come clean."

"The city council has already granted the N.C.O. a temporary franchise," he confessed.

Pennington sprang furiously to his feet. "Dammit." he snarled, "why did you do that without consulting me?"

"Didn't know you were remotely interested." Now that the ice was broken, Poundstone felt relieved and was prepared to defend his act vigorously. "And we did not commit ourselves irrevocably," he continued. "The temporary franchise will expire in twenty-eight days—and in that short time the N.C.O. cannot even get started."

"Have you any understanding as to an extension of that temporary franchise, in case the N.C.O. desires it?"

"Well, yes—not in writing, however. I gave Ogilvy to understand that if he was not ready in thirty days, an extension could readily be arranged."

"Any witnesses?"

"I am not such a fool, sir," Poundstone declared with asperity. "I had a notion—I might as well admit it—that you would have serious objection to having your tracks cut by a jump-crossing at B and Water streets." And for no reason in life except to justify himself and inculcate in Pennington an impression that the latter was dealing with a crafty and far-seeing mayor,

Poundstone smiled boldly and knowingly. "I repeat," he said, "that I did not put it in writing." He leaned back nonchalantly and blew smoke at the ceiling.

"You oily rascal!" Pennington soliloquized. "You're a smarter man than I thought. You're trying to play both ends against the middle." He recalled the report of his private detective and the incident of Ogilvy's visit to young Henry Poundstone's office with a small leather bag; he was more than ever convinced that this bag had contained the bribe, in gold coin, which had been productive of that temporary franchise and the verbal understanding for its possible extension.

"Ogilvy did business with you through your son Henry," he challenged. Poundstone started violently. "How much did Henry get out of it?" Pennington continued brutally.

"Two hundred and fifty dollars retainer, and not a cent more," Poundstone protested virtuously—and truthfully.

"You're not so good a business man as I gave you credit for being," the Colonel retorted mirthfully "Two hundred and fifty dollars! Oh, Lord! Poundstone, you're funny. Upon my word, you're a scream." And the Colonel gave himself up to a sincerely hearty laugh. "You call it a retainer," he continued presently, "but a grand jury might call it something else. However," he went on after a slight pause, "you're not in politics for your health; so let's get down to brass tacks. How much do you want to deny the N.C.O. not only an extension of that temporary franchise but also a permanent franchise when they apply for it?"

Poundstone rose with great dignity. "Colonel Pennington, sir," he said, "you insult me."

"Sit down. You've been insulted that way before now. Shall we say one thousand dollars per each for your three good councilmen and true, and for yourself that sedan of my niece's? It's a good car. Last year's model, but only run about four thousand miles and in tiptop condition. It's always had the best of care, and I imagine it will please Mrs. P. immensely and grant you surcease from sorrow. Of course, I will not give it to you. I'll sell it to you— five hundred down upon the signing of the agreement, and in lieu of the cash, I will take over that jitney Mrs. Poundstone finds so distasteful. Then I will employ your son Henry as the attorney for the Laguna Grande Lumber Company and give him a retainer of twenty-five hundred dollars for one year. I will leave it to you to get this twenty-five hundred dollars from Henry and pay my niece cash for the car. Doesn't that strike you as a perfectly safe and sane proposition?"

Had a vista of paradise opened up before Mr. Poundstone, he could not have been more thrilled. He had been absolutely honest in his plea to Mrs.

Poundstone that he could not afford a thirty-two-hundred-and-fifty-dollar sedan, much as he longed to oblige her and gain a greatly to be desired peace. And now the price was dangling before his eyes, so to speak. At any rate it was parked in the porte-cochere not fifty feet distant!

For the space of a minute the Mayor weighed his son's future as a corporation attorney against his own future as mayor of Sequoia—and Henry lost.

"It might be arranged, Colonel," he murmured in a low voice—the voice of shame.

"It is already arranged," the Colonel replied cheerfully. "Leave your jit at the front gate and drive home in Shirley's car. I'll arrange matters with her." He laughed shortly. "It means, of course, that I'll have to telegraph to San Francisco to-morrow and buy her a later model. Thank goodness, she has a birthday to-morrow! Have a fresh cigar, Mayor."

Riding home that night in Shirley Sumner's car Mrs. Poundstone leaned suddenly toward her husband, threw a fat arm around his neck and kissed him. "Oh, Henry, you darling!" she purred. "What did I tell you? If a person only wishes hard enough—"

"Oh, go to the devil!" he roared angrily. "You've nagged me into it. Shut up and take your arm away. Do you want me to wreck the car before we've had it an hour?"

As for Colonel Pennington, he had little difficulty in explaining the deal to Shirley, who was sleepy and not at all interested. The Poundstones had bored her to extinction, and upon her uncle's assurance that she would have a new car within a week, she thanked him and for the first time retired without offering her cheek for his good-night kiss. Shortly thereafter the Colonel sought his own virtuous couch and prepared to surrender himself to the first good sleep in three weeks. He laid the flattering unction to his soul that Bryce Cardigan had dealt him a poor hand from a marked deck and he had played it exceedingly well. "Lucky I blocked the young beggar from getting those rails out of the Laurel Creek spur," he mused, "or he'd have had his jump-crossing in overnight—and then where the devil would I have been? Up Salt Creek without a paddle—and all the courts in Christendom would avail me nothing."

He was dozing off, when a sound smote upon his ears. Instantly he was wide awake, listening intently, his head cocked on one side. The sound grew louder; evidently it was approaching Sequoia—and with a bound the Colonel sat up in bed, trembling in every limb.

Suddenly, out of the deep, rumbling diapason he heard a sharp click—then another and another. He counted them—six in all.

"A locomotive and two flat-cars!" he murmured. "And they just passed over the switch leading from the main-line tracks out to my log-dump. That means the train is going down Water Street to the switch into Cardigan's yard. By George, they've outwitted me!"

With the agility of a boy he sprang into his clothes, raced downstairs, and leaped into Mayor Poundstone's jitney, standing in the darkness at the front gate.

CHAPTER XXX

The success of Bryce Cardigan's plan for getting Ms rails down from Laurel Creek depended entirely upon the whimsy which might seize the crew of the big mogul that hauled the last load of logs out of Cardigan's redwoods on Thursday afternoon. Should the engineer and fireman decide to leave the locomotive at the logging-camp for the night, Bryce's task would be as simple as turning a hose down a squirrel-hole. On the other hand, should they run back to Sequoia with the engine, he and Ogilvy faced the alternative of "borrowing" it from the Laguna Grande Lumber Company's roundhouse; and that operation, in view of the fact that Pennington's night watchman would be certain to hear the engine leaving, offered difficulties.

Throughout the afternoon, after having sent his orders in writing to the woods-boss, via George Sea Otter (for he dared not trust to the telephone), be waited in his office for a telephone-call from the logging-camp as to what action the engine-crew had taken. He could not work; he could not think. He only knew that all depended upon the success of his coup to-night. Finally, at a quarter of six, Curtis, his woods-boss rang in.

"They're staying here all night, sir," he reported.

"House them as far from the log-landing as possible, and organize a poker-game to keep them busy in case they don't go to bed before eight o'clock," Bryce ordered. "In the meantime, send a man you can trust—Jim Harding, who runs the big bull-donkey, will do—down to the locomotive to keep steam up until I arrive."

He had scarcely hung up, when Buck Ogilvy came into the office. "Well?" he queried casually.

"Safe-o, Buck!" replied Bryce. "How about your end of the contract?"

"Crowbars, picks, shovels, hack-saws to cut the rails, lanterns to work by, and men to do the work will be cached in your lumber-yard by nine o'clock, waiting for the rails to arrive."

Bryce nodded his approval, "Then I suppose there's nothing to do but get a bite of dinner and proceed to business."

Buck insisted on keeping an engagement to dine with Moira, and Bryce agreed to call for him at the Bon Gusto restaurant. Then Bryce went home to dine with his father. Old Cardigan was happier than his son had seen him since the return of the latter to Sequoia.

"Well, sonny, I've had a mighty pleasant afternoon," he declared as Bryce led him to the dinner-table. "I've been up to the Valley of the Giants."

Bryce was amazed. "Why, how could you?" he demanded. "The old skid-road is impassable, and after you leave the end of the skid-road, the trail in to Mother's grave is so overgrown with buckthorn and wild lilac I doubt if a rabbit could get through it comfortably."

"Not a bit of it," the old man replied. "Somebody has gone to work and planked that old skid-road and put up a hand-railing on each side, while the trail through the Giants has been grubbed out and smoothed over. All that old logging-cable I abandoned in those choppings has been strung from tree to tree alongside the path on both sides. I can go up there alone now, once George sets me on the old skid-road; I can't get lost."

"How did you discover this?" Bryce demanded.

"Judge Moore, representing the new owner, called round this morning and took me in tow. He said his client knew the property held for me a certain sentimental value which wasn't transferred in the deed, and so the Judge had been instructed to have the skid-road planked and the forest trail grubbed out—for me. It appears that the Valley is going to be a public park, after all, but for the present and while I live, it is my private park."

"This is perfectly amazing, partner."

"It's mighty comforting," his father admitted. "Guess the new owner must be one of my old friends—perhaps somebody I did a favour for once—and this is his way of repaying. Remember the old sugar-pine windfall we used to sit on? Well, it's rotted through, and bears have clawed it into chips in their search for grubs, but the new owner had a seat put in there for me—just the kind of seat I like—a lumberjack's rocking-chair made from an old vinegar-barrel. I sat in it, and the Judge left me, and I did a right smart lot o' thinking. And while it didn't lead me anywhere, still I—er—"

"You felt better, didn't you?" his son suggested.

John Cardigan nodded. "I'd like to know the name of the owner," he said presently. "I'd like mighty well to say thank you to him. It isn't usual for people nowadays to have as much respect for sentiment in an old duffer like me as the fellow has. He sort of makes me feel as if I hadn't sold at all."

Buck Ogilvy came out of the Bon Gusto restaurant with Moira, just as Bryce, with George Sea Otter at the wheel of the Napier, drove up to the curb. They left Moira at her boarding-house, and rolled noiselessly away.

At nine o'clock they arrived at Cardigan's log-landing and found Jim Harding, the bull-donkey engineer, placidly smoking his pipe in the cab. Bryce hailed him.

"That you, Jim?"

"You bet."

"Run up to Jabe Curtis's shanty, and tell him we're here. Have him gather his gang and bring two pairs of overalls and two jumpers—large size—with him when he comes."

Harding vanished into the darkness, and Buck Ogilvy climbed up into the cab and glanced at the steam-gauge. "A hundred and forty," he announced. "Good enough!"

Presently the woods-boss, accompanied by thirty of his best men, came down to the log-landing. At Bryce's order they clambered aboard the engine and tender, hanging on the steps, on the roof of the cab, on the cowcatcher—anywhere they could find a toe-hold. Harding cast aside the two old ties which the careful engine-crew had placed across the tracks in front of the drivers as additional precaution; Buck Ogilvy cut off the air, and the locomotive and tender began to glide slowly down the almost imperceptible grade. With a slight click it cleared the switch and slid out onto the Cardigan lateral, swiftly gathering speed. A quarter of a mile down the line Buck Ogilvy applied the brakes and eased her down to twenty miles per hour.

At the junction with the main line Buck backed briskly up into the Laguna Grande woods, and coupled to the two loaded flat-cars. The woods-gang scrambled aboard the flats, and the train pulled out for Sequoia. Forty minutes later they rumbled down Water Street and slid to a grinding halt at the intersection of B Street.

From the darkness of Cardigan's drying-yard, where they had been waiting, twenty picked men of the mill-crew now emerged, bearing lanterns and tools. Under Buck Ogilvy's direction the dirt promptly began to fly, while the woods-crew unloaded the rails and piled them close to the sidewalk.

Suddenly a voice, harsh and strident with passion, rose above the thud of the picks and the clang of metal.

"Who's in charge here, and what in blazes do you mean by cutting my tracks?"

Bryce turned in time to behold Colonel Seth Pennington leap from an automobile and advance upon Buck Ogilvy. Ogilvy held a lantern up to the Colonel's face and surveyed Pennington calmly.

"Colonel," he began with exasperating politeness, "—I presume you are Colonel Pennington—my name is Buchanan P. Ogilvy, and I am in charge of these operations. I am the vice-president and general manager of the N.C.O., and I am engaged in the blithe task of making a jump-crossing of your rails. I had hoped to accomplish this without your knowledge or consent, but now that you are here, that hope, of course, has died a-bornin'. Have a cigar." And he thrust a perfecco under the Colonel's nose. Pennington struck it to the ground, and on the instant, half a dozen rough rascals emptied their shovels over him. He was deluged with dirt.

"Stand back, Colonel, stand back, if you please. You're in the way of the shovellers," Buck Ogilvy warned him soothingly.

Bryce Cardigan came over, and at sight of him Pennington choked with fury. "You—you—" he sputtered, unable to say more.

"I'm the N.C.O.," Bryce replied. "Nice little fiction that of yours about the switch-engine being laid up in the shops and the Laurel Creek bridge being unsafe for this big mogul." He looked Pennington over with frank admiration. "You're certainly on the job, Colonel. I'll say that much for you. The man who plans to defeat you must jump far and fast, or his tail will be trod on."

"You've stolen my engine," Pennington almost screamed. "I'll have the law on you for grand larceny."

"Tut-tut! You don't know who stole your engine. For all you know, your own engine-crew may have run it down here."

"I'll attend to you, sir," Pennington replied, and he turned to enter Mayor Poundstone's little flivver.

"Not to-night, at least," Bryce retorted gently. "Having gone this far, I would be a poor general to permit you to escape now with the news of your discovery. You'd be down here in an hour with a couple of hundred members of your mill-crew and give us the rush. You will oblige me, Colonel Pennington, by remaining exactly where you are until I give you permission to depart."

"And if I refuse—"

"Then I shall manhandle you, truss you up like a fowl in the tonneau of your car, and gag you."

To Bryce's infinite surprise the Colonel smiled. "Oh, very well!" he replied. "I guess you've got the bulge on me, young man. Do you mind if I sit in the warm cab of my own engine? I came away in such a hurry I quite forgot my overcoat."

"Not at all. I'll sit up there and keep you company."

Half an hour passed. An automobile came slowly up Water Street and paused half a block away, evidently reconnoitering the situation. Instantly the Colonel thrust his head out the cab window.

"Sexton!" he shouted. "Cardigan's cutting in a crossing. He's holding me here against my will. Get the mill-crew together and phone for Rondeau and his woods-crew. Send the switch-engine and a couple of flats up for them. Phone Poundstone. Tell him to have the chief of police—"

Bryce Cardigan's great hand closed over the Colonel's neck, while down Water Street a dark streak that was Buck Ogilvy sped toward the automobile, intending to climb in and make Pennington's manager a prisoner also. He was too late, however. Sexton swung his car and departed at full speed down Water Street, leaving the disappointed Buck to return panting to the scene of operations.

Bryce Cardigan released his hold on Pennington's neck. "You win, Colonel," he announced. "No good can come of holding you here any longer. Into your car and on your way."

"Thank you, young man," the Colonel answered, and there was a metallic ring in his voice. He looked at his watch in the glare of a torch. "Plenty of time," he murmured. "Curfew shall not ring to-night." Quite deliberately he climbed into the Mayor's late source of woe and breezed away.

Colonel Pennington did not at once return to his home, however. Instead, he drove up to the business centre of the town. The streets were deserted, but one saloon—the Sawdust Pile—was still open.

Pennington strode through the bar and into the back room, where a number of poker-games were in progress. For a moment he stood, his cold, ophidian glance circling the room until it came to rest on no less a personage than the Black Minorca, an individual with whom the reader has already had some slight acquaintance. It will be recalled that the Black Minorca led the futile rush against Bryce Cardigan that day in Pennington's woods.

The Colonel approached the table where the Black Minorca sat thumbing the edges of his cards, and touched the cholo on the shoulder. The Black Minorca turned, and Pennington nodded to him to follow; whereupon the latter cashed in his chips and joined his employer on the sidewalk. Here a whispered conversation ensued, and at its conclusion the Black Minorca nodded vigorously.

"Sure!" he assured the Colonel. "I'll fix 'em good and plenty."

Together Pennington and the Black Minorca entered the automobile and proceeded swiftly to the Laguna Grande Lumber Company's mill-office. From a locker the Colonel produced a repeating rifle and three boxes of cartridges, which he handed to the cholo, who departed without further ado into the night.

Twenty minutes later, from the top of a lumber-pile in Cardigan's drying-yard, Bryce Cardigan saw the flash of a rifle and felt a sudden sting on his left forearm. He leaped around in front of the cowcatcher to gain the shelter of the engine, and another bullet struck at his feet and ricocheted off into the night. It was followed by a fusillade, the bullets kicking up the freshly disturbed earth among the workers and sending them scurrying to various points of safety. In an instant the crossing was deserted, and work had been stopped, while from the top of the adjacent lumber-pile the Black Minorca poured a stream of lead and filthy invective at every point which he suspected of harbouring a Cardigan follower.

"I don't think he's hurt anybody," Buck Ogilvy whispered as he crouched with Bryce beside the engine, "but that's due to his marksmanship rather than his intentions."

"He tried hard enough to plug me," Bryce declared, and showed the hole through his sleeve. "They call him the Black Minorca, and he's a mongrel greaser who'd kill his own mother for a fifty-dollar bill."

"I'd like to plug him," Buck murmured regretfully.

"What would be the use? This will be his last night in Humboldt County—"

A rifle shot rang out from the side of B Street; from the lumber-pile across the street, Bryce and Ogilvy heard a suppressed grunt of pain, and a crash as of a breaking board. Instantly out of the shadows George Sea Otter came padding on velvet feet, rifle in hand—and then Bryce understood.

"All right, boss," said George simply as he joined Bryce and Ogilvy under the lee of the locomotive. "Now we get busy again."

"Safe-o, men," Ogilvy called. "Back to the job." And while Bryce, followed by the careless George Sea Otter, went into the lumber-yard to succour the enemy, Ogilvy set an example to the men by stepping into the open and starting briskly to work with a shovel.

At the bottom of the pile of lumber the Black Minorca was discovered with a severe flesh-wound in his right hip; also he was suffering from numerous bruises and contusions. George Sea Otter possessed himself of the fallen cholo's rifle, while Bryce picked the wretch up and carried him to his automobile.

"Take the swine over to the Laguna Grande Lumber Company's hospital and tell them to patch him up," he ordered George Sea Otter. "I'll keep both rifles and the ammunition here for Jules Rondeau and his woods-gang. They'll probably be dropping in on us about two a.m., if I know anything about Colonel Pennington's way of doing things."

CHAPTER XXXI

Having dispatched the Black Minorca to hold up the work until the arrival of reinforcements, Colonel Pennington fairly burned the streets en route to his home. He realized that there would be no more sleep for him that night, and he was desirous of getting into a heavy ulster before venturing forth again into the night air.

The violent slam with which he closed the front door after him brought Shirley, in dressing-gown and slippers, to the staircase.

"Uncle Seth!" she called.

"Here!" he replied from the hall below.

"What's the matter?"

"There's the devil to pay," he answered. "That fellow Cardigan is back of the N.C.O., after all, and he and Ogilvy have a gang of fifty men down at the intersection of Water and B streets, cutting in a jump-crossing of our line."

He dashed into the living room, and she heard him calling frantically into the telephone.

"At last!" she murmured, and crept down the stairs, pausing behind the heavy portieres at the entrance to the living room.

"That you, Poundstone?" she heard him saying rapidly into the transmitter. "Pennington speaking. Young Bryce Cardigan is behind that N.C.O. outfit, and it's a logging-road and not intended to build through to Grant's Pass at all. Cardigan and Ogilvy are at Water and B streets this very instant with a gang of fifty men cutting in a jump-crossing of my line, curse them! They'll have it in by six o'clock to-morrow morning if something isn't done—and once they get it in, the fat's in the fire.

"Telephone the chief of police and order him to take his entire force down there, if necessary, and stop that work. To blazes with that temporary franchise! You stop that work for two hours, and I'll do the rest. Tell the chief of police not to recognize that temporary franchise. He can be suspicious of it, can't he, and refuse to let the work go on until he finds you? And you can be hard to find for two hours, can you not? Delay, delay, man! That's all I want... Yes, yes, I understand. You get down about daylight and roast the chief of police for interfering, but in the meantime!... Thank you, Poundstone, thank you. Good-bye."

He stood at the telephone, the receiver still held to his ear and his right forefinger holding down the hook while the line cleared. When he spoke again, Shirley knew he was calling his mill-office. He got a response immediately, notwithstanding the lateness of the hour.

"Sexton? Pennington speaking. I've sent over the Black Minorca with a rifle and sixty rounds of ammunition... What? You can hear him shooting already? Bully boy with a crockery eye! He'll clean that gang out and keep them from working until the police arrive. You've telephoned Rondeau, have you?... Good! He'll have his men waiting at the log-landing, and there'll be no delay. As soon as you've seen the switch-engine started for the woods, meet me down at Water and B streets. Sexton, we've got to block them. It means a loss of millions to me if we fail!"

Shirley was standing in the doorway as he faced about from the telephone. "Uncle Seth," she said quietly, "use any honourable method of defeating Bryce Cardigan, but call off the Black Minorca. I shall hold you personally responsible for Bryce Cardigan's life, and if you fail me, I shall never forgive you."

"Silly, silly girl!" he soothed her. "Don't you know I would not stoop to bush-whacking? There's some shooting going on, but its wild shooting, just to frighten Cardigan and his men off the job."

"You can't frighten him," she cried passionately, "You know you can't. He'll kill the Black Minorca, or the Black Minorca will kill him. Go instantly and stop it."

"All right, all right!" he said rather humbly, and sprang down the front steps into the waiting car. "I'll play the game fairly, Shirley, never fear."

She stood in the doorway and watched the red tail-light, like a malevolent eye, disappear down the street. And presently as she stood there, down the boulevard a huge gray car came slipping noiselessly—so noiselessly, in fact, that Shirley recognized it by that very quality of silence. It was Bryce Cardigan's Napier.

"George!" she called. "Come here."

The car slid over to the gate and stopped at the sight of the slim white figure running down the garden walk.

"Is Mr. Cardigan hurt?" she demanded in an agony of suspense.

George Sea Otter grunted contemptuously. "Nobody hurt 'cept the Black Minorca. I am taking him to your company hospital, miss. He tried to shoot my boss, so I shoot him myself once through the leg. Now my boss says: 'Take him to the Laguna Grande hospital, George.' Me, I would drop this greaser in the bay if I was the boss."

She laughed hysterically. "On your way back from the hospital stop and pick me up, George," she ordered. "This senseless feud has gone far enough. I must stop it—at once."

He touched his broad hat, and she returned to the house to dress.

Meanwhile Colonel Pennington had reached the crossing once more, simultaneously with the arrival of Sam Perkins, the chief of police, accompanied by two automobiles crammed with patrolmen. Perkins strutted up to Bryce Cardigan and Buck Ogilvy.

"What's the meaning of all this row, Mr. Cardigan?" he demanded.

"Something has slipped, Sam," Bryce retorted pleasantly. "You've been calling me Bryce for the past twenty years, and now you're mistering me! The meaning of this row, you ask?" Bryce continued. "Well, I'm engaged in making a jump-crossing of Colonel Pennington's tracks, under a temporary franchise granted me by the city of Sequoia. Here's the franchise." And he thrust the document under the police chief's nose.

"This is the first I've heard about any franchise," Sam Perkins replied suspiciously. "Seems to me you been mighty secret about this job. How do I know this ain't a forgery?"

"Call up the mayor and ask him," Bryce suggested.

"I'll do that," quoth Mr. Perkins ponderously. "And in the meantime, don't do any more digging or rail-cutting." He hurried away to his automobile, leaving a lieutenant in charge of the squad.

"Also in the meantime, young man," Colonel Pennington announced, "you will pardon me if I take possession of my locomotive and flat-cars. I observe you have finished unloading those rails."

"Help yourself, Colonel," Bryce replied with an assumption of heartiness he was far from feeling.

"Thank you so much, Cardigan." With the greatest good nature in life, Pennington climbed into the cab, reached for the bell-cord, and rang the bell vigorously. Then he permitted himself a triumphant toot of the whistle, after which he threw off the air and gently opened the throttle. He was not a locomotive-engineer but he had ridden in the cab of his own locomotive and felt quite confident of his ability in a pinch.

With a creak and a bump the train started, and the Colonel ran it slowly up until the locomotive stood on the tracks exactly where Buck Ogilvy had been cutting in his crossing; whereupon the Colonel locked the brakes, opened his exhaust, and blew the boiler down. And when the last ounce of steam had escaped, he descended and smilingly accosted Bryce Cardigan.

"That engine being my property," he announced, "I'll take the short end of any bet you care to make, young man, that it will sit on those tracks until your temporary franchise expires. I'd give a good deal to see anybody not in my employ attempt to get up steam in that boiler until I give the word. Cut in your jump-crossing now, if you can, you whelp, and be damned to you. I've got you blocked!"

"I rather imagine this nice gentleman has it on us, old dear," chirped Buck Ogilvy plaintively. "Well! We did our damndest, which angels can't do no more. Let us gather up our tools and go home, my son, for something tells me that if I hang around here I'll bust one of two things—this sleek scoundrel's gray head or one of my bellicose veins! Hello! Whom have we here?"

Bryce turned and found himself facing Shirley Sumner. Her tender lip was quivering, and the tears shone in her eyes like stars. He stared at her in silence.

"My friend," she murmured tremulously, "didn't I tell you I would not permit you to build the N.C.O.?"

He bowed his head in rage and shame at his defeat. Buck Ogilvy took him by the arm. "'Tis midnight's holy hour,'" he quoted, "'and silence now is brooding like a gentle spirit o'er a still and pulseless world.' Bryce, old chap, this is one of those occasions where silence is golden. Speak not. I'll do it for you. Miss Sumner," he continued, bowing graciously, "and Colonel Pennington," favouring that triumphant rascal with an equally gracious bow, "we leave you in possession of the field—temporarily. However, if anybody should drive up in a hack and lean out and ask you, just tell him Buck Ogilvy has another trump tucked away in his kimono."

Bryce turned to go, but with a sudden impulse Shirley laid her hand on his arm—his left arm. "Bryce!" she murmured.

He lifted her hand gently from his forearm, led her to the front of the locomotive, and held her hand up to the headlight. Her fingers were crimson with blood.

"Your uncle's killer did that, Shirley," he said ironically. "It's only a slight flesh-wound, but that is no fault of your allies. Good-night."

And he left her standing, pale of face and trembling, in the white glare of the headlight.

CHAPTER XXXII

Shirley made no effort to detain Bryce Cardigan as he walked to his car and climbed into it. Ogilvy remained merely long enough to give orders to the foreman to gather up the tools, store them in the machine-shop of Cardigan's mill, and dismiss his gang; then he, too, entered the automobile, and at a word from Bryce, the car slid noiselessly away into the darkness. The track-cutting crew departed a few minutes later, and when Shirley found herself alone with her uncle, the tumult in her heart gave way to the tears she could no longer repress. Pennington stood by, watching her curiously, coldly.

Presently Shirley mastered her emotion and glanced toward him.

"Well, my dear?" he queried nervously.

"I—I think I had better go home," she said without spirit.

"I think so, too," he answered. "Get into the Mayor's flivver, my dear, and I'll drive you. And perhaps the least said about this affair the better, Shirley. There are many things that you do not understand and which cannot be elucidated by discussion."

"I can understand an attempt at assassination, Uncle Seth."

"That blackguard Minorca! I should have known better than to put him on such a job. I told him to bluff and threaten; Cardigan, I knew, would realize the grudge the Black Minorca has against him, and for that reason I figured the greaser was the only man who could bluff him. While I gave him orders to shoot, I told him distinctly not to hit anybody. Good Lord, Shirley, surely you do not think I would wink at a murder!"

"I do," she answered passionately. "With Bryce Cardigan out of the way, you would have a clear field before you—"

"Oh, my dear, my dear! Surely you do not realize what you are saying. You are beside yourself, Shirley. Please—please do not wound me so—so horribly. You do not—you cannot realize what a desperate fight I have been putting up for both our sakes. I am surrounded by enemies—the most implacable enemies. They force me to fight the devil with fire—and here you are, giving them aid and comfort."

"I want you to defeat Bryce Cardigan, if you can do it fairly."

"At another time and in a calmer mood we will discuss that villain," he said authoritatively. "If we argue the matter now, we are liable to misunderstandings; we may quarrel, and that is something neither of us can afford. Get into the car, and we will go home. There is nothing more to be done to-night."

"Your sophistry does not alter my opinion," she replied firmly. "However, as you say, this is neither the time nor the place to discuss it."

They drove home in silence. Shirley went at once to her room. For the Colonel, however, the night's work had scarcely begun. The instant he heard the door to his niece's room shut, he went to the telephone and called up the Laguna Grande roundhouse. Sexton, his manager, answered.

"Have you sent the switch-engine to the woods for Rondeau and his men?"

"Just left."

"Good! Now, then, Sexton, listen to me: As you know, this raid of Cardigan's has developed so suddenly I am more or less taken by surprise and have had no time to prepare the kind of counter-attack that will be most effective. However, with the crossing blocked, I gain time in which to organize—only there must be no weak point in my organization. In order to insure that, I am proceeding to San Francisco to-night by motor, via the coast road. I will arrive late to-morrow night, and early Saturday morning I will appear in the United States District Court with our attorneys and file a complaint and petition for an order temporarily restraining the N.C.O. from cutting our tracks.

"I will have to make an affidavit to support the complaint, so I had better be Johnny-on-the-spot to do it, rather than risk the delay of making the affidavit tomorrow morning here and forwarding it by mail to our attorneys. The judge will sign a restraining order, returnable in from ten to thirty days—I'll try for thirty, because that will knock out the N.C.O.'s temporary franchise— and after I have obtained the restraining order, I will have the United States marshal telegraph it to Ogilvy and Cardigan!"

"Bully!" cried Sexton heartily. "That will fix their clock."

"In the meantime," Pennington continued, "logs will be glutting our landings. We need that locomotive for its legitimate purposes. Take all that discarded machinery and the old boiler we removed from the mill last fall, dump it on the tracks at the crossing, and get the locomotive back on its run. Understand? The other side, having no means of removing these heavy obstructions, will be blocked until I return; by that time the matter will be in the District Court, Cardigan will be hung up until his temporary franchise expires—and the city council will not renew it. Get me?"

"Yes, sir."

"I'll be back Sunday forenoon. Good-bye."

He hung up, went to his chauffeur's quarters over the garage, and routed the man out of bed. Then he returned quietly to his room, dressed and packed a bag for his journey, left a brief note for Shirley notifying her of his departure, and started on his two-hundred-and-fifty mile trip over the mountains to the south. As his car sped through sleeping Sequoia and gained the open country, the Colonel's heart thrilled pleasurably. He held cards and spades, big and little casino, four aces and the joker; therefore he knew he could sweep the board at his pleasure. And during his absence Shirley would have opportunity to cool off, while he would find time to formulate an argument to lull her suspicions upon his return.

CHAPTER XXXIII

Quite oblivious of her uncle's departure for San Francisco, Shirley lay awake throughout the remainder of the night, turning over and over in her mind the various aspects of the Cardigan-Fennington imbroglio. Of one thing she was quite certain; peace must be declared at all hazards. She had been obsessed of a desire, rather unusual in her sex, to see a fight worth while; she had planned to permit it to go to a knockout, to use Bryce Cardigan's language, because she believed Bryce Cardigan would be vanquished—and she had desired to see him smashed—but not beyond repair, for her joy in the conflict was to lie in the task of putting the pieces together afterward! She realized now, however, that she had permitted matters to go too far. A revulsion of feeling toward her uncle, induced by the memory of Bryce Cardigan's blood on her white finger-tips, convinced the girl that, at all hazards to her financial future, henceforth she and her uncle must tread separate paths. She had found him out at last, and because in her nature there was some of his own fixity of purpose, the resolution cost her no particular pang.

It was rather a relief, therefore, when the imperturbable James handed her at breakfast the following note:

Shirley, Dear

After leaving you last night, I decided that in your present frame of mind my absence for a few days might tend to a calmer and clearer perception, on your part, of the necessary tactics which in a moment of desperation, I saw fit, with regret, to pursue last night. And in the hope that you will have attained your old attitude toward me before my return, I am leaving in the motor for San Francisco. Your terrible accusation has grieved me to such an extent that I do not feel equal to the task of confronting you until, in a more judicial frame of mind, you can truly absolve me of the charge of wishing to do away with young Cardigan. Your affectionate Uncle Seth.

Shirley's lip curled. With a rarer, keener intuition than she had hitherto manifested, she sensed the hypocrisy between the lines; she was not deceived.

"He has gone to San Francisco for more ammunition," she soliloquized. "Very well, Unkie-dunk! While you're away, I shall manufacture a few bombs myself."

After breakfast she left the house and walked to the intersection of B with Water Street. Jules Rondeau and his crew of lumberjacks were there, and with two policemen guarded the crossing.

Rondeau glanced at Shirley, surprised, then lifted his hat. Shirley looked from the woods bully to the locomotive and back to Rondeau.

"Rondeau," she said, "Mr. Cardigan is a bad man to fight. You fought him once. Are you going to do it again?"

He nodded.

"By whose orders?"

"Mr. Sexton, he tell me to do it."

"Well, Rondeau, some day I'll be boss of Laguna Grande and there'll be no more fighting," she replied, and passed on down B Street to the office of the Cardigan Redwood Lumber Company. Moira McTavish looked up as she entered.

"Where is he, dear?" Shirley asked. "I must see him."

"In that office, Miss Shirley," Moira replied, and pointed to the door. Shirley stepped to the door, knocked, and then entered. Bryce Cardigan, seated at his desk, looked up as she came in. His left arm was in a sling, and he looked harassed and dejected.

"Don't get up, Bryce," she said as he attempted to rise. "I know you're quite exhausted. You look it." She sat down. "I'm so sorry," she said softly.

His dull glance brightened. "It doesn't amount to that, Shirley." And he snapped his fingers. "It throbs a little and it's stiff and sore, so I carry it in the sling. That helps a little. What did you want to see me about?"

"I wanted to tell you," said Shirley, "that—that last night's affair was not of my making." He smiled compassionately. "I—I couldn't bear to have you think I'd break my word and tell him."

"It never occurred to me that you had dealt me a hand from the bottom of the deck, Shirley. Please don't worry about it. Your uncle has had two private detectives watching Ogilvy and me."

"Oh!" she breathed, much relieved. A ghost of the old bantering smile lighted her winsome features. "Well, then," she challenged, "I suppose you don't hate me."

"On the contrary, I love you," he answered. "However, since you must have known this for some time past, I suppose it is superfluous to mention it. Moreover, I haven't the right—yet."

She had cast her eyes down modestly. She raised them now and looked at him searchingly. "I suppose you'll acknowledge yourself whipped at last, Bryce?" she ventured.

"Would it please you to have me surrender?" He was very serious.

"Indeed it would, Bryce."

"Why?"

"Because I'm tired of fighting. I want peace. I'm—I'm afraid to let this matter go any further. I'm truly afraid."

"I think I want peace, too," he answered wearily. "I'd be glad to quit—with honour. And I'll do it, too, if you can induce your uncle to give me the kind of logging contract I want with his road."

"I couldn't do that, Bryce. He has you whipped—and he is not merciful to the fallen. You'll have to—surrender unconditionally." Again she laid her little hand timidly on his wounded forearm. "Please give up, Bryce—for my sake. If you persist, somebody will get killed."

"I suppose I'll have to," he murmured sadly. "I dare say you're right, though one should never admit defeat until he is counted out. I suppose," he continued bitterly, "your uncle is in high feather this morning."

"I don't know, Bryce. He left in his motor for San Francisco about one o'clock this morning."

For an instant Bryce Cardigan stared at her; then a slow, mocking little smile crept around the corners of his mouth, and his eyes lighted with mirth.

"Glorious news, my dear Shirley, perfectly glorious! So the old fox has gone to San Francisco, eh? Left in a hurry and via the overland route! Couldn't wait for the regular passenger-steamer to-morrow, eh? Great jumping Jehoshaphat! He must have had important business to attend to." And Bryce commenced to chuckle. "Oh, the poor old Colonel," he continued presently, "the dear old pirate! What a horrible right swing he's running into! And you want me to acknowledge defeat! My dear girl, in the language of the classic, there is nothing doing. I shall put in my crossing Sunday morning, and if you don't believe it, drop around and see me in action."

"You mustn't try," protested Shirley. "Rondeau is there with his crew—and he has orders to stop you. Besides, you can't expect help from the police. Uncle Seth has made a deal with the Mayor," Shirley pleaded frantically.

"That for the police and that venal Mayor Poundstone!" Bryce retorted, with another snap of his fingers. "I'll rid the city of them at the fall election."

"I came prepared to suggest a compromise, Bryce," she declared, but he interrupted her with a wave of his hand.

"You can't effect a compromise. You've been telling me I shall never build the N.C.O. because you will not permit me to. You're powerless, I tell you. I shall build it."

"You shan't!" she fired back at him, and a spot of anger glowed in each cheek. "You're the most stubborn and belligerent man I have ever known. Sometimes I almost hate you."

"Come around at ten to-morrow morning and watch me put in the crossing—watch me give Rondeau and his gang the run." He reached over suddenly, lifted her hand, and kissed it. "How I love you, dear little antagonist!" he murmured.

"If you loved me, you wouldn't oppose me," she protested softly. "I tell you again, Bryce, you make it very hard for me to be friendly with you."

"I don't want to be friendly with you. You're driving me crazy, Shirley. Please run along home, or wherever you're bound. I've tried to understand your peculiar code, but you're too deep for me; so let me go my way to the devil. George Sea Otter is outside asleep in the tonneau of the car. Tell him to drive you wherever you're going. I suppose you're afoot to-day, for I noticed the Mayor riding to his office in your sedan this morning."

She tried to look outraged, but for the life of her she could not take offense at his bluntness; neither did she resent a look which she detected in his eyes, even though it told her he was laughing at her.

"Oh, very well," she replied with what dignity she could muster. "Have it your own way. I've tried to warn you. Thank you for your offer of the car. I shall be glad to use it. Uncle Seth sold my car to Mayor Poundstone last night. Mrs. P. admired it so!"

"Ah! Then it was that rascally Poundstone who told your uncle about the temporary franchise, thus arousing his suspicions to such an extent that when he heard his locomotive rumbling into town, he smelled a rat and hurried down to the crossing?"

"Possibly. The Poundstones dined at our house last night."

"Pretty hard on you, I should say. But then I suppose you have to play the game with Uncle Seth. Well, good morning, Shirley. Sorry to hurry you away, but you must remember we're on a strictly business basis—yet; and you mustn't waste my time."

"You're horrid, Bryce Cardigan."

"You're adorable. Good morning."

"You'll be sorry for this," she warned him. "Good morning." She passed out into the general office, visited with Moira about five minutes, and drove away in the Napier. Bryce watched her through the window. She knew he was watching her, but nevertheless she could not forbear turning round to verify her suspicions. When she did, he waved his sound arm at her, and she flushed with vexation.

"God bless her!" he murmured. "She's been my ally all along, and I never suspected it! I wonder what her game can be."

He sat musing for a long time. "Yes," he concluded presently, "old Poundstone has double-crossed us—and Pennington made it worth his while. And the Colonel sold the Mayor his niece's automobile. It's worth twenty-five hundred dollars, at least, and since old Poundstone's finances will not permit such an extravagance, I'm wondering how Pennington expects him to pay for it. I smell a rat as big as a kangaroo. In this case two and two don't make four. They make six! Guess I'll build a fire under old Poundstone."

He took down the telephone-receiver and called up the Mayor. "Bryce Cardigan speaking, Mr. Poundstone," he greeted the chief executive of Sequoia.

"Oh, hello, Bryce, my boy," Poundstone boomed affably. "How's tricks?"

"So-so! I hear you've bought that sedan from Colonel Pennington's niece. Wish I'd known it was for sale. I'd have outbid you. Want to make a profit on your bargain?"

"No, not this morning, Bryce. I think we'll keep it. Mrs. P. has been wanting a closed car for a long time, and when the Colonel offered me this one at a bargain, I snapped it up. Couldn't afford a new one, you know, but then this one's just as good as new."

"And you don't care to get rid of it at a profit?" Bryce repeated.

"No, sirree!"

"Oh, you're mistaken, Mr. Mayor. I think you do. I would suggest that you take that car back to Pennington's garage and leave it there. That would be the most profitable thing you could do."

"Wha—what—what in blue blazes are you driving at?" the Mayor sputtered.

"I wouldn't care to discuss it over the telephone. I take it, however, that a hint to the wise is sufficient; and I warn you, Mayor, that if you keep that car it will bring you bad luck. To-day is Friday, and Friday is an unlucky day. I'd get rid of that sedan before noon if I were you."

There was a long, fateful silence. Then in a singularly small, quavering voice: "You think it best, Cardigan?"

"I do. Return it to No. 38 Redwood Boulevard, and no questions will be asked. Good-bye!"

When Shirley reached home at noon, she found her car parked in front of the porte cochere; and a brief note, left with the butler, informed her that after thinking the matter over, Mrs. Poundstone had decided the Poundstone family could not afford such an extravagance, and accordingly the car was returned with many thanks for the opportunity to purchase it at such a ridiculously low figure. Shirley smiled, and put the car up in the garage. When she returned to the house her maid Thelma informed her that Mr. Bryce Cardigan had been calling her on the telephone. So she called Bryce up at once.

"Has Poundstone returned your car?" he queried.

"Why, yes. What makes you ask?"

"Oh, I had a suspicion he might. You see, I called him up and suggested it; somehow His Honour is peculiarly susceptible to suggestions from me, and—"

"Bryce Cardigan," she declared, "you're a sly rascal—that's what you are. I shan't tell you another thing."

"I hope you had a stenographer at the dictograph when the Mayor and your uncle cooked up their little deal," he continued. "That was thoughtful of you, Shirley. It was a bully club to have up your sleeve at the final show-down, for with it you can make Unkie-dunk behave himself and force that compromise you spoke of. Seriously, however, I don't want you to use it, Shirley. We must avoid a scandal by all means; and praise be, I don't need your club to beat your uncle's brains out. I'm taking HIS club away from him to use for that purpose."

"Really, I believe you're happy to-day."

"Happy? I should tell a man! If the streets of Sequoia were paved with eggs, I could walk them all day without making an omelette."

"It must be nice to feel so happy, after so many months of the blues."

"Indeed it is, Shirley. You see until very recently I was very much worried as to your attitude toward me. I couldn't believe you'd so far forget yourself as to love me in spite of everything—so I never took the trouble to ask you. And now I don't have to ask you. I know! And I'll be around to see you after I get that crossing in!"

"You're perfectly horrid," she blazed, and hung up without the formality of saying good-bye.

CHAPTER XXXIV

Shortly after Shirley's departure from his office, Bryce had a visit from Buck Ogilvy. The latter wore a neatly pressed suit of Shepherd plaid, with a white carnation in his lapel, and he was, apparently, the most light-hearted young man in Humboldt County. He struck an attitude and demanded:

"Boss, what do you think of my new suit?"

"You lunatic! Don't you know red blonds should never wear light shades? You're dressed like a Negro minstrel."

"Well, I feel as happy as an end-man. And by the way, you're all chirked up yourself. Who's been helping you to the elixir of life. When we parted last night, you were forty fathoms deep in the slough of despond."

"No less a divinity than Miss Shirley Sumner! She called this morning to explain that last night's fiasco was none of her making, and quite innocently she imparted the information that old Pennington lighted out for San Francisco at one o'clock this morning. Wherefore I laugh. Te-he! Ha-hah!"

"Three long, loud raucous cheers for Uncle. He's gone to rush a restraining order through the United States District Court. Wonder why he didn't wire his attorneys to attend to the matter for him."

"He has the crossing blocked, and inasmuch as the Mayor feeds out of Pennington's hand, the Colonel is quite confident that said crossing will remain blocked, As for the restraining order—well, if one wants a thing well done, one should do it oneself."

"All that doesn't explain your cheerful attitude, though."

"Oh, but it does. I've told you about old Duncan McTavish, Moira's father, haven't I?" Ogilvy nodded, and Bryce continued: "When I fired the old scoundrel for boozing, it almost broke his heart; he had to leave Humboldt, where everybody knew him, so he wandered down into Mendocino County and got a job sticking lumber in the drying-yard of the Willits Lumber Company. He's been there two months now, and I am informed by his employer that old Mac hasn't taken a drink in all that time. And what's more, he isn't going to take one again."

"How do you know?"

"Because I make it my business to find out. Mac was the finest woods-boss this county ever knew; hence you do not assume that I would lose the old scoundrel without making a fight for him, do you? Why, Buck, he's been on the Cardigan pay-roll thirty years, and I only fired him in order to reform him. Well, last week I sent one of Mac's old friends down to Willits purposely to call on him and invite him out 'for a time'; but Mac wouldn't drink with him. No, sir, he couldn't be tempted. On the contrary, he told the tempter that I had promised to give him back his job if he remained on the water wagon for one year; he was resolved to win back his job and his self-respect."

"I know what your plan is," Ogilvy interrupted. "You're going to ask Duncan McTavish to waylay Pennington on the road at some point where it runs through the timber, kidnap him, and hold him until we have had time to clear the crossing and cut Pennington's tracks.

"We will do nothing of the sort," Buck continued seriously. "Listen, now, to Father's words of wisdom. This railroad-game is an old one to me; I've fought at crossings before now, and whether successful or defeated, I have always learned something in battle. Didn't you hear me tell that girl and her villainous avuncular relative last night that I had another ace up my kimono?"

Bryce nodded.

"That was not brag, old dear. I had the ace, and this morning I played it— wherefore in my heart there is that peace that passeth understanding— particularly since I have just had a telegram informing me that my ace took the odd trick."

He opened a drawer in Bryce's desk and reached for the cigars he knew were there.

"Not at all a bad cigar for ten cents. However—you will recall that from the very instant we decided to cut in that jump-crossing, we commenced to plan against interference by Pennington; in consequence we kept, or tried to keep, our decision a secret. However, there existed at all times the possibility that Pennington might discover our benevolent intentions and block us with his only weapon—a restraining order issued by the judge of the United States District Court.

"Now, one of the most delightful things I know about a court is that it is open to all men seeking justice—or injustice disguised as justice. Also there is a wise old saw to the effect that battles are won by the fellow who gets there first with the most men. The situation from the start was absurdly simple. If Pennington got to the District Court first, we were lost!"

"You mean you got there first?" exclaimed Bryce.

"I did—by the very simple method of preparing to get there first in case anything slipped. Something did slip—last night! However, I was ready; so all I had to do was press the button, for as Omar Khayyam remarked: 'What shall it avail a man if he buyeth a padlock for his stable after his favourite stallion hath been lifted?' Several days ago, my boy, I wrote a long letter to our attorney in San Francisco explaining every detail of our predicament; the instant I received that temporary franchise from the city council, I mailed a certified copy of it to our attorney also. Then, in anticipation of our discovery by Pennington, I instructed the attorney to prepare the complaint and petition for a restraining order against Seth Pennington et al. and stand by to rush the judge with it the instant he heard from me!

"Well, about the time old Pennington started for San Francisco this morning, I had our attorney out of bed and on the long-distance telephone; at nine o'clock this morning he appeared in the United States District Court; at nine-fifteen the judge signed a restraining order forbidding our enemies to interfere with us in the exercise of a right legally granted us by the city of Sequoia, and at nine-thirty a deputy United States marshal started in an automobile for Sequoia, via the overland route. He will arrive late to-morrow night, and on Sunday we will get that locomotive out of our way and install our crossing."

"And Pennington—"

"Ah, the poor Pennington! Mon pauvre Seth!" Buck sighed comically. "He will be just twenty-four hours late."

"You old he-fox!" Bryce murmured. "You wicked, wicked man!"

Buck Ogilvy lifted his lapel and sniffed luxuriously at his white carnation, the while a thin little smile played around the corners of his humorous mouth. "Ah," he murmured presently, "life's pretty sweet, isn't it!"

CHAPTER XXXV

Events followed each other with refreshing rapidity. While the crew of the big locomotive on the crossing busied themselves getting up steam, Sexton and Jules Rondeau toiled at the loading of the discarded boiler and heavy castings aboard two flat-cars. By utilizing the steel derrick on the company's wrecking-car, this task was completed by noon, and after luncheon the mogul backed up the main line past the switch into the Laguna Grande yards; whereupon the switch-engine kicked the two flat-cars and the wrecking-car out of the yard and down to the crossing, where the obstructions were promptly unloaded. The police watched the operation with alert interest but forebore to interfere in this high-handed closing of a public thoroughfare.

To Sexton's annoyance and secret apprehension, Bryce Cardigan and Buck Ogilvy promptly appeared on the scene, both very cheerful and lavish with expert advice as to the best method of expediting the job in hand. To Bryce's surprise Jules Rondeau appeared to take secret enjoyment of this good-natured chaffing of the Laguna Grande manager. Occasionally he eyed Bryce curiously but without animus, and presently he flashed the latter a lightning wink, as if to say: "What a fool Sexton is to oppose you!"

"Well, Rondeau," Bryce hailed the woods-boss cheerfully, "I see you have quite recovered from that working over I gave you some time ago. No hard feelings, I trust. I shouldn't care to have that job to do over again. You're a tough one."

"By gar, she don' pay for have hard feelings wiz you, M'sieur," Rondeau answered bluntly. "We have one fine fight, but"—he shrugged—"I don' want some more."

"Yes, by gar, an' she don' pay for cut other people's trees, M'sieur," Bryce mimicked him. "I shouldn't wonder if I took the value of that tree out of your hide."

"I t'enk so, M'sieur." He approached Bryce and lowered his voice. "For one month I am no good all ze tam. We don' fight some more, M'sieur. And I have feel ashame' for dose Black Minorca feller. Always wiz him eet is ze knife or ze club—and now eet is ze rifle. COCHON! W'en I fight, I fight wiz what le bon Dieu give me."

"You appear to have a certain code, after all," Bryce laughed. "I am inclined to like you for it. You're sporty in your way, you tremendous scoundrel!"

"Mebbeso," Rondeau suggested hopefully, "M'sieur likes me for woods-boss?"

"Why, what's the matter with Pennington? Is he tired of you?"

The colour mounted slowly to the woods bully's swarthy cheek. "Mademoiselle Sumnair, he's tell me pretty soon he's goin' be boss of Laguna Grande an' stop all thees fight. An' w'en Mademoiselle, he is in the saddle, good-bye Jules Rondeau. Thees country—I like him. I feel sad, M'sieur, to leave dose beeg trees." He paused, looking rather wistfully at Bryce. "I am fine woods-boss for somebody," he suggested hopefully.

"You think Miss Sumner dislikes you then, Rondeau?"

"I don' theenk. I know." He sighed; his huge body seemed to droop. "I am out of zee good luck now," he murmured bitterly. "Everybody, she hate Jules Rondeau. Colonel—she hate because I don' keel M'sieur Cardigan; Mademoiselle, he hate because I try to keel M'sieur Cardigan; M'sieur Sexton, she hate because I tell her thees mornin' she is one fool for fight M'sieur Cardigan."

Again he sighed. "Dose beeg trees! In Quebec we have none. In zee woods, M'sieur, I feel—here!" And he laid his great calloused, hairy hand over his heart. "W'en I cut your beeg trees, M'sieur, I feel like hell."

"That infernal gorilla of a man is a poet," Buck Ogilvy declared. "I'd think twice before I let him get out of the country, Bryce."

"'Whose salt he eats, his song he sings,'" quoth Bryce. "I forgive you, Rondeau, and when I need a woods-boss like you, I'll send for you."

CHAPTER XXXVI

At eleven o'clock Saturday night the deputy United States marshal arrived in Sequoia. Upon the advice of Buck Ogilvy, however, he made no attempt at service that night, notwithstanding the fact that Jules Rondeau and his bullies still guarded the crossing. At eight o'clock Sunday morning, however, Bryce Cardigan drove him down to the crossing. Buck Ogilvy was already there with his men, superintending the erection of a huge derrick close to the heap of obstructions placed on the crossing. Sexton was watching him uneasily, and flushed as Ogilvy pointed him out to the marshal.

"There's your meat, Marshal," he announced. The marshal approached and extended toward Sexton a copy of the restraining order. The latter struck it aside and refused to accept it—whereupon the deputy marshal tapped him on the shoulder with it. "Tag! You're out of the game, my friend," he said pleasantly.

As the document fluttered to Sexton's feet, the latter turned to Jules Rondeau. "I can no longer take charge here, Rondeau," he explained. "I am forbidden to interfere."

"Jules Rondeau can do ze job," the woods-boss replied easily. "Ze law, she have not restrain' me. I guess mebbeso you don' take dose theengs away, eh, M'sieur Cardigan. Myself, I lak see."

The deputy marshal handed Rondeau a paper, at the same time showing his badge. "You're out, too, my friend," he laughed. "Don't be foolish and try to buck the law. If you do, I shall have to place a nice little pair of handcuffs on you and throw you in jail—and if you resist arrest, I shall have to shoot you. I have one of these little restraining orders for every able-bodied man in the Laguna Grande Lumber Company's employ—thanks to Mr. Ogilvy's foresight; so it is useless to try to beat this game on a technicality."

Sexton, who still lingered, made a gesture of surrender. "Dismiss your crew, Rondeau," he ordered. "We're whipped to a frazzle."

A gleam of pleasure, not unmixed with triumph, lighted the dark eyes of the French-Canadian. "I tol' M'sieur Sexton she cannot fight M'sieur Cardigan and win," he said simply, "Now mebbe he believe that Jules Rondeau know somet'ing."

"Shut up," Sexton roared petulantly. Rondeau shrugged contemptuously, turned, and with a sweep of his great arm indicated to his men that they were to go; then, without a backward glance to see that they followed, the woods-boss strode away in the direction of the Laguna Grande mill. Arrived at the mill-office, he entered, took down the telephone, and called up Shirley Sumner.

"Mademoiselle," he said, "Jules Rondeau speaks to you. I have for you zee good news. Bryce Cardigan, she puts in the crossing to-day. One man of the law she comes from San Francisco with papers, and M'sieur Sexton say to me: 'Rondeau, we are whip'. Deesmess your men.' So I have deesmess doze men, and now I deesmess myself. Mebbeso bimeby I go to work for M'sieur Cardigan. For Mademoiselle I have no weesh to make trouble to fire me. I queet. I will not fight dose dirty fight some more. Au revoir, mademoiselle. I go."

And without further ado he hung up.

"What's this, what's this?" Sexton demanded. "You re going to quit? Nonsense, Rondeau, nonsense!"

"I will have my time, M'sieur," said Jules Rondeau. "I go to work for a man. Mebbeso I am not woods-boss for heem, but—I work."

"You'll have to wait until the Colonel returns, Rondeau."

"I will have my time," said Jules Rondeau patiently.

"Then you'll wait till pay-day for it, Rondeau. You know our rules. Any man who quits without notice waits until the regular pay-day for his money."

Jules advanced until he towered directly over the manager. "I tol' M'sieur I would have my time," he repeated once more. "Is M'sieur deaf in zee ears?" He raised his right hand, much as a bear raises its paw; his blunt fingers worked a little and there was a smoldering fire in his dark eyes.

Without further protest Sexton opened the safe, counted out the wages due, and took Rondeau's receipt.

"Thank you, M'sieur," the woods-boss growled as he swept the coin into his pocket. "Now I work for M'sieur Cardigan; so, M'sieur, I will have zee switchengine weeth two flat-cars and zee wrecking-car. Doze dam trash on zee crossing—M'sieur Cardigan does not like, and by gar, I take heem away. You onderstand, M'sieur? I am Jules Rondeau, and I work for M'sieur Cardigan. La la, M'sieur!" The great hand closed over Sexton's collar. "Not zee pistol—no, not for Jules Rondeau."

Quite as easily as a woman dresses a baby, he gagged Sexton with Sexton's own handkerchief, laid him gently on the floor and departed, locking the door behind him and taking the key. At the corner of the building, where the telephone-line entered the office, he paused, jerked once at the wire, and passed on, leaving the broken ends on the ground.

In the round-house he found the switch-engine crew on duty, waiting for steam in the boiler. The withdrawal of both locomotives, brief as had been their absence, had caused a glut of logs at the Laguna Grande landings, and

Sexton was catching up with the traffic by sending the switch-engine crew out for one train-load, even though it was Sunday. The crew had been used to receiving orders from Rondeau, and moreover they were not aware of his recent action; hence at his command they ran the switch-engine out of the roundhouse, coupled up the two flat-cars and the wrecking-car, and backed down to the crossing. Upon arrival, Jules Rondeau leaned out of the cab window and hailed Bryce. "M'sieur," he said, "do not bozzer to make zee derrick. I have here zee wrecking-car—all you need; pretty soon we lift him off zee crossing, I tell you, eh, M'sieur Cardigan?"

Bryce stepped over to the switch-engine and looked up at his late enemy. "By whose orders is this train here?" he queried.

"Mine," Rondeau answered. "M'sieur Sexton I have tie like one leetle pig and lock her in her office. I work now for M'sieur."

And he did. He waited not for a confirmation from his new master but proceeded to direct operations like the born driver and leader of men that he was. With his late employer's gear he fastened to the old castings and the boiler, lifted them with the derrick on the wrecking-car, and swung them up and around onto the flat-cars. By the middle of the afternoon the crossing was once more clear. Then the Cardigan crew fell upon it while Jules Rondeau ran the train back to the Laguna Grande yards, dismissed his crew, returned to the mill-office, and released the manager.

"You'll pay through the nose for this, you scoundrel," Sexton whimpered. "I'll fix you, you traitor."

"You feex nothing, M'sieur Sexton," Rondeau replied imperturbably. "Who is witness Jules Rondeau tie you up? Somebody see you, no? I guess you don' feex me. Sacre! I guess you don' try."

CHAPTER XXXVII

Colonel Pennington's discovery at San Francisco that Bryce Cardigan had stolen his thunder and turned the bolt upon him, was the hardest blow Seth Pennington could remember having received throughout thirty-odd years of give and take. He was too old and experienced a campaigner, however, to permit a futile rage to cloud his reason; he prided himself upon being a foeman worthy of any man's steel.

On Tuesday he returned to Sequoia. Sexton related to him in detail the events which had transpired since his departure, but elicited nothing more than a noncommittal grunt.

"There is one more matter, sir, which will doubtless be of interest to you," Sexton continued apologetically. "Miss Sumner called me on the telephone yesterday and instructed me formally to notify the board of directors of the Laguna Grande Company of a special meeting of the board, to be held here at two o'clock this afternoon. In view of the impossibility of communicating with you while you were en route, I conformed to her wishes. Our by-laws, as you know, stipulate that no meeting of the board shall be called without formal written notice to each director mailed twenty-four hours previously."

"What the devil do you mean, Sexton, by conforming to her wishes? Miss Sumner is not a director of this company." Pennington's voice was harsh and trembled with apprehension.

"Miss Sumner controls forty per cent. of the Laguna Grande stock, sir. I took that into consideration."

"You lie!" Pennington all but screamed. "You took into consideration your job as secretary and general manager. Damnation!"

He rose and commenced pacing up and down his office. Suddenly he paused. Sexton still stood beside his desk, watching him respectfully. "You fool!" he snarled. "Get out of here and leave me alone."

Sexton departed promptly, glancing at his watch as he did so. It lacked five minutes of two. He passed Shirley Sumner in the general office.

"Shirley," Pennington began in a hoarse voice as she entered his office, "what is the meaning of this directors' meeting you have requested?"

"Be seated, Uncle Seth," the girl answered quietly. "If you will only be quiet and reasonable, perhaps we can dispense with this directors' meeting which appears to frighten you so."

He sat down promptly, a look of relief on his face.

"I scarcely know how to begin, Uncle Seth," Shirley commenced sadly. "It hurts me terribly to be forced to hurt you, but there doesn't appear to be any other way out of it. I cannot trust you to manage my financial affairs in the future—this for a number of reasons, the principal one being—"

"Young Cardigan," he interrupted in a low voice.

"I suppose so," she answered, "although I did think until very recently that it was those sixteen townships of red cedar—that crown grant in British Columbia in which you induced me to invest four hundred thousand dollars. You will remember that you purchased that timber for me from the Caribou Timber Company, Limited. You said it was an unparalleled investment. Quite recently I learned—no matter how—that you were the principal owner of the Caribou Timber Company, Limited! Smart as you are, somebody swindled you with that red cedar. It was a wonderful stand of timber—so read the cruiser's report—but fifty per cent. of it, despite its green and flourishing appearance, is hollow-butted! And the remaining fifty per cent. of sound timber cannot be logged unless the rotten timber is logged also and gotten out of the way also. And I am informed that logging it spells bankruptcy."

She gazed upon him steadily, but without malice; his face crimsoned and then paled; presently his glance sought the carpet. While he struggled to formulate a verbal defense against her accusation Shirley continued:

"You had erected a huge sawmill and built and equipped a logging-road before you discovered you had been swindled. So, in order to save as much as possible from the wreck, you decided to unload your white elephant on somebody else. I was the readiest victim. You were the executor of my father's estate—you were my guardian and financial adviser, and so you found it very, very easy to swindle me!"

"I had my back to the wall," he quavered. "I was desperate—and it wasn't at all the bad investment you have been told it is. You had the money—more money than you knew what to do with—and with the proceeds of the sale of those cedar lands, I knew I could make an investment in California redwood and more than retrieve my fortunes—make big money for both of us."

"You might have borrowed the money from me. You know I have never hesitated to join in your enterprises."

"This was too big a deal for you, Shirley. I had vision. I could see incalculable riches in this redwood empire, but it was a tremendous gamble and required twenty millions to swing it at the very start. I dreamed of the control of California redwood; and if you will stand by me, Shirley, I shall yet make my dream come true—and half of it shall be yours. It has always been my intention to buy back from you secretly and at a nice profit to you that Caribou red cedar, and with the acquisition of the Cardigan properties I would have been in position to do so. Why, that Cardigan tract in the San Hedrin which we will buy in within a year for half a million is worth five millions at least. And by that time, I feel certain—in fact, I know—the Northern Pacific will commence building in from the south, from Willits."

She silenced him with a disdainful gesture. "You shall not smash the Cardigans," she declared firmly.

"I shall—" he began, but he paused abruptly, as if he had suddenly remembered that tact and not pugnacity was the requirement for the handling of this ticklish situation.

"You are devoid of mercy, of a sense of sportsmanship. Now, then, Uncle Seth, listen to me: You have twenty-four hours in which to make up your mind whether to accept my ultimatum or refuse it. If you refuse, I shall prosecute you for fraud and a betrayal of trust as my father's executor on that red-cedar timber deal."

He brightened a trifle. "I'm afraid that would be a long, hard row to hoe, my dear, and of course, I shall have to defend myself."

"In addition," the girl went on quietly, "the county grand jury shall be furnished with a stenographic report of your conversation of Thursday night with Mayor Poundstone. That will not be a long, hard row to hoe, Uncle Seth, for in addition to the stenographer, I have another very reliable witness, Judge Moore. Your casual disposal of my sedan as a bribe to the Mayor will be hard to explain and rather amusing, in view of the fact that Bryce Cardigan managed to frighten Mr. Poundstone into returning the sedan while you were away. And if that is not sufficient for my purposes, I have the sworn confession of the Black Minorca that you gave him five hundred dollars to kill Bryce Cardigan. Your woods-boss, Rondeau, will also swear that you approached him with a proposition to do away with Bryce Cardigan. I think, therefore, that you will readily see how impossible a situation you have managed to create and will not disagree with me when I suggest that it would be better for you to leave this county."

His face had gone gray and haggard. "I can't," he murmured, "I can't leave this great business now. Your own interests in the company render such a course unthinkable. Without my hand at the helms, things will go to smash."

"I'll risk that. I want to get rid of that worthless red-cedar timber; so I think you had better buy it back from me at the same figure at which, you sold it to me."

"But I haven't the money and I can't borrow it. I—I——"

"I will have the equivalent in stock of the Laguna Grande Lumber Company. You will call on Judge Moore to complete the transaction and leave with him your resignation as president of the Laguna Grande Lumber Company."

The Colonel raised his glance and bent it upon her in cold appraisal. She met it with firmness, and the thought came to him: "She is a Pennington!" And hope died out in his heart. He began pleading in maudlin fashion for mercy, for compromise. But the girl was obdurate.

"I am showing you more mercy than you deserve—you to whom mercy was ever a sign of weakness, of vacillation. There is a gulf between us, Uncle Seth—a gulf which for a long time I have dimly sensed and which, because of my recent discoveries, has widened until it can no longer be bridged."

He wrung his hands in desperation and suddenly slid to his knees before her; with hypocritical endearments he strove to take her hand, but she drew away from him. "Don't touch me," she cried sharply and with a breaking note in her voice. "You planned to kill Bryce Cardigan! And for that—and that alone—I shall never forgive you."

She fled from the office, leaving him cringing and grovelling on the floor. "There will be no directors' meeting, Mr. Sexton," she informed the manager as she passed through the general office. "It is postponed."

CHAPTER XXXVIII

That trying interview with her uncle had wrenched Shirley's soul to a degree that left her faint and weak. She at once set out on a long drive, in the hope that before she turned homeward again she might regain something of her customary composure.

Presently the asphaltum-paved street gave way to a dirt road and terminated abruptly at the boundaries of a field that sloped gently upward—a field studded with huge black redwood stumps showing dismally through coronets of young redwoods that grew riotously around the base of the departed parent trees. From the fringe of the thicket thus formed, the terminus of an old skid-road showed and a signboard, freshly painted, pointed the way to the Valley of the Giants.

Shirley had not intended to come here, but now that she had arrived, it occurred to her that it was here she wanted to come. Parking her car by the side of the road, she alighted and proceeded up the old skid, now newly planked and with the encroaching forestration cut away so that the daylight might enter from above. On over the gentle divide she went and down toward the amphitheatre where the primeval giants grew. And as she approached it, the sound that is silence in the redwoods—the thunderous diapason of the centuries—wove its spell upon her; quickly, imperceptibly there faded from her mind the memory of that grovelling Thing she had left behind in the mill-office, and in its place there came a subtle peace, a feeling of awe, of wonder—such a feeling, indeed, as must come to one in the realization that man is distant but God is near.

A cluster of wild orchids pendent from the great fungus-covered roots of a giant challenged her attention. She gathered them. Farther on, in a spot where a shaft of sunlight fell, she plucked an armful of golden California poppies and flaming rhododendron, and with her delicate burden she came at length to the giant-guarded clearing where the halo of sunlight fell upon the grave of Bryce Cardigan's mother. There were red roses on it—a couple of dozen, at least, and these she rearranged in order to make room for her own offering.

"Poor dear!" she murmured audibly. "God didn't spare you for much happiness, did He?"

A voice, deep, resonant, kindly, spoke a few feet away. "Who is it?"

Shirley, startled, turned swiftly. Seated across the little amphitheatre in a lumberjack's easy-chair fashioned from an old barrel, John Cardigan sat, his sightless gaze bent upon her. "Who is it?" he repeated.

"Shirley Sumner," she answered. "You do not know me, Mr. Cardigan."

"No," replied he, "I do not. That is a name I have heard, however. You are Seth Pennington's niece. Is someone with you?"

"I am quite alone, Mr. Cardigan."

"And why did you come here alone?" he queried.

"I—I wanted to think."

"You mean you wanted to think clearly, my dear. Ah, yes, this is the place for thoughts." He was silent a moment. Then: "You were thinking aloud, Miss Shirley Sumner. I heard you. You said: 'Poor dear, God didn't spare you for much happiness, did He?' And I think you rearranged my roses. Didn't I have them on her grave?"

"Yes, Mr. Cardigan. I was merely making room for some wild flowers I had gathered."

"Indeed. Then you knew—about her being here."

"Yes, sir. Some ten years ago, when I was a very little girl, I met your son Bryce. He gave me a ride on his Indian pony, and we came here. So I remember."

"Well, I declare! Ten years ago, eh? You've met, eh? You've met Bryce since his return to Sequoia, I believe. He's quite a fellow now."

"He is indeed."

John Cardigan nodded sagely. "So that's why you thought aloud," he remarked impersonally. "Bryce told you about her. You are right, Miss Shirley Sumner. God didn't give her much time for happiness—just three years; but oh, such wonderful years! Such wonderful years!

"It was mighty fine of you to bring flowers," he announced presently. "I appreciate that. I wish I could see you. You must be a dear, nice, thoughtful girl. Won't you sit down and talk to me?"

"I should be glad to," she answered, and seated herself on the brown carpet of redwood twigs close to his chair.

"So you came up here to do a little clear thinking," he continued in his deliberate, amiable tones. "Do you come here often?"

"This is the third time in ten years," she answered. "I feel that I have no business to intrude here. This is your shrine, and strangers should not profane it."

"I think I should have resented the presence of any other person, Miss Sumner. I resented you—until you spoke."

"I'm glad you said that, Mr. Cardigan. It sets me at ease."

"I hadn't been up here for nearly two years until recently. You see I—I don't own the Valley of the Giants any more."

"Indeed. To whom have you sold it?"

"I do not know, Miss Sumner. I had to sell; there was no other way out of the jam Bryce and I were in; so I sacrificed my sentiment for my boy. However, the new owner has been wonderfully kind and thoughtful. She reorganized that old skid-road so even an old blind duffer like me can find his way in and out without getting lost—and she had this easy-chair made for me. I have told Judge Moore, who represents the unknown owner, to extend my thanks to his client. But words are so empty, Shirley Sumner. If that new owner could only understand how truly grateful I am—how profoundly her courtesy touches me—"

"HER courtesy?" Shirley echoed. "Did a woman buy the Giants?"

He smiled down at her. "Why, certainly. Who but a woman—and a dear, kind, thoughtful woman—would have thought to have this chair made and brought up here for me?"

Fell a long silence between them; then John Cardigan's trembling hand went groping out toward the girl's. "Why, how stupid of me not to have guessed it immediately!" he said. "You are the new owner. My dear child, if the silent prayers of a very unhappy old man will bring God's blessing on you—there, there, girl! I didn't intend to make you weep. What a tender heart it is, to be sure!"

She took his great toil-worn hand, and her hot tears fell on it, for his gentleness, his benignancy, had touched her deeply. "Oh, you must not tell anybody! You mustn't," she cried.

He put his hand on her shoulder as she knelt before him. "Good land of love, girl, what made you do it? Why should a girl like you give a hundred thousand dollars for my Valley of the Giants? Were you"—hesitatingly—"your uncle's agent?"

"No, I bought it myself—with my own money. My uncle doesn't know I am the new owner. You see, he wanted it—for nothing."

"Ah, yes. I suspected as much a long time ago. Your uncle is the modern type of business man. Not very much of an idealist, I'm afraid. But tell me why you decided to thwart the plans of your relative."

"I knew it hurt you terribly to sell your Giants; they were dear to you for sentimental reasons. I understood, also, why you were forced to sell; so I—well, I decided the Giants would be safer in my possession than in my uncle's.

In all probability he would have logged this valley for the sake of the clear seventy-two-inch boards he could get from these trees."

"That does not explain satisfactorily, to me, why you took sides with a stranger against your own kin," John Cardigan persisted. "There must be a deeper and more potent reason, Miss Shirley Sumner."

"Well," Shirley made answer, glad that he could not see the flush of confusion and embarrassment that crimsoned her cheek, "when I came to Sequoia last May, your son and I met, quite accidentally. The stage to Sequoia had already gone, and he was gracious enough to invite me to make the journey in his car. Then we recalled having met as children, and presently I gathered from his conversation that he and his John-partner, as he called you, were very dear to each other. I was witness to your meeting that night— I saw him take you in his big arms and hold you tight because you'd—gone blind while he was away having a good time. And you hadn't told him! I thought that was brave of you; and later, when Bryce and Moira McTavish told me about you—how kind you were, how you felt your responsibility toward your employees and the community—well, I just couldn't help a leaning toward John-partner and John-partner's boy, because the boy was so fine and true to his father's ideals."

"Ah, he's a man. He is indeed," old John Cardigan murmured proudly. "I dare say you'll never get to know him intimately, but if you should—"

"I know him intimately," she corrected him. "He saved my life the day the log-train ran away. And that was another reason. I owed him a debt, and so did my uncle; but Uncle wouldn't pay his share, and I had to pay for him."

"Wonderful," murmured John Cardigan, "wonderful! But still you haven't told me why you paid a hundred thousand dollars for the Giants when you could have bought them for fifty thousand. You had a woman's reason, I dare say, and women always reason from the heart, never the head. However, if you do not care to tell me, I shall not insist. Perhaps I have appeared, unduly inquisitive."

"I would rather not tell you," she answered.

A gentle, prescient smile fringed his old mouth; he wagged his leonine head as if to say: "Why should I ask, when I know?" Fell again a restful silence. Then:

"Am I allowed one guess, Miss Shirley Sumner?"

"Yes, but you would never guess the reason."

"I am a very wise old man. When one sits in the dark, one sees much that was hidden from him in the full glare of the light. My son is proud, manly, independent, and the soul of honour. He needed a hundred thousand dollars; you knew it. Probably your uncle informed you. You wanted to loan him some money, but—you couldn't. You feared to offend him by proffering it; had you proffered it, he would have declined it. So you bought my Valley of the Giants at a preposterous price and kept your action a secret." And he patted her hand gently, as if to silence any denial, while far down the skid-road a voice—a half-trained baritone—floated faintly to them through the forest. Somebody was singing—or rather chanting—a singularly tuneless refrain, wild and barbaric.

"What is that?" Shirley cried.

"That is my son, coming to fetch his old daddy home," replied John Cardigan. "That thing he's howling is an Indian war-song or paean of triumph—something his nurse taught him when he wore pinafores. If you'll excuse me, Miss Shirley Sumner, I'll leave you now. I generally contrive to meet him on the trail."

He bade her good-bye and started down the trail, his stick tapping against the old logging-cable stretched from tree to tree beside the trail and marking it.

Shirley was tremendously relieved. She did not wish to meet Bryce Cardigan to-day, and she was distinctly grateful to John Cardigan for his nice consideration in sparing her an interview. She seated herself in the lumberjack's easy-chair so lately vacated, and chin in hand gave herself up to meditation on this extraordinary old man and his extraordinary son.

A couple of hundred yards down the trail Bryce met his father. "Hello, John Cardigan!" he called. "What do you mean by skallyhooting through these woods without a pilot? Eh? Explain your reckless conduct."

"You great overgrown duffer," his father retorted affectionately, "I thought you'd never come." He reached into his pocket for a handkerchief, but failed to find it and searched through another pocket and still another. "By gravy, son," he remarked presently, "I do believe I left my silk handkerchief—the one Moira gave me for my last birthday—up yonder. I wouldn't lose that handkerchief for a farm. Skip along and find it for me, son. I'll wait for you here. Don't hurry."

"I'll be back in a pig's whisper," his son replied, and started briskly up the trail, while his father leaned against a madrone tree and smiled his prescient little smile.

Bryce's brisk step on the thick carpet of withered brown twigs aroused Shirley from her reverie. When she looked up, he was standing in the centre of the little amphitheatre gazing at her.

"You—you!" she stammered, and rose as if to flee from him.

"The governor sent me back to look for his handkerchief, Shirley," he explained. "He didn't tell me you were here. Guess he didn't hear you." He advanced smilingly toward her. "I'm tremendously glad to see you to-day, Shirley," he said, and paused beside her. "Fate has been singularly kind to me. Indeed, I've been pondering all day as to just how I was to arrange a private and confidential little chat with you, without calling upon you at your uncle's house."

"I don't feel like chatting to-day," she answered a little drearily—and then he noted her wet lashes. Instantly he was on one knee beside her; with the amazing confidence that had always distinguished him in her eyes, his big left arm went around her, and when her hands went to her face, he drew them gently away.

"I've waited too long, sweetheart," he murmured. "Thank God, I can tell you at last all the things that have been accumulating in my heart. I love you, Shirley. I've loved you from that first day we met at the station, and all these months of strife and repression have merely served to make me love you the more. Perhaps you have been all the dearer to me because you seemed so hopelessly unattainable."

He drew her head down on his breast; his great hand patted her hot cheek; his honest brown eyes gazed earnestly, wistfully into hers. "I love you," he whispered. "All that I have—all that I am—all that I hope to be—I offer to you, Shirley Sumner; and in the shrine of my heart I shall hold you sacred while life shall last. You are not indifferent to me, dear. I know you're not; but tell me—answer me—"

Her violet eyes were uplifted to his, and in them he read the answer to his cry. "Ah, may I?" he murmured, and kissed her.

"Oh, my dear, impulsive, gentle big sweetheart," she whispered—and then her arms went around his neck, and the fullness of her happiness found vent in tears he did not seek to have her repress. In the safe haven of his arms she rested; and there, quite without effort or distress, she managed to convey to him something more than an inkling of the thoughts that were wont to come to her whenever they met.

"Oh, my love!" he cried happily, "I hadn't dared dream of such happiness until to-day. You were so unattainable—the obstacles between us were so many and so great—"

"Why to-day, Bryce?" she interrupted him.

He took her adorable little nose in his great thumb and forefinger and tweaked it gently. "The light began to dawn yesterday, my dear little enemy, following an interesting half-hour which I put in with His Honour the Mayor. Acting upon suspicion only, I told Poundstone I was prepared to send him to the rock-pile if he didn't behave himself in the matter of my permanent franchise for the N.C.O.—and the oily old invertebrate wept and promised me anything if I wouldn't disgrace him. So I promised I wouldn't do anything until the franchise matter should be definitely settled—after which I returned to my office, to find awaiting me there no less a person than the right-of-way man for the Northwestern Pacific. He was a perfectly delightful young fellow, and he had a proposition to unfold. It seems the Northwestern Pacific has decided to build up from Willits, and all that powwow and publicity of Buck Ogilvy's about the N.C.O. was in all probability the very thing that spurred them to action. They figured the C.M. & St.P. was back of the N.C.O.—that it was to be the first link of a chain of coast roads to be connected ultimately with the terminus of the C.M. & St.P. on Gray's Harbour, Washington, and if the N.C.O. should be built, it meant that a rival road would get the edge on them in the matter of every stick of Humboldt and Del Norte redwood—and they'd be left holding the sack."

"Why did they think that, dear?"

"That amazing rascal Buck Ogilvy used to be a C. M. me that the money had been deposited in escrow there awaiting formal deed. That money puts the Cardigan Redwood Lumber Company in the clear—no receivership for us now, my dear one. And I'm going right ahead with the building of the N.C.O.—while our holdings down on the San Hedrin double in value, for the reason that within three years they will be accessible and can be logged over the rails of the Northwestern Pacific!"

"Bryce," Shirley declared, "haven't I always told you I'd never permit you to build the N.C.O.?"

"Of course," he replied, "but surely you're going to withdraw your objections now."

"I am not. You must choose between the N.C.O. and me." And she met his surprised gaze unflinchingly.

"Shirley! You don't mean it?"

"I do mean it. I have always meant it. I love you, dear, but for all that, you must not build that road."

He stood up and towered above her sternly. "I must build it, Shirley. I've contracted to do it, and I must keep faith with Gregory of the Trinidad Timber Company. He's putting up the money, and I'm to do the work and operate the line. I can't go back on him now."

"Not for my sake?" she pleaded. He shook his head. "I must go on," he reiterated.

"Do you realize what that resolution means to us?" The girl's tones were grave, her glance graver.

"I realize what it means to me!"

She came closer to him. Suddenly the blaze in her violet eyes gave way to one of mirth. "Oh, you dear big booby!" she cried. "I was just testing you." And she clung to him, laughing. "You always beat me down—you always win. Bryce, dear, I'm the Laguna Grande Lumber Company—at least, I will be to-morrow, and I repeat for the last time that you shall NOT build the N.C.O.—because I'm going to—oh, dear, I shall die laughing at you—because I'm going to merge with the Cardigan Redwood Lumber Company, and then my railroad shall be your railroad, and we'll extend it and haul Gregory's logs to tidewater for him also. And—silly, didn't I tell you you'd never build the N.C.O.?"

"God bless my mildewed soul!" he murmured, and drew her to him.

In the gathering dusk they walked down the trail. Beside the madrone tree John Cardigan waited patiently.

"Well," he queried when they joined him, "did you find my handkerchief for me, son?"

"I didn't find your handkerchief, John Cardigan," Bryce answered, "but I did find what I suspect you sent me back for—and that is a perfectly wonderful daughter-in-law for you."

John Cardigan smiled and held out his arms for her. "This," he said, "is the happiest day that I have known since my boy was born."

CHAPTER XXXIX

Colonel Seth Pennington was thoroughly crushed. Look which way he would, the bedevilled old rascal could find no loophole for escape.

"You win, Cardigan," he muttered desperately as he sat in his office after Shirley had left him. "You've had more than a shade in every round thus far, and at the finish you've landed a clean knockout. If I had to fight any man but you—"

He sighed resignedly and pressed the push-button on his desk. Sexton entered. "Sexton," he said bluntly and with a slight quiver in his voice, "my niece and I have had a disagreement. We have quarrelled over young Cardigan. She's going to marry him. Now, our affairs are somewhat involved, and in order to straighten them out, we spun a coin to see whether she should sell her stock in Laguna Grande to me or whether I should sell mine to her— and I lost. The book-valuation of the stock at the close of last year's business, plus ten per cent. will determine the selling price, and I shall resign as president. You will, in all probability, be retained to manage the company until it is merged with the Cardigan Redwood Lumber Company—when, I imagine, you will be given ample notice to seek a new job elsewhere. Call Miss Sumner's attorney, Judge Moore, on the telephone and ask him to come to the office at nine o'clock to-morrow, when the papers can be drawn up and signed. That is all."

The Colonel did not return to his home in Redwood Boulevard that night. He had no appetite for dinner and sat brooding in his office until very late; then he went to the Hotel Sequoia and engaged a room. He did not possess sufficient courage to face his niece again.

At four o'clock the next day the Colonel, his baggage, his automobile, his chauffeur, and the solemn butler James, boarded the passenger steamer for San Francisco, and at four-thirty sailed out of Humboldt Bay over the thundering bar and on into the south. The Colonel was still a rich man, but his dream of a redwood empire had faded, and once more he was taking up the search for cheap timber. Whether he ever found it or not is a matter that does not concern us.

At a moment when young Henry Poundstone's dream of legal opulence was fading, when Mayor Poundstone's hopes for domestic peace had been shattered beyond repair, the while his cheap political aspirations had been equally devastated because of a certain damnable document in the possession of Bryce Cardigan, many events of importance were transpiring. On the veranda of his old-fashioned home, John Cardigan sat tapping the floor with his stick and dreaming dreams which, for the first time in many years, were rose-tinted. Beside him Shirley sat, her glance bent musingly out across the roofs of Sequoia and on to the bay shore, where the smoke and exhaust-steam floated up from two sawmills—her own and Bryce Cardigan's. To her came at regularly spaced intervals the faint whining of the saws and the rumble of log-trains crawling out on the log-dumps; high over the piles of bright, freshly sawed lumber she caught from time to time the flash of white spray as the great logs tossed from the trucks, hurtled down the skids, and crashed into the Bay. At the docks of both mills vessels were loading, their tall spars cutting the skyline above and beyond the smokestacks; far down the Bay a steam schooner, loaded until her main-deck was almost flush with the water, was putting out to sea, and Shirley heard the faint echo of her siren as she whistled her intention to pass to starboard of a wind-jammer inward bound in tow of a Cardigan tug.

"It's wonderful," she said presently, apropos of nothing.

"Aye," he replied in his deep, melodious voice, "I've been sitting here, my dear, listening to your thoughts. You know something, now, of the tie that binds my boy to Sequoia. This"—he waved his arm abroad in the darkness— "this is the true essence of life—to create, to develop the gifts that God has given us—to work and know the blessing of weariness—to have dreams and see them come true. That is life, and I have lived. And now I am ready to rest." He smiled wistfully. "'The king is dead. Long live the king.' I wonder if you, raised as you have been, can face life in Sequoia resolutely with my son. It is a dull, drab sawmill town, where life unfolds gradually without thrill—where the years stretch ahead of one with only trees, among simple folk. The life may be hard on you, Shirley; one has to acquire a taste for it, you know."

"I have known the lilt of battle, John-partner," she answered; "hence I think I can enjoy the sweets of victory. I am content."

"And what a run you did give that boy Bryce!"

She laughed softly. "I wanted him to fight; I had a great curiosity to see the stuff that was in him," she explained.

CHAPTER XL

Next day Bryce Cardigan, riding the top log on the end truck of a long train just in from Cardigan's woods in Township Nine, dropped from the end of the log as the train crawled through the mill-yard on its way to the log-dump. He hailed Buck Ogilvy, where the latter stood in the door of the office.

"Big doings up on Little Laurel Creek this morning, Buck."

"Do tell!" Mr. Ogilvy murmured morosely.

"It was great," Bryce continued. "Old Duncan McTavish returned. I knew he would. His year on the mourner's-bench expired yesterday, and he came back to claim his old job of woods-boss."

"He's one year too late," Ogilvy declared. "I wouldn't let that big Canadian Jules Rondeau quit for a farm. Some woods-boss, that—and his first job with this company was the dirtiest you could hand him—smearing grease on the skid-road at a dollar and a half a day and found. He's made too good to lose out now. I don't care what his private morals may be. He CAN get out the logs, hang his rascally hide, and I'm for him."

"I'm afraid you haven't anything to say about it, Buck," Bryce replied dryly.

"I haven't, eh? Well, any time you deny me the privilege of hiring and firing, you're going to be out the service of a rattling good general manager, my son. Yes, sir! If you hold me responsible for results, I must select the tools I want to work with."

"Oh, very well," Bryce laughed. "Have it your own way. Only if you can drive Duncan McTavish out of Cardigan's woods, I'd like to see you do it. Possession is nine points of the law, Buck—and Old Duncan is in possession."

"What do you mean—in possession?"

"I mean that at ten o'clock this morning Duncan McTavish appeared at our log-landing. The whisky-fat was all gone from him, and he appeared forty years old instead of the sixty he is. With a whoop he came jumping over the logs, straight for Jules Rondeau. The big Canuck saw him coming and knew what his visit portended—so he wasn't taken unawares. It was a case of fight for his job—and Rondeau fought."

"The devil you say!"

"I do—and there was the devil to pay. It was a rough and tumble and no grips barred—just the kind of fight Rondeau likes. Nevertheless old Duncan floored him. While he's been away somebody taught him the hammer-lock and the crotch-hold and a few more fancy ones, and he got to work on

Rondeau in a hurry. In fact, he had to, for if the tussle had gone over five minutes, Rondeau's youth would have decided the issue."

"And Rondeau was whipped?"

"To a whisper. Mac floored him, climbed him, and choked him until he beat the ground with his free hand in token of surrender; whereupon old Duncan let him up, and Rondeau went to his shanty and packed his turkey. The last I saw of him he was headed over the hill to Camp Two on Laguna Grande. He'll probably chase that assistant woods-boss I hired after the consolidation, out of Shirley's woods and help himself to the fellow's job. I don't care if he does. What interests me is the fact that the old Cardigan woods-boss is back on the job in Cardigan's woods, and I'm mighty glad of it. The old horsethief has had his lesson and will remain sober hereafter. I think he's cured."

"The infamous old outlaw!"

"Mac knows the San Hedrin as I know my own pocket. He'll be a tower of strength when we open up that tract after the railroad builds in. By the way, has my dad been down this morning?"

"Yes. Moira read the mail to him and then took him up to the Valley of the Giants. He said he wanted to do a little quiet figuring on that new steam schooner you're thinking of building. He thinks she ought to be bigger—big enough to carry two million feet."

Bryce glanced at his watch. "It's half after eleven," he said. "Guess I'll run up to the Giants and bring him home to luncheon."

He stepped into the Napier standing outside the office and drove away. Buck Ogilvy waited until Bryce was out of sight; then with sudden determination he entered the office.

"Moira," he said abruptly, approaching the desk where she worked, "your dad is back, and what's more, Bryce Cardigan has let him have his old job as woods-boss. And I'm here to announce that you're not going back to the woods to keep house for him. Understand? Now, look here, Moira. I've shilly-shallied around you for months, protesting my love, and I haven't gotten anywhere. To-day I'm going to ask you for the last time. Will you marry me? I need you worse than that rascal of a father of yours does, and I tell you I'll not have you go back to the woods to take care of him. Come, now, Moira. Do give me a definite answer."

"I'm afraid I don't love you well enough to marry you, Mr. Ogilvy," Moira pleaded. "I'm truly fond of you, but—"

"The last boat's gone," cried Mr. Ogilvy desperately. "I'm answered. Well, I'll not stick around here much longer, Moira. I realize I must be a nuisance, but I can't help being a nuisance when you're near me. So I'll quit my good job here and go back to my old game of railroading."

"Oh, you wouldn't quit a ten-thousand-dollar job," Moira cried, aghast.

"I'd quit a million-dollar job. I'm desperate enough to go over to the mill and pick a fight with the big bandsaw. I'm going away where I can't see you. Your eyes are driving me crazy."

"But I don't want you to go, Mr. Ogilvy."

"Call me Buck," he commanded sharply.

"I don't want you to go, Buck," she repeated meekly. "I shall feel guilty, driving you out of a fine position."

"Then marry me and I'll stay."

"But suppose I don't love you the way you deserve—"

"Suppose! Suppose!" Buck Ogilvy cried. "You're no longer certain of yourself. How dare you deny your love for me? Eh? Moira, I'll risk it."

Her eyes turned to him timidly, and for the first time he saw in their smoky depths a lambent flame. "I don't know," she quavered, "and it's a big responsibility in case—"

"Oh, the devil take the case!" he cried rapturously, and took her hands in his. "Do I improve with age, dear Moira?" he asked with boyish eagerness; then, before she could answer, he swept on, a tornado of love and pleading. And presently Moira was in his arms, he was kissing her, and she was crying softly because—well, she admired Mr. Buck Ogilvy; more, she respected him and was genuinely fond of him. She wondered, and as she wondered, a quiet joy thrilled her in the knowledge that it did not seem at all impossible for her to grow, in time, absurdly fond of this wholesome red rascal.

"Oh, Buck, dear," she whispered, "I don't know, I'm sure, but perhaps I've loved you a little bit for a long time."

"I'm perfectly wild over you. You're the most wonderful woman I ever heard of. Old rosy-cheeks!" And he pinched them just to see the colour come and go.

John Cardigan was seated in his lumberjack's easy-chair as his son approached. His hat lay on the litter of brown twigs beside him; his chin was sunk on his breast, and his head was held a little to one side

in a listening attitude; a vagrant little breeze rustled gently a lock

of his fine, long white hair. Bryce stooped over the old man and shook

him gently by the shoulder.

"Wake up, partner," he called cheerfully. But John Cardigan did not wake, and again his son shook him. Still receiving no response, Bryce lifted the leonine old head and gazed into his father's face. "John Cardigan!" he cried sharply. "Wake up, old pal."

The old eyes opened, and John Cardigan smiled up at his boy. "Good son," he whispered, "good son!" He closed his sightless eyes again as if the mere effort of holding them open wearied him. "I've been sitting here—waiting," he went on in the same gentle whisper. "No, not waiting for you, boy—waiting—"

His head fell over on his son's shoulder; his hand went groping for Bryce's. "Listen," he continued. "Can't you hear it—the Silence? I'll wait for you here, my son. Mother and I will wait together now—in this spot she fancied. I'm tired—I want rest. Look after old Mac and Moira—and Bill Dandy, who lost his leg at Camp Seven last fall—and Tom Ellington's children—and—all the others, son. You know, Bryce. They're your responsibilities. Sorry I can't wait to see the San Hedrin opened up, but—I've lived my life and loved my love. Ah, yes, I've been happy—so happy just doing things—and—dreaming here among my Giants—and—"

He sighed gently. "Good son," he whispered again; his big body relaxed, and the great heart of the Argonaut was still. Bryce held him until the realization came to him that his father was no more—that like a watch, the winding of which has been neglected, he had gradually slowed up and stopped.

"Good-bye, old John-partner!" he murmured.

"You've escaped into the light at last. We'll go home together now, but we'll come back again."

And with his father's body in his strong arms he departed from the little amphitheatre, walking lightly with his heavy burden down the old skid-road to the waiting automobile. And two days later John Cardigan returned to rest forever—with his lost mate among the Giants, himself at last an infinitesimal portion of that tremendous silence that is the diapason of the ages.

When the funeral was over, Shirley and Bryce lingered until they found themselves alone beside the freshly turned earth. Through a rift in the great branches two hundred feet above, a patch of cerulean sky showed faintly; the sunlight fell like a broad golden shaft over the blossom-laden grave, and from the brown trunk of an adjacent tree a gray squirrel, a descendant, perhaps, of the gray squirrel that had been wont to rob Bryce's pockets of pine-nuts twenty years before, chirped at them inquiringly.

"He was a giant among men," said Bryce presently. "What a fitting place for him to lie!" He passed his arm around his wife's shoulders and drew her to him. "You made it possible, sweetheart."

She gazed up at him in adoration. And presently they left the Valley of the Giants to face the world together, strong in their faith to live their lives and love their loves, to dream their dreams and perchance when life should be done with and the hour of rest at hand, to surrender, sustained and comforted by the knowledge that those dreams had come true.

THE END

Milton Keynes UK
Ingram Content Group UK Ltd.
UKHW040831071024
449371UK00007B/713